Study Guide
for use with
Price Theory
and Applications

Second Edition

Peter Pashigian
University of Chicago

Boston, Massachusetts   Burr Ridge, Illinois   Dubuque, Iowa
Madison, Wisconsin   New York, New York   San Francisco, California   St. Louis, Missouri

Irwin/McGraw-Hill

A Division of The McGraw·Hill Companies

Study Guide for use with
PRICE THEORY AND APPLICATIONS

1 2 3 4 5 6 7 8 9 0 BBC/BBC 9 0 9 8 7

ISBN 0-07-048781-2

http://www.mhhe.com

How to Use This Book

This study guide is designed to help you succeed in your intermediate microeconomic theory class. The goal is to help you master and apply the material in *Price Theory and Applications* by B. Peter Pashigian. Just as a map gives you a sense of the land, but can never replace the experience of actually going on a trip, this guide is a complement to the textbook, not a substitute.

Economics is a mental discipline–a way of understanding the world and solving many of life's problems. Economics is neither a cookbook nor a religion; it is better understood than memorized. To remember your economics lessons first try to understand a small set of key concepts; then practice applying those concepts to a wide variety of problems. Some of these applications are provided in the textbook. More are supplied in this study guide.

A good strategy is to read each chapter of the text when your instructor assigns it. After you have read through the chapter once, refer to the Learning Objectives and Chapter Overview in this study guide. Did you catch the major points? Do you understand them well enough to try your hand at a few problems? If not, reread the textbook chapter, pausing when necessary to think about important ideas. Work through the study-guide material for each chapter, checking the answer *after* you have answered them in the guide.

After you have tackled the problems and questions in this guide, return to the chapter in the textbook. Try the Review Questions, Exercises, and Problem Sets. Develop your confidence by working through these questions and problems before you check your answers.

Chapter 1

PRICING AND THE DEMAND AND SUPPLY MODEL

• LEARNING OBJECTIVES

After completing this chapter, you should be able to

1. Define and explain the law of demand and the law of supply.

2. Understand the distinction between a change in quantity demanded and a change in demand, and between a change in quantity supplied and a change in supply.

3. Draw a graph showing market equilibrium, and describe how the equilibrium comes about.

4. Demonstrate how changes in demand or supply cause price changes, and how price changes adjust quantity to reestablish equilibrium.

5. Explain how shortages and surpluses would persist if laws or other impediments prevented price adjustments.

6. Calculate price elasticity of demand, and use this concept to predict how revenue and expenditure change in response to a price change.

7. Compute price elasticity of supply, and comprehend how the amount offered for sale reacts to a change in market price.

• CHAPTER OVERVIEW

Demand

The **law of demand** states that quantity demanded varies inversely with price. If price increases, the quantity that buyers are willing and able to buy decreases. If price decreases, the quantity that buyers are willing and able to buy increases, *other factors remaining constant.* The demand curve is plotted under the condition that other influences on the amount demanders wish to buy - income, prices of related goods, tastes, number of buyers - remain constant. If the price of a good increases, the relevant point on the demand curve moves upward to the left; if the price decreases, the relevant point on the demand curve moves downward to the right. As long as a demand curve is stationary, a change in price leads to a **change in quantity demanded.**

If income, the prices of substitutes or complements, or the tastes or number of buyers change, the entire demand curve is displaced. An increase in income normally causes consumers to buy more of a good even though its price has not decreased. The only way to depict this on a diagram is if the entire graph shifts location. An **increase in demand** happens when buyers wish to purchase more of a good *at each price*; the entire demand curve shifts to the right. A **decrease in demand** occurs when buyers wish to purchase less of a good *at each price*; the entire demand curve shifts to the left.

Supply

The same distinction must be made between a **change in quantity supplied** and a **change in supply.** A *change in quantity supplied* refers to the movement of quantity along a stationary supply curve in response to a price change. Given technology, the prices of inputs, and the number of sellers, an increase in price means that suppliers desire to sell more of a good. A decrease in price means that suppliers desire to sell less of a good. A *change in supply* happens only when something besides the good's own price changes. If the prices of factors of production increase, or if firms leave the market, then the amount the (remaining) suppliers wish to sell decreases *at every price*. This is a **decrease in supply** - a leftward shift in the supply curve. If the prices of inputs fall, or if new technology enhances efficiency, or if the number of firms increases, then the supply curve will shift to the right. An **increase in supply** means that suppliers offer to sell more at each price.

Market Equilibrium

Professor Pashigian demonstrates that market prices are not arbitrary. Markets adjust prices until quantity demanded equals quantity supplied at the prevailing price. Allowed to function, a competitive market will establish the **equilibrium** price and quantity at the point where the demand curve and the supply curve intersect. At the equilibrium price, the quantity that buyers wish to purchase equals the quantity that suppliers wish to sell, so there is no tendency for price, and therefore quantity, to change.

Figure 1-1 depicts Professor Pashigian's example of the demand and supply of wood throughout American history. During America's colonial period, wood was plentiful, (supply curve S_0) and demand (D_0) was relatively modest because population was small. Price P_0 and quantity Q_0 prevailed at time 0. Due to the relatively low price of wood, most bridges, railroad ties, and even large buildings were built with wood. As the population grew, the demand for wood increased. This is shown as a shift in the demand curve from D_0 to D_1. Had the price stayed at P_0, a **shortage** equal to $Q' - Q_0$ would have persisted. Rather than do without, buyers of wood bid its price up, until, at P_1, quantity demanded again equaled quantity supplied at Q_1.

As more and more timberland was cleared to make room for farms and cities, the supply of wood decreased. The decrease in supply is depicted as a shift from supply curve S_0 to supply curve S_1. Now, at price P_1, there is again a shortage of wood equal to $Q_1 - Q''$. Price must again rise until, at price P_2, quantity demanded equals quantity supplied, Q_2.

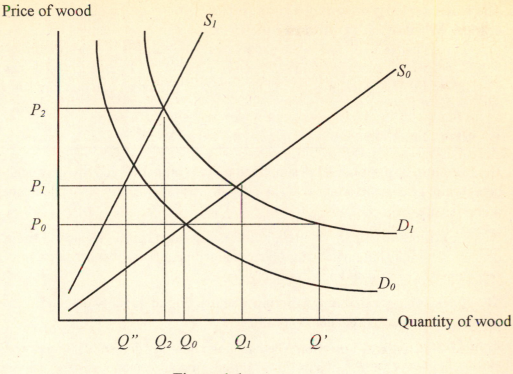

Figure 1-1

Note what happened in the above example. The market remains in equilibrium until or unless either the demand curve or the supply curve shifts. A change in demand or a change in supply occurs *before* a price change. Indeed, a change in demand or a change in supply *causes* a temporary shortage or surplus until price adjusts. If price were prevented from changing, the shortage or surplus would persist. When the demand curve shifted from D_0 to D_1, the equilibrium quantity and the price moved along the supply curve, the curve that did not shift. When the supply curve shifted from S_0 to S_1, the equilibrium price and quantity moved along demand curve D_1, the curve that did not shift. Remember that an increase in demand increases equilibrium price, but an increase in price reduces quantity demanded.

Price Elasticity of Demand

The **price elasticity of demand** measures the responsiveness of quantity demanded to a price change. If demand is **price-elastic,** the percentage change in quantity is greater, in absolute value, than the percentage change in price; expenditure moves in the opposite direction to the change in price. If demand is **price-inelastic**, the percentage change in quantity is smaller, in absolute terms, than the percentage change in price; expenditure changes in the same direction as price. If demand is **unit price-elastic**, then the percentage change in price is exactly balanced by the percentage change in quantity, so that expenditure does not change.

The **price elasticity of supply** measures the sensitivity of the quantity supplied to a price change. When supply is **unit price-elastic**, the percentage change in quantity equals the percentage change in price. When supply is **price-inelastic**, a 1 percent price change will be followed by a change in quantity supplied of less than 1 percent. When supply is **price-elastic**, a 1 percent price change will be followed by a change in quantity supplied that is larger than 1 percent.

• KEY TERMS

Demand and supply model A simplified picture of market activity in which the equilibrium price is determined at the point where the quantity demanded equals the quantity supplied.

Demand function The inverse relationship between quantity demanded and price. The demand function shifts when other factors--income, prices of substitutes, prices of complements, tastes, and number of buyers--change.

Movement along a demand function The reaction of quantity demanded to a price change, other factors remaining constant.

Shift in the Demand Function The change in quantity demanded at *every price* due to a change in income, prices of substitutes, prices of complements, tastes, or the number of buyers.

Substitutes Commodities a consumer would purchase to fulfill the same desires as the good in question. Chicken is a substitute for beef, so an increase in the price of beef would increase the demand for chicken.

Complements Commodities a consumer would purchase to go with a good in question. Lemon is a complement to tea, so an increase in the price of tea would reduce the demand for lemons.

Supply function The direct relationship between quantity supplied and price. The supply function shifts when other factors--prices of inputs, technology, or the number of sellers--change.

Movement along the supply function The reaction of quantity supplied to a price change, other factors remaining constant.

Shift in the supply function The change in quantity supplied at *every price* due to a change in prices of inputs, technology, or the number of firms.

Equilibrium price and quantity The market is in equilibrium when, at the prevailing price, the quantity demanded equals the quantity supplied. At equilibrium, there is no tendency for either price or quantity to change.

Excess demand A condition that exists when, at the prevailing price, quantity demanded exceeds quantity supplied. Excess demand is also known as a **shortage** and causes market price to increase until equilibrium is restored.

Excess supply A condition when, at the prevailing price, quantity supplied exceeds quantity demanded. Excess supply is also known as a **surplus** and causes market price to decrease until equilibrium is restored.

Price Elasticity of Demand The percentage change in quantity demanded divided by the percentage change in price.

- **Price-elastic demand** The percentage change in quantity demanded is greater (in absolute value) than the percentage change in price. When demand is price-elastic, expenditure moves in the opposite direction to price.

- **Price-inelastic demand** The percentage change in quantity demanded is smaller (in absolute value) than the percentage change in price. When demand is price-inelastic, expenditure moves in the same direction as price.

- **Unitary-elastic demand** The percentage change in quantity demanded equals (in absolute value) the percentage change in price. When demand is unitary price-elastic, expenditure does not change when price changes.

Price elasticity of supply The percent change in quantity supplied divided by the percentage change in price

- **Price-elastic supply** The percentage change in quantity is greater than the percentage change in price.

- **Price-inelastic supply** The percentage change in quantity is smaller than the percentage change in price.

- **Unitary-elastic supply** The percentage change in quantity equals the percentage change in price.

- ## PROBLEMS

1. **Figure 1-2** is a supply and demand model depicting an initial equilibrium in the U. S. strawberry market. For each of the following events, indicate whether the demand curve shifts or the supply curve shifts, the direction of the shift, and what happens to equilibrium price and quantity.

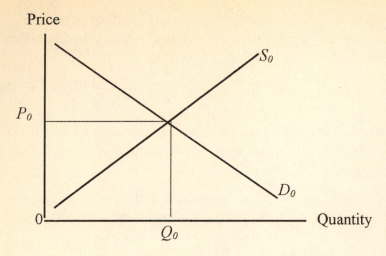

Price

P_0

S_0

D_0

0

Q_0

Quantity

Figure 1-2

a. The wage rate for strawberry pickers increases relative to the wage rate for workers in general. _____

    _____

b. The price of cream decreases; cream is a complement for strawberries.

    _____

    _____

c. Blight wipes out half the European strawberry plants; strawberry plants in the United States are unaffected.

    _____

    _____

d. The price of blueberries, a substitute for strawberries, declines.

    _____

    _____

2. The demand equation for strawberries has been estimated as $Q_D = 500 - 100P$. Where Q_D is the quantity of strawberries demanded, in quarts, and P is the price per quart. For each of the following prices, compute the quantity of strawberries demanded, the expenditure on strawberries, and the point price elasticity of demand.

Price	Quantity Demanded	Total Expenditure	Point Price Elasticity
$5.00	_____	_____	_____
$4.00	_____	_____	_____
$3.00	_____	_____	_____
$2.00	_____	_____	_____
$1.00	_____	_____	_____
$0.00	_____	_____	_____

3. The demand equation for blueberries is unknown, but below are some observed price/quantity pairs ($ per quart, and number of quarts demanded). Calculate the arc price elasticity over each pair of prices

Price per quart	Number of Quarts Demanded	Arc Price Elasticity
$5.00	100	
$4.00	200	_____
$3.00	400	_____
$2.00	750	_____
$1.00	1200	_____

4. A more extensive investigation of the strawberry market reveals that the quantity of strawberries demanded (Q_D) depends on the price of strawberries (P_s), the price of blueberries (P_b), and the price of cream (P_c) $Q_D = 500 - 100P_s + 50P_b - 20P_c$

a. If $P_b = \$2.00$ and $P_c = \$1.00$, indicate the quantity of strawberries demanded, total expenditure, and the point elasticity of demand for strawberries at each of the following prices.

Price	Quantity Demanded	Total Expenditure	Point Price Elasticity
$5.00	_____	_____	_____
$4.00	_____	_____	_____
$3.00	_____	_____	_____
$2.00	_____	_____	_____
$1.00	_____	_____	_____
$0.00	_____	_____	_____

b. If P_c increases to $1.50 while P_b = $2.00, indicate the quantity of strawberries demanded, total expenditure, and the point elasticity of demand for strawberries, at each of the following prices

Price	Quantity Demanded	Total Expenditure	Point Price Elasticity
$5.00			
$4.00			
$3.00			
$2.00			
$1.00			
$0.00			

c. If P_c = $1.50, and P_b = $1.00, indicate the quantity of strawberries demanded, total expenditure, and the point elasticity of demand for strawberries, at of the following prices

Price	Quantity Demanded	Total Expenditure	Point Price Elasticity
$5.00			
$4.00			
$3.00			
$2.00			
$1.00			
$0.00			

5. Suppose that the demand equation for strawberries is $Q_D = 600 - 100P$ and that the supply equation for strawberries is $Q_S = 100P$. For each of the following prices, determine the quantity demanded, the quantity supplied, and whether there would be a surplus, a shortage, or equilibrium in the strawberry market.

Price	Quantity Demanded	Quantity Supplied	State of Market
$5.00			
$4.00			
$3.00			
$2.00			
$1.00			
$0.00			

6. Suppose that the strawberry market in question #5 was subjected to price controls. Answer the following questions assuming that the demand equation is $Q_D = 600 - 100P$ and the supply equation is $Q_S = 100P$:

a. If a price ceiling of $2 were placed on strawberries, what would be the quantity demanded? _____ At this ceiling price, what would be the quantity supplied? _____ Would there be a shortage or a surplus of strawberries at this price? _____

b. If lucky buyers could resell their strawberries to disappointed buyers, what is the market clearing price of the quantity of strawberries supplied in your answer to part a? _____

c. From your analysis in parts a and b, does the ceiling price on strawberries actually make strawberry consumers better off or worse off? Explain: _____

_____

_____

_____

- **TRUE - FALSE QUESTIONS** _____

For each of the following statements, indicate whether the statement is true (agrees with economic theory), false (is contradicted by economic theory), or uncertain (could be true or false; not enough information is given), and briefly explain your answer.

1. According to the law of demand, consumers purchase more at lower prices than they would at higher prices.

_____

_____

_____

_____

2. If the price of strawberries increases from $3 to $4 per quart, and the quantity of strawberries purchased increased from 2,000 to 3,000, the demand curve for strawberries must have shifted to the right.

_____

_____

_____

_____

3. If demand for a good increases while the supply of that good decreases, equilibrium price must increase, but equilibrium quantity might increase or decrease.

_____

_____

_____

_____

4. Inelastic demand means that the quantity of a good demanded is constant at all prices.

_____

_____

_____

_____

5. For a linear demand curve, the point of unit elasticity occurs at one-half of that price where quantity demanded becomes zero.

_____

_____

_____

_____

• MULTIPLE-CHOICE QUESTIONS

1. A rise in the price of tomatoes due to poor growing conditions will cause

   a. an increase in the demand for tomatoes.

   b. a decrease in the demand for tomatoes.

   c. an increase in the quantity of tomatoes demanded.

   d. a decrease in the quantity of tomatoes demanded.

2. If the government were to abolish child labor laws, the effect on the market for men's shirts would be to

   a. increase demand and raise price.

   b. increase demand and lower price.

   c. increase supply and lower price.

   d. decrease supply and raise price.

3. A rise in the wages of all workers in the economy will cause

   a. an increase in the demand for haircuts.

   b. a decrease in the supply of haircuts.

   c. an increase in the demand for haircuts and a decrease in the supply of haircuts.

   d. a decrease in the demand for haircuts and an increase in the supply of haircuts.

4. A fall in the demand for drugs will cause

   a. a decrease in the price of drugs.

   b. an increase in the price of drugs.

   c. a decrease in the supply of drugs.

   d. an increase in the supply of drugs.

5. If the price of good X rises and, as a result, the demand for good Y falls, then goods X and Y must be

   a. complements.

   b. substitutes.

   c. inferior.

   d. normal.

6. If we observe a fall in the price of cars accompanied by an increase in car sales, we would suspect

   a. an increase in demand.

   b. a decrease in demand.

   c. an increase in supply.

   d. a decrease in supply.

7. The introduction of rent controls in a previously unregulated rental market would

   a. create a shortage of rental units.

   b. create a surplus of rental units.

   c. shift the demand curve for rental units outward.

   d. shift the demand curve for rental units inward.

8. If the price of shoes rose 10 percent and the quantity of shoes purchased fell by 12 percent, then

    a. the demand for shoes is price elastic.

    b. the demand for shoes is price inelastic.

    c. the demand for shoes is unitary elastic.

    d. any of the above may be true; it is impossible to tell without additional information.

9. If a price of $90 is associated with a quantity of 600 and a price of $110 is associated with a quantity of 400, arc price elasticity of demand over this range is

    a. -0.1.   b. -1.

    c. -2.   d. -10.

10. If Jean, the barber, raised the price of his nose hair clippers and total revenue is unchanged, then

    a. demand is price elastic.

    b. demand is price inelastic.

    c. demand is unitary elastic.

    d. any of the above may be true; it is impossible to tell without additional information.

- **ANSWERS TO PROBLEMS, TRUE-FALSE QUESTIONS, AND MULTIPLE-CHOICE QUESTIONS**

Answers to Problems

1.   a. A rise in the wage of strawberry pickers would shift the supply curve to the left, equilibrium price would increase and equilibrium quantity would decrease.

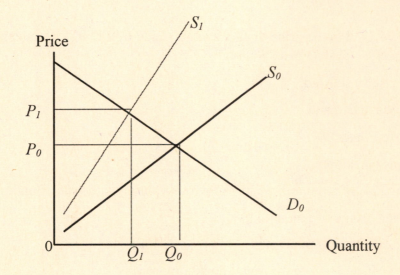

b. A reduction in the price of a complement will increase demand, increasing both equilibrium price and equilibrium quantity.

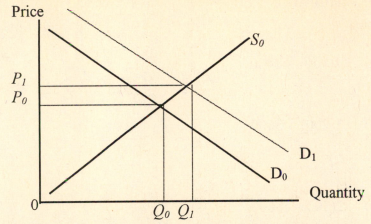

c. Blight in Europe would cause European countries to import strawberries from the United States. This increase in demand causes the quantity exchanged and price to both rise.

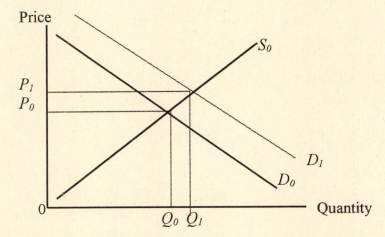

d. A reduction in the price of blueberries, a substitute for strawberries, would reduce the demand for strawberries, reducing the equilibrium price and quantity exchanged.

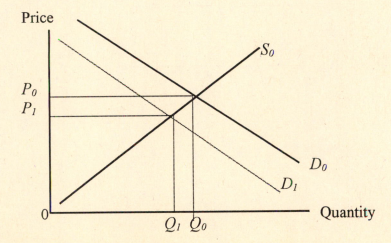

2.

Price	Quantity Demanded	Total Expenditure	Point Price Elasticity
$5.00	$Q_D = 500 - 100(5) = 0$	$5(0) = 0$	$E_P = -100\dfrac{5}{0} = -\infty$
$4.00	$Q_D = 500 - 100(4) = 100$	$4(100) = \$400$	$E_P = -100\dfrac{4}{100} = -4$
$3.00	$Q_D = 500 - 100(3) = 200$	$3(200) = \$600$	$E_P = -100\dfrac{3}{200} = -\dfrac{3}{2} = -1.$
$2.00	$Q_D = 500 - 100(2) = 300$	$2(300) = \$600$	$E_P = -100\dfrac{2}{300} = -\dfrac{2}{3} = -0.$
$1.00	$Q_D = 500 - 100(1) = 400$	$1(400) = \$400$	$E_P = -100\dfrac{1}{400} = -\dfrac{1}{4} = -0.$
$0.00	$Q_D = 500 - 100(0) = 500$	$0(500) = 0$	$E_P = -100\dfrac{0}{500} = -0 = 0$

3.

Price Pairs	Quantity Pairs	Arc Price Elasticity
$5.00 to $4.00	100 to 200	$E_P = \dfrac{100-200}{5-4} \times \dfrac{5+4}{100+200} = \dfrac{-100}{1} \times \dfrac{9}{300} = -3$
$4.00 to $3.00	200 to 400	$E_P = -100\dfrac{1}{400} = -\dfrac{1}{4} = -0.25$
$3.00 to $2.00	400 to 750	$E_P = \dfrac{400-750}{3-2} \times \dfrac{3+2}{400+750} = \dfrac{-350}{1} \times \dfrac{5}{1150} = -1.52$
$2.00 to $1.00	750 to 1,200	$E_P = \dfrac{750-1200}{2-1} \times \dfrac{2+1}{750+1200} = \dfrac{-450}{1} \times \dfrac{3}{1950} = -0.6923$

4. a. Note, the demand equation becomes $Q_D = 500 - 100P_s + 50(2) - 20(1) = 500 - 100P_s$

Price	Quantity Demanded	Total Expenditure	Point Price Elasticity
$5.00	$Q_D = 580 - 100(5) = 80$	$5(80) = 400$	$E_P = -100\dfrac{5}{80} = -6.25$
$4.00	$Q_D = 580 - 100(4) = 180$	$4(180) = \$720$	$E_P = -100\dfrac{4}{180} = -2.22$
$3.00	$Q_D = 580 - 100(3) = 280$	$3(280) = \$840$	$E_P = -100\dfrac{3}{280} = -1.07$
$2.00	$Q_D = 580 - 100(2) = 380$	$2(300) = \$760$	$E_P = -100\dfrac{2}{380} = -0.526$
$1.00	$Q_D = 580 - 100(1) = 480$	$1(480) = \$480$	$E_P = -100\dfrac{1}{480} = -0.2083$
$0.00	$Q_D = 580 - 100(0) = 580$	$0(500) = 0$	$E_P = -100\dfrac{0}{580} = -0 = 0$

b. If P_c increases to $1.50, while $P_b = \$2.00$, the demand equation becomes

$Q_D = 500 - 100P_s + 50(2) - 20(1.5) = 570 - 100P_s$, that is, quantity demanded decreases by 10 at each price

Price	Quantity Demanded	Expenditure	Point Price Elasticity
$5.00	70	$350	-7.14
$4.00	170	$680	-2.35
$3.00	270	$810	-1.11
$2.00	370	$740	-0.54
$1.00	470	$470	-0.21
$0.00	570	$0	0.00

c. If $P_c = \$1.50$, and $P_b = \$1.00$, $Q_D = 500 - 100P_s + 50(1) - 20(1.5) = 530 - 100P_s$, that is, quantity demanded decreases by 40 at each price, relative to part b

Price	Quantity Demanded	Expenditure	Point Price Elasticity
$5.00	30	$150	-16.67
$4.00	130	$520	-3.08
$3.00	230	$690	-1.30
$2.00	330	$660	-0.61
$1.00	430	$430	-0.23
$0.00	530	$0	0.00

5.

Price	Quantity Demanded	Quantity Supplied	State of Market
$5.00	100	500	surplus
$4.00	200	400	surplus
$3.00	300	300	equilibrium
$2.00	400	200	shortage
$1.00	500	100	shortage

6. a. With a price ceiling = $2, quantity demanded = <u>400</u> and quantity supplied = <u>200</u>. There would be a <u>shortage</u> of strawberries at this price.

   b. If lucky buyers could sell their strawberries, the market clearing price would equal <u>$4.00.</u>

   c. Price controls actually make strawberry consumers worse off, because ultimate consumers pay $4 under price controls, but the equilibrium price would be $3 without controls.

Answers to True-False Questions

1. *False.* According to the law of demand, consumers *demand a larger quantity* at lower prices than they would at higher prices. In order for consumers to *purchase* the quantity they demand, sellers must be willing to supply that quantity or more. That is, just because quantity demanded increases as price decreases does not necessarily mean that consumers will actually be able to buy more; there could be a shortage if price controls or other impediments to market functioning prevent equilibrium.

2. *True.* According to the law of demand, an increase in the price of strawberries should decrease the quantity demanded. If we observe more being purchased at a higher price, we can infer that some other factor (e.g., an increase in income, a decrease in the price of a substitute, an increase in the price of a complement, an increase in the number of buyers) caused demand to increase, which caused price to increase until quantity demanded and quantity supplied were again equal.

3. *True.* Both an increase in demand and a decrease in supply would increase equilibrium price. By itself, however, an increase in demand would increase quantity exchanged, and a decrease in supply would reduce quantity exchanged, so the overall effect on quantity is ambiguous.

4. *False.* This is a common mistake. Inelastic demand means that the percentage change in quantity is smaller (in absolute value) than the percentage change in price; inelastic demand does not mean that quantity does not change. This would happen only in the extreme case of zero elastic demand, and few, if any, products exhibit this extreme lack of responsiveness of quantity demanded to price.

5. *True.* A linear demand curve has an equation like $Q_d = a - bP$, where a is the quantity demanded when $P = 0$, and $-b$ is $\dfrac{\Delta Q_d}{\Delta P}$. Solving for $Q_d = 0$, we find

$P_{max} = \dfrac{a}{b}$. Applying the formula for point elasticity, we have

$$E_P = \frac{\Delta Q_d}{\Delta P} \times \frac{P}{Q_d} = -b\frac{P}{a-bP} = -1 \rightarrow -bP = -a+bP \rightarrow 2bP = a \rightarrow P = \frac{a}{2b} = \frac{1}{2}P_{max}$$

That is, the point of unit price elasticity occurs at the midpoint of the demand curve, or at one-half the highest price consumers would pay.

Answers to Multiple Choice Questions

1. d 2. d 3. c 4. a 5. a 6. c 7. a 8. a
9. c 10. c

Chapter 2

CONSUMER BEHAVIOR AND MARKET DEMAND

• LEARNING OBJECTIVES

After completing this chapter, you should be able to

1. Explain the assumptions necessary to construct the economic model of consumer preferences.

2. Draw an indifference curve and explain the reasons underlying its shape.

3. Construct an indifference curve map and use it to depict consumer preferences.

4. Appreciate how consumer preferences are revealed through the marginal rate of substitution.

5. Employ a budget constraint to depict the options a consumer confronts in the market.

6. Juxtapose an indifference map and a budget line to illustrate how an individual maximizes utility subject to an income constraint.

7. Construct an individual demand function from the price-consumption path.

8. Aggregate individual demand curves to develop the market demand curve.

9. Distinguish between substitutes and complements and calculate the arc cross-price elasticity of demand.

• CHAPTER OVERVIEW

Consumer Preferences and Utility

This chapter explains how individuals make choices in an environment of scarcity. We assume that people seek to maximize their satisfaction or **utility.** The alternative collections of goods from which they choose are called **market baskets.** When consumers consider their options, we assume that they (1) can rank all consumption prospects (the completeness assumption), (2) make the same choices whenever confronted with the same options (consistency), (3) avoid contradictions in their choices (transitivity), and (4) prefer more to less.

Indifference Curves

To depict market baskets containing combinations of two commodities, economists construct **indifference curves.** Because more is preferred to less, consumers will be indifferent only among market baskets that contain more of one good and less of other goods. The exception to this rule occurs for **perfect complements**, commodities that must be consumed in fixed proportions. Because a typical person derives no additional satisfaction from an extra left shoe unless it is matched with an extra right shoe, the indifference curves for left and right shoes are L-shaped. Otherwise indifference curves are negatively sloped. If a consumer does not discriminate between two goods, such as two brands of writing paper, those goods will be considered **perfect substitutes**, and their indifference curves will be negatively sloped, straight lines.

The slope of the indifference curve is the **marginal rate of substitution**, indicating the maximum amount of one good a consumer would sacrifice in order to acquire another unit of the other good. Most pairs of commodities lie between the two extremes of perfect substitutes and perfect complements. This causes the marginal rate of substitution, the **slope of the indifference curve**, to become progressively flatter as one good increases (and the other good decreases). If I like sporting events and movies, and I have many season tickets to sporting events and few movie tickets, I may be willing to give up several sports tickets for one movie ticket. But as I continue to substitute movie tickets for sports tickets, I begin to get stingy with those sports tickets. Eventually, when I have few sports tickets and many movie tickets, it may take quite a few extra movie tickets to induce me to part with a sports ticket.

Indifference maps depict levels of (ordinal) utility associated with higher and lower orders of consumer options. In **Figure 2-1**, points **A** and **C** are both on seven-year-old Jennie's indifference curve U_0. This means that Jennie would not care if her best friend or the class bully chose between those two prospects. Note that point **A** has more stuffed toys and fewer clothes than point **C**. If she received more clothes and kept all her stuffed toys, she would attain indifference curve U_1 at point **B**. Her gain in satisfaction could be depicted

as $\Delta U = \dfrac{\Delta U}{\Delta q_1} \Delta q_1$, that is, the change in utility is the additional utility per unit of good 1,

clothes (the **marginal utility** of clothes) times the additional amount of that good. To bring her back to the same level of satisfaction, she must give up enough of good 2 (stuffed toys) to achieve point **C**. From **B** to **C**, the change in satisfaction is

$\Delta U = \dfrac{\Delta U}{\Delta q_2} \Delta q_2$. Between point **A** and point **C**, satisfaction did not change, so

$\dfrac{\Delta U}{\Delta q_1} \Delta q_1 = -\dfrac{\Delta U}{\Delta q_2} \Delta q_2$, or $MU_1 \Delta q_1 = -MU_2 \Delta q_2$. It follows that the marginal rate of

substitution $(-\Delta q_2 / \Delta q_1)$, must equal the ratio of marginal utilities (MU_1 / MU_2). The maximum amount of good 2 a person will give up to get another unit of good 1 equals the ratio of the marginal utility of good 1 divided by the marginal utility of good 2. **Marginal utility** is the additional amount of satisfaction obtained from one more of one good, the consumption of all other goods remaining constant.

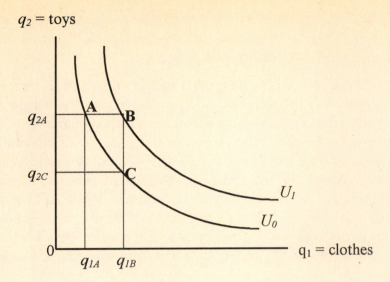

Figure 2-1

Figure 2-1 depicts two indifference curves out of all possible indifference curves, which constitute the consumer's indifference map. Because of the assumption that more is preferred to less, indifference curves further away from the origin (up and to the right) represent increasingly preferred market baskets. We could assign numbers of *utils* (a subjective measure of utility or satisfaction) to each indifference curves, with those curves nearest the origin having the lowest numbers. However, for our purposes, consumers don't need to know exactly how much satisfaction they get from particular market baskets; they just need to be able to rank market baskets. Because of the assumption of *transitivity*, indifference curves cannot intersect.

The Budget Constraint Line

Whereas the indifference map depicts what a consumer would *like* to have, the budget constraint shows what the consumer can actually purchase. The budget constraint divides the graph into those market baskets that the consumer can afford (below and on the budget constraint line) and those market baskets that he or she cannot afford (above the budget line). If we assume that the commodities in the market basket exhaust consumption opportunities (we will allow the possibilities of saving and borrowing in a later chapter), the consumer will choose a market basket that lies along the budget constraint (i.e., one that exhausts the consumer's entire income). The budget constraint line is obtained by first solving the budget equation, $I = P_x X + P_y Y$, for one of the

commodities, say Y: $Y = \dfrac{I}{P_Y} - \dfrac{P_x}{P_y} X$. The *y*-intercept, $\dfrac{I}{P_y}$, is the maximum amount of

good Y that could be purchased if all income were spent on good Y. The slope of the budget constraint line is $-\dfrac{P_x}{P_y}$; if the consumer wishes to purchase one more unit of good

X, he or she must sacrifice $\dfrac{P_x}{P_y}$ units of good Y.

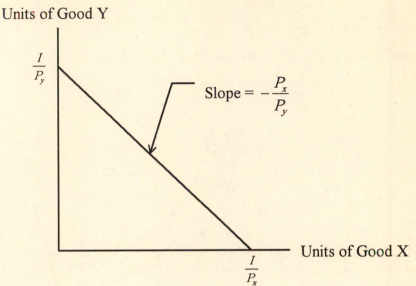

Figure 2-2

The budget constraint line in **Figure 2-2** is drawn under the assumption that the consumer's income, I, and the prices of the two goods, P_x and P_y, remain constant regardless of which market basket is chosen. Budget constraint lines will be kinked or curved if prices depend on quantity purchased. Discount schemes will kink the budget line out; if prices increase with consumption, budget lines would bend in toward the origin. An increase in income, prices constant, will cause a parallel, rightward (or upward) shift in the budget line; a decrease in income, prices constant, causes a parallel leftward (or downward) shift in the budget line. An increase in the price of good X, holding income and the price of Y constant, will cause the x-intercept to move closer to the origin; the new budget line will be steeper than the previous budget line.

Consumer Choice

We assume that the consumer wishes to reach a point on the highest indifference curve consistent with the budget constraint; that is, the consumer wishes to achieve the maximum satisfaction, given his/her income and the prices of goods. Laying the consumer's indifference map over the budget constraint line as shown in **Figure 2-3** solves the utility maximization problem. Note that the budget line intersects indifference curve U_0 at point **A** and point **A'**. These market baskets are feasible (they are on the budget constraint line), but they are not the best options. At point **A,** the consumer is willing to sacrifice more units of good Y than the market requires. That is, the consumer's $\text{MRS}_{Y \text{ for } X}$ exceeds the market's $\text{MRS} = -P_X/P_Y$. Substituting good X for good Y along the budget line allows the consumer to achieve higher satisfaction. At point **B** the consumer has achieved a point on indifference curve U_1, but this is still not a utility maximum. Further substitution of X for

Y eventually moves the consumer to point **C**, where indifference curve U_2 is *tangent* to the budget constraint line. Here the consumer has reconciled the marginal rate of substitution with the ratio of the market prices; further substitution (e.g., to point **B'** or point **A'**) would make the consumer worse off. Mathematically, at point **C**:

$-\dfrac{MU_x}{MU_y} = -\dfrac{P_x}{P_y}$, or $\dfrac{MU_x}{P_x} = \dfrac{MU_y}{P_y}$. The consumer maximizes satisfaction by purchasing

that bundle which offers the same marginal utility per dollar spent on all goods purchased.

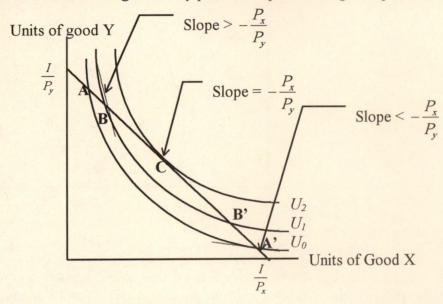

Figure 2-3

Changes in Price

Imagine that the consumer is initially maximizing utility at point **C**, when the price of good X falls, while money income, the price of good Y, and tastes remain constant. Note that in **Figure 2-4,** the decrease in the price of X causes the budget line to become flatter; each unit of X purchased now requires a smaller sacrifice of good Y. Referring to the original price as P_{x0}, and the new price as P_{x1}, we have $P_{x0} > P_{x1}$. Before the price change, at

point **C**, $\dfrac{MU_x}{P_{x0}} = \dfrac{MU_y}{P_y}$; after the price decrease, $\dfrac{MU_x}{P_{x1}} > \dfrac{MU_y}{P_y}$ at point **C** because

$P_{x0} > P_{x1}$. The consumer accommodates the price change by increasing the consumption of X (and changing the consumption of Y) until $\dfrac{MU_x}{P_{x1}} = \dfrac{MU_y}{P_y}$ at point **D**.

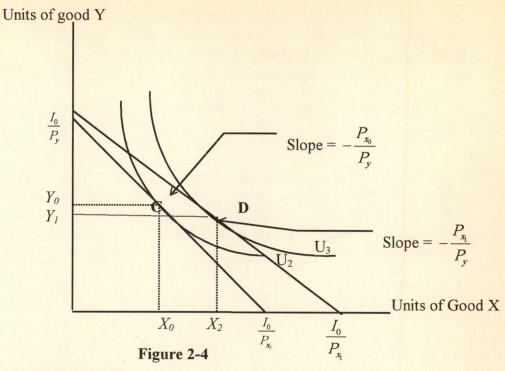

Units of good Y

Slope $= -\dfrac{P_{x_0}}{P_y}$

Slope $= -\dfrac{P_{x_1}}{P_y}$

$\dfrac{I_0}{P_y}$

Y_0
Y_1

C

D

U_3

U_2

Units of Good X

X_0 X_2 $\dfrac{I_0}{P_{x_0}}$ $\dfrac{I_0}{P_{x_1}}$

Figure 2-4

The Consumer Demand Curve

If we plot the prices of good X on the vertical axis, and the associated quantities of X that would maximize utility on the horizontal axis, we obtain the **consumer demand curve**, as shown in **Figure 2-5**. Note that the consumer demand curve reflects all the purchases a consumer would be willing and able to make at alternative prices, *if* **income, the prices of the other good, and tastes are constant.** Note that this is exactly how the demand curve was defined in Chapter 1.

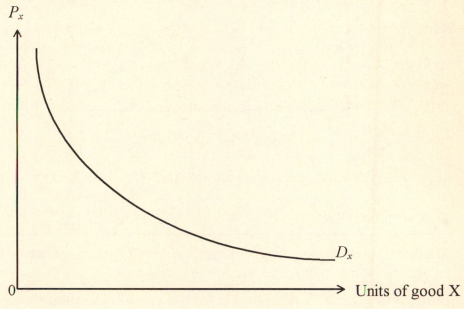

P_x

D_x

0   Units of good X

Figure 2-5

Page 24

The response of consumers to relative price changes can also be used to determine whether goods are substitutes or complements. In Figure 2-4, good Y is a substitute for good X, because when the price of good X decreased, the consumption of good Y also decreased. Substitutes have an arc cross-price elasticity that is negative; if X and Y are substitutes, $E_{YP_x} = \dfrac{\Delta Y}{\Delta P_x} \times \dfrac{P_x^1 + P_x^2}{Y_1 + Y_2} > 0$ because Y increases when P_x increases.

Figure 2-6 shows how goods X and Y can be complements. An increase in the price of X would cause the consumer to decrease consumption of X. If expenditure on X increases (the demand for X is price inelastic), then the expenditure on Y will have to fall. This means that the consumption on X must decrease. The consumption of Y moves in the opposite direction to the price of X. The arc cross-price elasticity is negative:

$$E_{YP_x} = \dfrac{\Delta Y}{\Delta P_x} \times \dfrac{P_x^1 + P_x^2}{Y_1 + Y_2} < 0 \,.$$

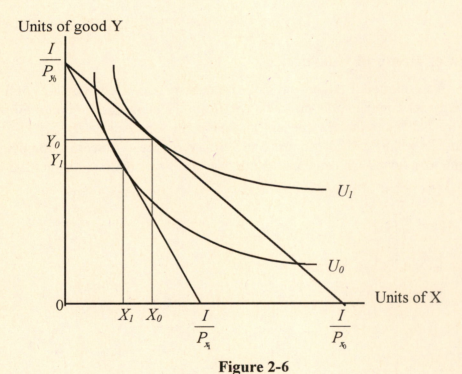

Figure 2-6

• KEY TERMS

Market basket A combination of commodities that represents one option on the indifference curve map or the budget constraint line.

Indifference curve A set of market baskets providing a consumer with the same level of satisfaction or utility.

Diminishing marginal rate of substitution As the consumer substitutes goods along an indifference curve, less and less of one good will be sacrificed to obtain more units of the other good.

Indifference map A diagram showing a set of difference curves, representing higher levels of satisfaction as consumption prospects move further from the origin.

Affordable market baskets Market baskets that lie on or below the budget constraint line.

Specialization in consumption When the consumer elects to purchase only one of two commodities because the marginal utility to price ratio of the first unit of the good not consumed is less than the marginal utility to price ratio of the last unit of the good that is consumed.

Consumer demand function The function or diagram obtained by plotting the price of a good on the vertical axis, and the associated quantities of that good that maximize utility on the horizontal axis, holding money income, the price of the other good(s), and tastes constant.

Substitutes Commodities whose consumption moves in opposite directions in response to a price change. If the price of butter rises, people consume less butter. Because they are consuming less butter, they consume more margarine, even though the price of margarine has not changed.

Complements Commodities whose consumption moves in the same direction when the price of a commodity changes. If the price of tea rises, people consume less tea. Because they are consuming less tea, they also consume less lemon, even if the price of lemon does not change. Lemon is a complementary good for tea.

Transitivity The assumption that if market basket **A** is preferred to market basket **B**, and if market basket **B** is preferred to market basket **C**, then **A** is preferred to **C**.

Marginal rate of substitution The maximum amount of one good a consumer would sacrifice to obtain another unit of some other good: $MRS_{yx} = -\dfrac{\Delta Y}{\Delta X}\Big|_{U=\text{constant}} = \dfrac{MU_x}{MU_y}$.

Perfect substitutes Pairs of commodities whose indifference curves are negatively sloped straight lines (constant MRS).

Perfect complements Pairs of commodities whose indifference curves are L-shaped; the marginal rate of substitution is undefined.

Budget constraint A line depicting the combination of commodities that exhaust the consumer's income.

Maximal utility The level of satisfaction achieved when the consumer purchases that bundle where the (highest) indifference curve is tangent to the budget constraint line.

Composite good A good depicting all other commodities that could be purchased instead of the good in question. Usually plotted on the y-axis, the composite good has a price of

1, so it is measured as purchasing power remaining after a specific quantity of the other good (plotted on the *x*-axis) is purchased.

Market demand function The function or curve obtained by adding up the total quantity demanded by all consumers at each price of a particular good.

Earmarked subsidies Income subsidies that must be spent on specified goods or services.

Unrestricted subsidies Income subsidies that can be spent as the recipient desires.

• PROBLEMS

1. For each of the following situations, indicate what of the assumptions of consumer preference theory, if any, are being violated:

   a. I can't make up my mind between chocolate and vanilla ice cream.

   _____

   b. Monday I eat donuts instead of bagels. Tuesday I eat bagels instead of donuts. Neither price has changed.

   _____

   c. I prefer fish to chicken, I prefer chicken to steak, and I prefer steak to fish.

   _____

   d. I consider one more can of Coke equivalent to one more can of Pepsi, no matter how much soda I have already drunk.

   _____

   e. Another pretzel is useless to me unless I also get another beer.

   _____

Chart 2-1 refers to Maria's indifference map between books and CDs. Use it to answer Problems 2 and 3.

Chart 2-1

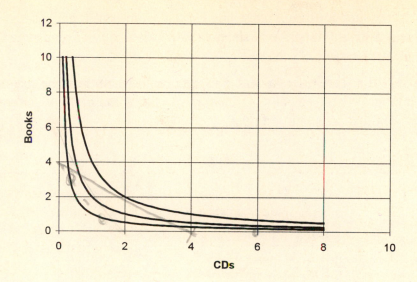

2. Suppose that Maria has a budget of $40 per month to spend on these items; the price of books is $10 each, and each CD has a price of $20.

   a. Draw Maria's budget constraint line; label the y-intercept I_0/P_{b0}, and label the x-intercept I_0/P_{c0}.

   b. What market basket of books and CDs maximizes utility, given Maria's income and the prices of the commodities?

   _____

   c. What is the price ratio (P_c/P_b) at the optimal market basket?

   _____

   d. What is the marginal rate of substitution at the optimal market basket?

   _____

3. a. Redraw Maria's budget constraint assuming that her income remains $60 per month and the price of CD's falls to $10. Label the y-intercept I_0/P_{b0} and label the x-intercept I_0/P_{c1}.

   b. What market basket maximizes Maria's utility?

   _____

   c. What is the price ratio (P_c/P_b) at the optimal market basket?

   _____

   d. What is the marginal rate of substitution at the optimal market basket?

   _____

4. The graph below shows an indifference map between shoes and pants.

    a. Draw the budget constraint line when income equals $120 per month and the price of pants is $30 and the price of shoes is $30. Also draw the consumer's optimum point.

    b. Suppose that a store offers a deal: Buy one pair of pants, get the second pair free (with a limit of two free pairs per customer). Draw the new budget constraint and the new optimal consumption point.

Chart 2-2

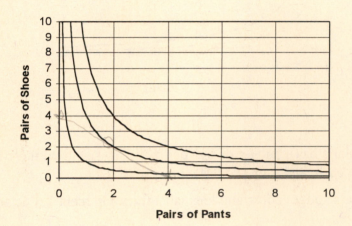

5. The arc cross-price elasticity between lemon and tea is –0.5. Are tea and lemon substitutes or complements? Explain.

   _____

   _____

   _____

6. Suppose that the price of cabbage rises from $0.50 per pound to $0.75 per pound and that this causes the sales of corned beef to fall from 1,000 pounds per week to 800 pounds per week.

    a. What is the arc cross-price elasticity of demand?

   _____

    b. Are the goods complements or substitutes? Why?

   _____

   _____

   _____

• TRUE - FALSE QUESTIONS

For each of the following statements, indicate whether the statement is true (agrees with economic theory), false (is contradicted by economic theory), or uncertain (could be true or false; not enough information is given), and briefly explain your answer.

1. Indifference curves are negatively sloped because more is preferred to less.

_____

_____

_____

_____

2. Consumers who buy new cars instead of used cars are not behaving rationally, since they fail to buy the least expensive car.

_____

_____

_____

_____

3. If monthly income and in all prices increased by ten percent, the consumer would not change his or her purchases, as long as preferences remained constant.

_____

_____

_____

_____

4. If the demand for good X is price inelastic, an increase in the price of X will lead to a decrease in the consumption of the composite good, if money income, tastes, and the price of the composite good remain constant.

_____

_____

_____

_____

5. In deciding between movie tickets and sports tickets, Jacques chooses only sports tickets. Jacques is not maximizing utility.

_____

_____

_____

_____

• MULTIPLE CHOICE QUESTIONS

1. Indifference curves typically have a negative slope because

   a. more of commodity X makes the consumer better off, whereas more of commodity Y makes the consumer worse off.

   b. loss of X requires compensation with more Y to keep utility constant.

   c. the consumer prefers some market baskets to others.

   d. the willingness to give up X to obtain Y diminishes as more Y is consumed.

2. The case of perfect substitutes means that the indifference curves will be

   a. L-shaped.

   b. bowed from the origin.

   c. bowed to the origin.

   d. straight lines.

3. If Jill is willing to sacrifice up to 10 units of Y to get 2 units of X, her marginal rate of substitution (MRS_{yx}) is

   a. −5

   b. −2

   c. −1/2

   d. −1/5

4. If indifference curve I_1 is assigned 100 utils and indifference curve I_2 is assigned 200 utils by the consumer,

   a. I_2 has twice the utility of I_1.

   b. I_1 has twice the utility of I_2.

   c. I_1 is preferred to I_2.

   d. I_2 is preferred to I_1.

5. Angelo has $150 to spend on entertainment each month and theater tickets cost $50 while movie tickets cost $10. He typically attends the theater twice and attends the movies five times per month.

   a. Angelo is maximizing utility if his marginal rate of substitution of theater tickets to movie tickets is $MRS_{tm} = -0.4$.

   b. Angelo is maximizing utility if his marginal rate of substitution of theater tickets to movie tickets is $MRS_{tm} = -0.2$.

   c. Angelo is maximizing utility if his marginal rate of substitution of theater tickets to movie tickets is $MRS_{tm} = -2.5$.

   d. Angelo is maximizing utility if his marginal rate of substitution of theater tickets to movie tickets is $MRS_{tm} = -5$.

6. If $P_x = \$12$ and $\$P_y = \$24$ and income is $240 per month, utility is maximized when

   a. the consumer buys only good Y.

   b. the consumer buys only good X.

   c. the consumer buys so that her $MRS_{yx} = -1/2$.

   d. any of the above could be true.

7. If the price of good X increases, while the price of Y and income remain constant, and the consumer buys less of both goods.

   a. the consumer did not maximize utility.

   b. X and Y must be complements.

   c. X and Y must be substitutes.

   d. any of the above could be true; we cannot tell without more information.

8. The price of membership in a snooker club is $50; thereafter, the price of each game is $0.50. Alternatively, nonmembers can pay $2.50 per game. How many games would you have to play to be just indifferent to joining or not joining?

   a. 20

   b. 25

   c. 30

   d. 35

9. If shoes are discounted 10 percent and socks are discounted 20 percent, then

   a. the budget constraint shifts outward, parallel to the original budget constraint.

   b. the budget constraint shifts inward, parallel to the original budget constraint.

   c. the budget constraint shifts outward and has a different slope than the original budget constraint.

   d. the budget constraint shifts inward and has a different slope than the original budget constraint.

10. If the consumer purchases good X at $20 each, good Y at $10 each, but purchases no units of good Z at $5 each,

   a. the consumer is behaving irrationally.

   b. the consumer is behaving rationally but is still not maximizing utility.

   c. the first unit of good Z must have a marginal utility less than half the marginal utility last unit of good Y.

   d. the first unit of good Z must have a marginal utility greater than one-fourth the marginal utility of the last unit of good X.

• ANSWERS TO PROBLEMS, TRUE-FALSE, AND MULTIPLE-CHOICE QUESTIONS

Answers to Problems:

1. a. Violates completeness assumption.

   b. Violates consistency assumption.

   c. Violates transitivity assumption.

   d. Violates no assumptions; Coke and Pepsi are perfect substitutes.

   e. Violates no assumptions; pretzels and beers are perfect complements.

Chart 2-1a

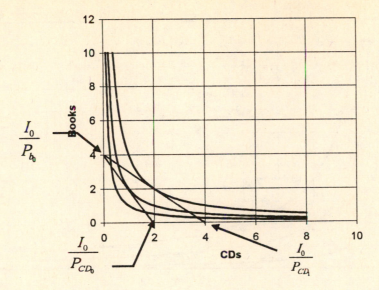

2. a. $\dfrac{I_0}{P_{b_0}}$ = 4 books; $\dfrac{I_0}{P_{CD_0}}$ = 2 CDs

   b. Approximately 1 CD and 2 books per month.

   c. $-\dfrac{P_{CD}}{P_b} = -\dfrac{20}{10} = -2$

   d. $MRS_{bCD} = -\dfrac{P_{CD}}{P_b} = -\dfrac{20}{10} = -2$

3. a. The new budget line connects $\dfrac{I_0}{P_{b_0}}$ and $\dfrac{I_0}{P_{CD_1}}$ in Chart 2-1a.

   b. Approximately 2 books and 2 CDs.

   c. $-\dfrac{P_{CD}}{P_b} = -\dfrac{10}{10} = -1$

   d. $MRS_{bCD} = -\dfrac{P_{CD}}{P_b} = -\dfrac{10}{10} = -1$

Chart 2-2a

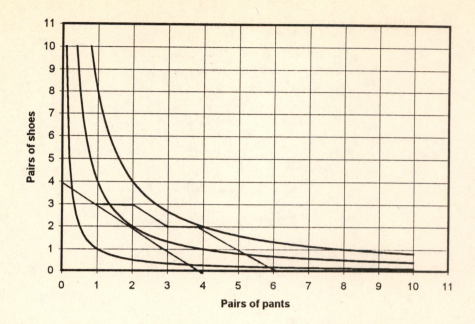

4. a. The budget constraint line is a straight line connecting 4 pairs of shoes and 4 pairs of pants. The optimal market basket is 2 pairs of shoes and 2 pairs of pants.

    b. The budget constraint line is kinked, with the new optimal market basket at 4 pairs of pants and 2 pairs of shoes.

5. Commodities with negative arc cross-price elasticities are complements; therefore, tea and lemon are complementary goods.

6. a. $E_{cb,c} = \dfrac{\Delta Q_b}{\Delta P_{cb}} \times \dfrac{P_{cb_1} + P_{cb_2}}{Q_{b_1} + Q_{b_1}} = \dfrac{-200}{0.25} \times \dfrac{0.50 + 0.75}{1,000 + 800} = \dfrac{-200}{0.25} \times \dfrac{1.25}{1,800} = -0.56$

    b. Corned beef and cabbage are complementary goods because they have a negative cross price elasticity.

Answers to True-False Questions

1. *True*. Because more is preferred to less, an increase in one commodity while the other commodity remained constant would increase satisfaction (raise the consumer to a higher indifference curve). Accordingly, if one commodity increases, the other commodity must decrease in order for the consumer to remain on the same indifference curve. This causes the indifference curve to have a negative slope ($\dfrac{\Delta Y}{\Delta X} < 0$).

2. *False*. This is a case of specialization in consumption. The ratio of marginal utility to price is greater for the new car than for the used car; this consumer maximizes utility by purchasing the new car and not purchasing a used car.

3. *True*. With income and prices changing by the same percentage, neither the intercepts nor the slope of the budget constraint line would change. Given the same indifference map (tastes do not change), the tangency point on the highest indifference curve would not change.

4. *True*. An increase in the price of X will increase expenditure on X when the demand for X is price inelastic. This leaves less income for other goods, which is the composite good. The consumption of the composite good must decrease.

5. *False*. Economists never have a basis for concluding that individuals did not maximize utility. This is a simple case of a corner solution, where the marginal utility of the last dollar spent on sports tickets exceeds the marginal utility of the first dollar spent on movie tickets.

Answers to Multiple Choice Questions

1. b	2. d	3. a	4. d	5. b	6. d	7. b	8. b
9. c	10. c						

Chapter 3

EXTENDING THE THEORY OF CONSUMER BEHAVIOR

• LEARNING OBJECTIVES

After completing this chapter, you should be able to

1. Distinguish between normal goods and inferior goods.

2. Separate the consumer's response to a change in the price of a good into the substitution effect and the income effect.

3. Understand how the slope of the demand curve is related to the size of the income and substitution effects.

4. List and explain the determinants of the elasticity of demand.

5. Understand, explain, and calculate consumer surplus.

6. Understand, explain, and calculate expected income.

7. Understand, explain, and calculate expected utility.

8. Explain how the relation between expected utility and expected income predicts risk preference.

• CHAPTER OVERVIEW

Income Effects

In Chapter 2 we saw that a consumer maximizes utility by allocating income so that the ratio of marginal utility to price is the same for all commodities. We saw that a change in the price of a good changes the optimal consumption of that good because (1) the opportunity cost of consuming a good has changed and (2) because the consumer's real income has changed. In this chapter we formalize this distinction. The change in consumption due to the change in the consumer's real income is called, appropriately, the **income effect** of a price change. The change in consumption due to the change in the relative price of that commodity is known as the **substitution effect**.

First we consider the effect of a change in real income, with the relative prices of commodities remaining constant. In **Figure 3-1** we imagine that income has increased from I_0 to I_1. Note that the new budget constraint line is parallel to the original budget constraint line; this is because the ratio of the prices, $\dfrac{P_x}{P_y}$, did not change, so the slopes of the two budget lines are the same. What did change are the number of market baskets the consumer can afford. Point **C** is no longer the optimal point because the consumer still has $I_1 - I_0$ income left over. By purchasing $(X_1 - X_0)$ extra units of X and $(Y_1 - Y_0)$ extra units of good Y, satisfaction has increased from U_2 to U_3 at point **C'**.

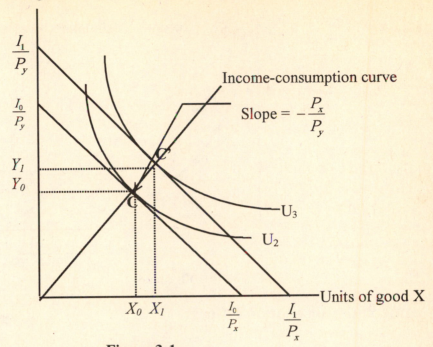

Figure 3-1

In Figure 3-1, goods X and Y are both **normal goods** because the consumption of each good increased when real income increased. In this case, real income increased because money income grew and prices remained constant; real income could also increase if money income remained constant and both prices fell proportionately. If the consumption of either good decreased after real income increased, then that good would be an **inferior good**. Not all the goods that a consumer purchases could be inferior goods, however, because if real income increases, the consumption of at least one good must increase.

A normal good's **income consumption curve** and its **Engel curve** will have a positive slopes. An inferior good's income consumption curve and its Engel curve will have negative slopes (**Figure 3-2**). The **income elasticity of demand** measures the percentage change in the quantity demanded due to a 1 percent increase in income. A normal good has a positive income elasticity of demand, and an inferior good has negative income elasticity.

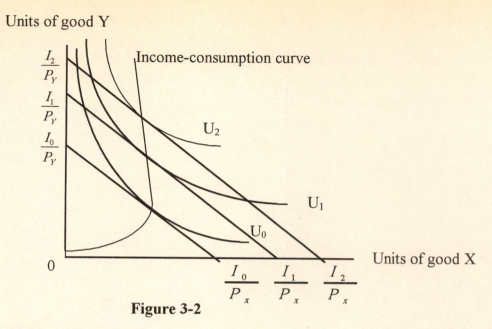

Figure 3-2

Income and Substitution Effects

In **Figure 3-3,** we consider the response of a consumer to the change in the price of one good. The consumer is initially maximizing utility at point **C** before the price of good X falls, while money income, the price of good Y, and tastes remain constant. Note that the decrease in the price of X causes the budget line to become flatter. Each unit of X purchased now requires a smaller sacrifice of good Y. Referring to the original price as P_{x0}, and the new price as P_{x1}, we have $P_{x0} > P_{x1}$. Before the price change, at point **C**,

$\dfrac{MU_x}{P_{x0}} = \dfrac{MU_y}{P_y}$; after the price decrease, $\dfrac{MU_x}{P_{x1}} > \dfrac{MU_y}{P_y}$ at point **C**, because $P_{x0} > P_{x1}$.

The consumer adjusts to the price change by increasing the consumption of X (and

changing the consumption of Y) until $\dfrac{MU_x}{P_{x1}} = \dfrac{MU_y}{P_y}$ at point **E**.

If the consumer were forced to remain on the same indifference curve, say, by reducing money income to I', the optimal point on indifference curve U_2 would be point **D**, where

$\dfrac{MU_x}{P_{x1}} = \dfrac{MU_y}{P_y}$. A movement from point **C** to point **D** along indifference curve U_2, is

called the **substitution effect** of the relative price change. Because of the curvature of indifference curves, the substitution effect always results in more consumption of the good whose relative price decreased and less consumption of the other good, whose relative price increased. Because real income increases when the price of a good decreases, the consumer would have unused purchasing power at point **D** and could increase utility by moving to point **E** on indifference curve U_3. Because, in this example, X and Y are normal goods, the increase in real income led to an increase in the consumption of both goods relative to point **D,** after the substitution effect is taken into account. For good X (whose relative price decreased), the income effect reinforces the substitution effect. For good Y (whose relative price increased), the income effect works in the opposite direction of the substitution effect. In this case, the substitution effect was stronger than the income effect, so that the overall consumption of good Y decreased when.

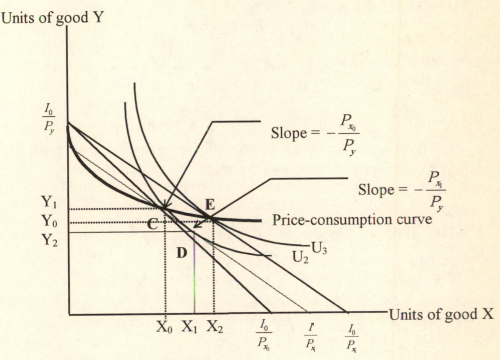

Figure 3.3

The Slutsky Equation

The substitution effect measures the change in the quantity demanded of X due to a change in the relative price of X, holding utility constant. The sign of the substitution effect is negative because quantity demanded changes in the opposite direction to the change in the price of X. The **Slutsky equation**, $\dfrac{\Delta X}{\Delta P} = \dfrac{\Delta X}{\Delta P}\Big|_{U=c} - X\left(\dfrac{\Delta X}{\Delta I}\right)$, breaks the total change in quantity demanded, $\dfrac{\Delta X}{\Delta P}$, into the substitution effect, $\dfrac{\Delta X}{\Delta P}\Big|_{U=c}$, and the income effect, $-X\left(\dfrac{\Delta X}{\Delta I}\right)$.

If the good is normal, the slope of the demand function will always be negative since the substitution effect is reinforced by the income effect. The demand function for an inferior good could be either negatively or positively sloped, depending on whether the income effect (which in this case leads quantity demanded to increase as the price rises) is larger or smaller than the substitution effect. For typical goods, the substitution effect is stronger the closer the two goods are to being perfect substitutes, and weaker the closer the two goods are to being complements. The income effect is larger for goods that consume a large part of the consumer's budget and for goods with a large income elasticity of demand.

Consumer Surplus

Consumer surplus is the difference between the maximum amount a consumer would be willing to pay to consume a given quantity and the amount the consumer actually pays. The consumer's **marginal value function** shows the maximum amount a consumer is willing to pay for an extra unit of a good. If there are no income effects, the marginal value function corresponds to the consumer's demand curve. In this case, the area under the demand curve represents the maximum amount the consumer would be willing to pay for each quantity of X. Consumer surplus is the area under the demand curve minus the amount the consumer actually pays for X (spending on $X = P_x Q_x$).

Producers often perceive consumer surplus as an additional source of revenue and profit. Government policies that set minimum price above the market equilibrium price transfer consumer surplus from consumers to producers. That part of consumer surplus, which is neither retained nor transferred, is the **dead weight loss**; dead weight loss is a waste.

Decision Making under Uncertainty

Although it is often convenient to imagine that economic decisions occur in an environment of **certainty** (each option has only one known outcome), many economic decisions occur in an environment of **uncertainty.** Economists deal with uncertainty by computing average or **expected** outcomes. The **expected income hypothesis** assumes that individuals evaluate uncertain prospects by their expected value. Suppose a baseball player has a 1 percent chance of making a major league baseball team and earning $400,000 per year. He also has a 99 percent chance of remaining on a minor league team and earning $40,000 per year. His expected income is obtained by multiplying each outcome by its probability and summing:

$$E(I) = .01(\$400,000) + .99(\$40,000) = \$4,000 + \$39,600 = \$43,600$$

Individuals who maximize expected income are called **risk-neutral** because they behave *as if* options are ranked strictly by their expected income. In our baseball example, a risk-neutral athlete would be indifferent between signing a contract to play baseball (not knowing whether he would play in the minor leagues or major leagues), or taking a coaching job that paid $43,600 with certainty. If he accepted a coaching job at less than $43,600, the athlete would display **risk-averse** behavior, since he paid a premium to avoid risk. If the athlete turned chose a professional baseball career over a coaching job paying more than $43,600 would display **risk-taking** behavior, since he paid a premium to accept risk.

Economists employ the **expected utility hypothesis** to explain and predict behavior under uncertain situations. Expected utility for a risk neutral person is proportional to expected income; marginal utility of income is constant. For a risk averse person, marginal utility of income decreases as income increases, so that certain prospects are preferred over uncertain prospects with the same expected income. Risk averse people typically buy insurance to reduce the cost of uncertainty. A **risk taking** person behaves as if the marginal utility of income increases as income increases; a risk taking person would prefer an uncertain prospect (because of the possiblity of a more favorable outcome) to a certain prospect with the same expected income. Risk taking people are more likely to gamble than risk-neutral or risk-averse people.

- ## KEY TERMS

Income effect The change in the consumption of a good due to the change in money income.

Substitution effect The measure of the change in quantity demanded due to a change in the relative price of a good holding utility constant, that is, while remaining on the same indifference curve.

Normal good A good whose consumption changes in the same direction as real income, tastes and relative prices remaining constant.

Inferior good A good whose consumption changes the opposite direction as real income, tastes and relative prices remaining constant.

Income elasticity of demand The percentage change in quantity demanded divided by the percentage change in income. As with price elasticity of demand, either the **arc income elasticity of demand,** $E_{I_{arc}} = \dfrac{\Delta X}{\Delta I} \times \dfrac{I_1 + I_2}{X_1 + X_2}$, or the **point income elasticity of demand,** $E_{I_{point}} = \dfrac{\Delta X}{\Delta I} \times \dfrac{I}{X}$, can be used.

Giffin good An inferior good whose income effect is stronger than its substitution effect, so that quantity demanded changes in the same direction as its price. Most economists consider the Giffin good an anomaly.

Marginal value function The expression for the maximum amount a consumer would pay for each unit of a good. When there is no income effect of a price change, the marginal value function is the same as the demand curve.

Consumer surplus The difference between the total value a consumer imputes to consuming a particular quantity of a good, and the amount actually paid to consume that quantity. Consumer surplus equals the sum of the difference between the marginal value function and the price that the consumer pays for each unit.

Dead weight loss The difference between the consumer surplus under ideal market conditions and the surplus transferred to others after the market process is distorted.

Probability The chance or likelihood that a particular state of nature will come to pass. Under certainty, outcomes have probabilities of 100 percent. Under uncertainty, outcomes have probabilities between 0 percent and 100 percent.

Expected income The sum of the probability of income in each possible state of nature times the value of that income: $E(I) = p_1 I_1 + p_2 I_2 + \cdots + p_n I_n$.

Expected utility   The sum of the probability of income in each possible state of nature times the value of the utility of that income: $E(I) = p_1U(I_1) + p_2U(I_2) + \cdots + p_nU(I_n)$.

Risk neutral   A person who makes decisions *as if* expected utility were proportional to expected income. This is equivalent to assuming that the marginal utility of income is constant.

Risk averse   Making decisions *as if* expected utility for certain prospects were greater than the expected utility of uncertain prospects with the same expected income. This is equivalent to assuming that the marginal utility of income decreases as income increases.

Risk taker   A person who makes decisions *as if* expected utility for uncertain prospects were greater than the expected utility of certain prospects with the same expected income. This is equivalent to assuming that the marginal utility of income increases as income increases.

Insurance A contract or policy that awards the policyholder a specified amount of money (or percent of a loss) in the event that a calamity (e.g., death, automobile accident, earthquake) occurs.

Premium What a policy holder actually pays for insurance coverage.

Load factor The difference between the premium and the expected loss from a calamity. The load factor covers the cost of administering policies (commissions to sales people, the cost of investigating claims) plus profit.

• PROBLEMS

1. Suppose that a consumer's income rises from $20,000 to $21,000 per year. Her purchases of gourmet ice cream, whose price is constant at $2.00 per pint, increase from 20 to 25 pints per year.

    a.   What is her arc income elasticity of demand?

    _____

    b.   Is gourmet ice cream a normal or inferior good for this customer?   Explain.

    _____

    c.   What happens to the share of income she spends on gourmet ice cream?

    _____

2. **Chart 3-1** is the indifference map for Clyde, a country-western fanatic. On the horizontal axis we plot the number of country-western recordings (CWCDs) and on the vertical axis we plot the composite good.

    a.   Assuming an income of $1,000 per month, with a price of $20 per CWCD, plot Clyde's budget constraint line and identify his optimal purchase of CWCDs. Label the initial tangency point **A**.

Chart 3-1

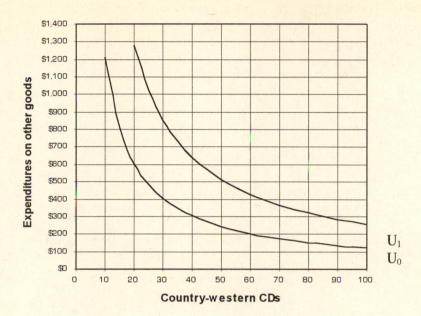

Country-western CDs

b. Now imagine that the price of CWCD's falls by 50% to $10 each, with income remaining at $1,000 per month. Show the substitution effect along indifference curve U_0 and label the consumption point at the new price ratio point **B**. ⁓

c. Using the data in part b, show the new budget constraint line, and show the income effect of this price change on indifference curve U_1. Label the optimal point that incorporates the income effect point **C**. Are CWCD's normal or inferior goods? Explain.

_____

_____

_____

d. Do Clyde's purchases of CWCDs follow the law of demand, according to your answer to part b of this question? Briefly explain.

_____

_____

_____

e. Did the income effect reinforce or counteract the substitution effect for Clyde? Explain how this is reflected in your answer to part c.

_____

_____

_____

3. **Chart 3-2** below shows Yvonne's demand curve for eclairs. You will need to calculate areas on the graph. The market price for eclairs is $4/lb. [Hint: It will help to remember that the area of a triangle is ½(LxW), where L is the length (quantity) and W is width (price).]

   a. What quantity of eclairs does Yvonne consume per month?

   _____

   b. What is her monthly expenditure on eclairs?

   _____

   c. What is the most that she would be willing to pay for that quantity?

   _____

Chart 3-2

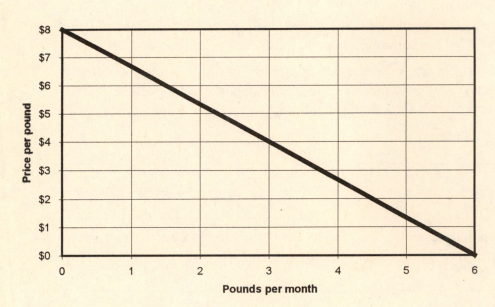

   d. What is her consumer surplus on the quantity consumed?

   _____

   d. If the Eclair Palace charged a cover charge of $5.50 to buy eclairs, would Yvonne continue to purchase there? Explain.

   _____

e. What assumption did you have to make to use the demand curve instead of the marginal value function to estimate consumer surplus? Does this assumption seem reasonable in this case?

_____

_____

_____

4. The government decides to impose a tax of $1 per pound on eclairs because they are bad for people's teeth. Illustrate the impact of the tax on **Chart 3-3**:

Chart 3-3

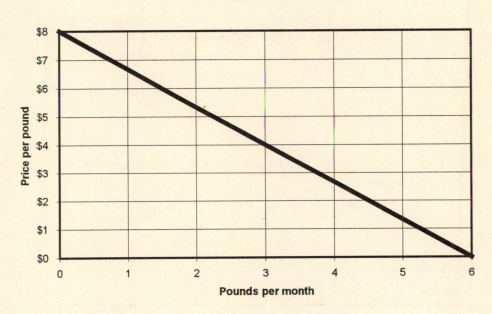

a. What happens to Yvonnne's monthly eclair purchases?

_____

b. What is the size of the consumer surplus after the tax?

_____

c. How much of the consumer surplus was lost as a result of the tax?

_____

d. How much tax revenue does the government receive from Yvonne?

_____

e. What is the size of the dead weight loss associated with the tax?

_____

5. You are thinking about buying your Aunt Violet's gift shop. You are guaranteed $50,000 per year if you do. Alternatively, you could put your money into Freefall Industries. You figure that there is a 50 percent chance you will make nothing and a 50 percent chance that you will make $80,000 per year in Freefall Industries.

a. If you wished to maximize **expected income**, which investment would you make? Briefly explain.

_____

_____

_____

b. Suppose you have a utility function such that you get 0 utils of satisfaction out of $0, 10 utils of satisfaction out of $50,000 and 30 utils of satisfaction out of $80,000. If you wished to maximize **expected utility**, which investment would you make? Show your calculations supporting your answer.

_____

_____

_____

c. According to your answers to part a and b, are you risk neutral, risk averse, or a risk taker? Explain.

_____

_____

_____

• TRUE-FALSE QUESTIONS

For each of the following statements, indicate whether the statement is true (agrees with economic theory), false (is contradicted by economic theory), or uncertain (could be true or false; not enough information is given), and briefly explain your answer.

1. All normal goods have negatively sloped demand curves.

_____

_____

_____

_____

2. All inferior goods have positively sloped demand curves.

_____

_____

_____

_____

3. When a consumer is purchasing goods X and Y and the price of X increases, the price of Y and income remain constant, the change in the consumption of good Y depends on whether the income or substitution effect of X is stronger.

_____

_____

_____

_____

4. James consumes two beers each Saturday night at either one of two bars near campus. He pays $2 per bottle at either bar. He would be willing to pay as much as $10 for two beers. One bar initiates a $5 per night cover charge. James' consumer surplus declines to $1 per Saturday night.

_____

_____

_____

_____

5. Risk averse people never gamble.

_____

_____

_____

_____

- **MULTIPLE CHOICE QUESTIONS**

1. Which of the following statements is *always* true?

   a. The income effect is negative.

   b. The substitution effect is negative.

   c. The income effect is positive.

   d. The substitution effect is positive.

2. Demand curves for normal goods have negative slopes because

   a. the substitution effect is greater than the income effect.

   b. the income effect is greater than the substitution effect.

   c. the substitution and income effects reinforce each other.

   d. the substitution and income effects offset each other.

3. If tofu has an income elasticity of demand equal to +0.7, then:

   a. tofu is a normal good.

   b. tofu is an inferior good.

   c. the *share* of income spent on tofu increases as income increases.

   d. the demand curve for tofu is positively sloped.

4. For an inferior good

   a. the income consumption curve has a negative slope and the Engel curve has a positive slope.

   b. the income consumption curve has a positive slope and the Engel curve has a negative slope.

   c. both the income consumption curve the Engel curve have a positive slope.

   d. both the income consumption curve the Engel curve have a negative slope.

5. Suppose that your income increased from $1,000 per month to $2,000 per month and that the number of restaurant meals you consumed rose from 5 to 15 per month. Your arc income elasticity of demand for restaurant meals is

   a. +0.67.

   b. +1.50.

   c. +2.00.

   d. +3.00.

6. If Sam were willing to pay up to $100 for a ticket to watch the finals of the U. S. Scrabble Championship, but he is lucky enough to buy a ticket for $15, then his consumer surplus on the ticket is

   a. $115.

   b. $100.

   c. $85.

   d. $15.

7. If the U. S. government imposes a quota on the importation of Japanese cars, then

   a. the price of Japanese cars will increase.

   b. Japanese car companies will gain surplus.

   c. U. S. buyers of Japanese cars will lose surplus.

   d. all of the above will occur.

8. Elizabeth owns an apartment building valued at $3 million. Because the building is located in an older part of town, she calculates that the probability that the building will be destroyed by fire is 1 percent per year. She buys government subsidized fire insurance for an annual premium of $10,000. Elizabeth must be:

   a. risk-averse.

   b. risk-neutral.

   c. a risk taker.

   d. one of the above, but it is impossible to tell without additional information.

9. Option 1 has a certain outcome of +$5,000. Option 2 has a 20 percent chance of $0, a 40 percent chance of +$2,500 and a 40 percent chance of +$10,000. A risk neutral investor would

   a. select 1.

   b. select 2.

   c. be indifferent.

   d. possibly due any of the above could be true.

10. If Bob's utility associated with $10,000 is 10 utils and his utility associated with $20,000 is 18 utils, Bob must be

   a. risk-averse.

   b. risk-neutral.

   c. risk-loving.

   d. one of the above, but it is impossible to say without additional information.

- ## ANSWERS TO PROBLEMS, TRUE-FALSE AND MULTIPLE CHOICE QUESTIONS

Problems

1. a. $E_{I_{arc}} = \dfrac{5}{1000} \times \dfrac{41,000}{45} = \dfrac{205}{45} = 4.56$.

   b. This is a normal good; the income elasticity is positive.

   c. The share of income spent on gourmet ice cream increases from 0.2 percent to 0.238 percent.

2. a. Point **A** occurs at approximately 25 CWCDs, leaving $700 for other goods.

   b. Point **B** occurs at approximately 35 CWCDs, leaving $350 for other goods.

   c. Point **C** occurs at approximately 50 CWCDs, leaving $500 for other goods. Since the income effect increased the consumption of CWCDs, they are normal goods.

Chart 3-1a

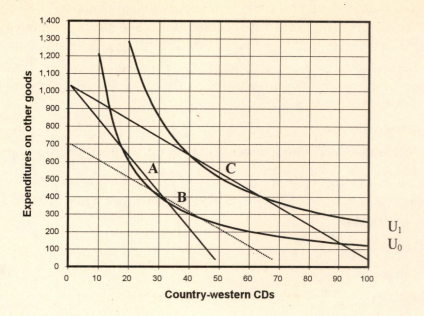

d. Clyde's CWCD consumption does follow the law of demand. The decrease in price was followed by an increase in consumption.

e. Because CWCDs are normal goods, the income effect reinforced the substitution effect.

3. a. Yvonne consumes <u>3 lbs</u> of eclairs per month.

Chart 3-2a

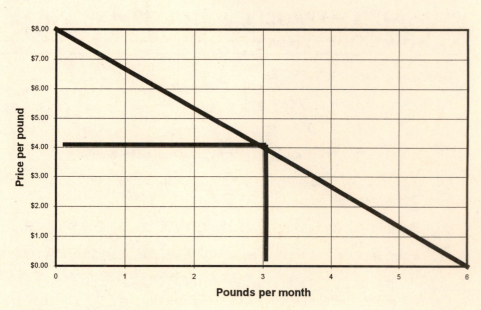

b. Yvonne spends $4 \times 3 = \$12$ per month on eclairs.

c. $12 + \frac{1}{2}(\$8 - \$4)3 = \$12 + \$6 = \$18$ She would pay a maximum of $18 for 4 eclairs.

d.   Her consumer surplus is: $18 – $12 = $6.

e.   Because the cover charge is less than her consumer surplus, Yvonne *might* pay the cover charge, if there were no other place to buy eclairs that provided a consumer surplus greater than $0.50.

f.   We are assuming that the marginal utility of income remains constant, which is a reasonable assumption in this case because eclair expenditure is only a small proportion of her budget.

4.

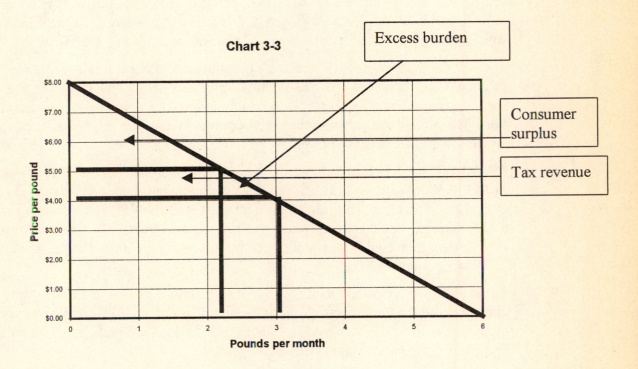

Chart 3-3

a.   Quantity purchased falls to $6 – 0.75(5) = 2.25$ eclairs per month.

b.   Consumer surplus $= \frac{1}{2}(\$8 – \$5)2.25 = \$3.75$.

c.   Loss of consumer surplus $= 6 – 3.75 = 2.625$.

d.   Tax revenue $= \$1 \times 2.25 = \$2.25$.

e.   Deadweight loss $= 2.625 - 2.25 = \$0.375$.

5. a.   The expected income of the gift shop is $50,000. The expected income from Freefall Industries is $E(I) = \frac{1}{2}(0) + \frac{1}{2}(\$80,000) = \$40,000$. Investing in the gift shop would maximize expected income.

b. The expected utility from the gift shop is 10. The expected utility from Freefall Industries is $E(I) = \frac{1}{2}(0) + \frac{1}{2}(30) = 15$ utils. Investing in Freefall Industries would maximize expected utility.

c. You are a risk taker since the uncertain option with the lower expected income was selected over the certain option with the higher expected income.

True-False Questions

1. *True*. For normal goods, a price increase has a negative substitution effect, and the reduction in real income also causes consumption of the goods to decrease.

2. *False*. For inferior goods, the substitution effect of a price increase is negative, while the reduction in real income causes consumption to increases; the income and substitution effects operate in opposite directions. However, the demand curve for an inferior good will be positively sloped only if the income effect is stronger than the substitution effect, which happens only in the unlikely case of a Giffin good.

3. *True*. If the price of good X increases, the substitution effect causes the consumption of good Y to increase as the consumption of good X decreases. However, the reduction in real income causes the consumption of Y, a normal good, to decrease. Since the income and substitution effects operate in opposite directions, the overall impact on good Y's consumption depends on the relative strength of the income and substitution effects.

4. *False (or uncertain)*. If only one bar has a cover charge, James will switch his patronage to that bar and preserve his consumer surplus of $6. Only if both bars have a cover charge, and there is no place else where he can receive a consumer surplus greater than $1 would James continue to patronize those bars and suffer a reduction in consumer surplus to $1.

5. *False*. Risk averse people might gamble if they believe that the expected utility of the gamble exceeded the expects utility of keeping their money. This could be explained by the existence of favorable odds, the miscalculation of the odds, or the possibility that playing the game is a form of entertainment.

Multiple Choice Questions

1. b   2. c   3. a   4. d   5. B   6. c   7. d

8. d   (Risk takers, risk neutral, and risk averse individuals would all consider this insurance policy an attractive prospect. The fact that she bought the insurance doesn't tell us whether she is risk averse, risk neutral, or a risk taker.)

9. d   (A risk neutral person would be indifferent between the prospects, meaning that he or she *might* pick either option 1 or 2.)

10. a

Chapter 4

THE COST OF TIME AND THE THEORY OF CONSUMER BEHAVIOR

• LEARNING OBJECTIVES

After completing this chapter you should be able to

1. Understand and draw a full budget constraint.

2. Calculate the full price of a good.

3. Predict how changes in nonwage income will shift the full price budget.

4. Predict how changes in the wage rate will shift the full price budget.

5. Understand why consumers who earn higher wage rates will substitute goods with lower time-price ratios for goods with higher time-price ratios.

6. Understand why consumers with higher wage rates will pay higher prices to economize on time.

7. Understand how observed differences in shopping behavior by men and women result from different opportunity costs of time, rather than to gender differences per se.

• CHAPTER OVERVIEW

Full Income Budget Constraint

This chapter relaxes the simplifying assumption that the money price is the only cost of consuming a good for the more realistic observation that the **full price** of a good is the sum of its money price and the opportunity cost of the time required to consume that good. **Full income** is the consumer income if all available time (e.g., time not spent eating or sleeping) is spent working. It follows that time spent consuming could have been spent earning more labor income. Economists assume that consumer-workers maximize utility by allocating time between consuming and working. The optimal point of consumption occurs where the consumer's highest attainable indifference curve is tangent to the **full income budget constraint**.

Utility Maximization under Full Income Budget Constraint

As in previous chapters, an increase in nonwage income (e.g., rental, dividend, or royalty income) causes a parallel shift in the full income budget constraint. The change in the optimal consumption point reflects a pure income effect of that income change. In **Figure 4-1**, $\dfrac{V + wT}{F_Y}$ is the maximum amount of good Y that can be consumed, once both the money price and the foregone wage cost of time have been included, $F_Y = P_Y + wt_Y$. Here P_Y is the money price of Y, t_Y is the time required to consume a unit of Y, and w is the hourly wage rate. By similar logic, the maximum X that can be consumed is $\dfrac{V + wT}{F_X}$.

Point **A** maximizes utility for this full price budget line and the consumer's preferences.

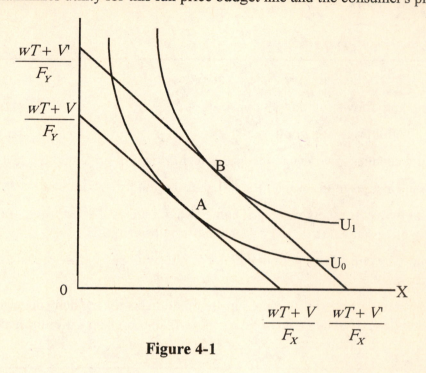

Figure 4-1

Wage Changes

Figure 4-2 illustrates the impact of a wage-rate change on the consumption of X and Y. If $\dfrac{t_Y}{P_Y} = \dfrac{t_X}{P_X}$, then the wage change would affect the full price of each good proportionately, leading to the same result as in Figure 4-1. It is more likely that one good is more **time intensive** than the other is. Figure 4-2 is drawn under the assumption that $\dfrac{t_Y}{P_Y} > \dfrac{t_X}{P_X}$: Good Y is more time-intensive than good X. This means that the wage increase is more effective at increasing the consumption of X than Y; the *y*-intercept moves up more than the *x*-intercept moves out. This causes the full-price budget constraint line to become flatter. The wage increase effectively reduces the *relative price* of good X.

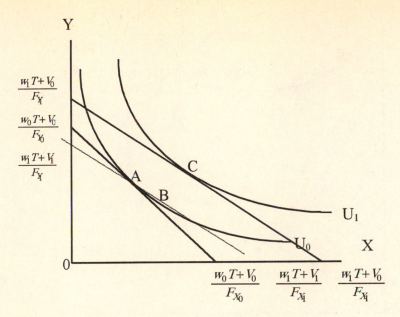

Figure 4-2

Minimizing the Full Price of Commodities

For simplicity, we have assumed that forces beyond the consumer's control determine the full price of each commodity. In reality, the consumer *determines* the full price of each product by selecting from a menu of alternatives for consuming the same good. Options that are time-consuming and low in price will appeal to consumers earning low wage rates. Options that are timesaving but higher in money price will appeal to consumers receiving higher wage rates. The consumer seeks to minimize the full price of each commodity by searching among stores until the gain in timesaving equals the increase in the product price. This approach to consumer behavior reveals that many so-called differences in shopping behavior, often attributed to differences in tastes, can actually be traced to differences in the opportunity cost of time. In Figure 4.3, line **b** shows the tendency of the opportunity cost of time to decrease as the price of X increases. Line **a** has a slope of 1, that translates the price on the horizontal axis to the vertical axis. Line **c** is the full price, the sum of P_X and wt_X. Note that the full price line reaches its minimum point when

$$\frac{\Delta F_X}{\Delta P_X} = 0 \text{, implying } -\Delta wt_X = \Delta P_X.$$

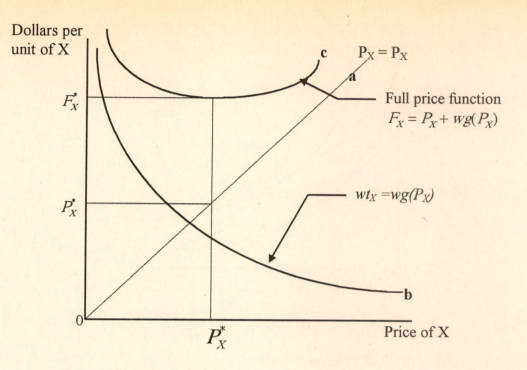

Figure 4-3

• KEY TERMS

Time constraint The limit of time availability between working and consuming derived from the fact that some time must be spent in sleeping and other personal maintenance activities, so that time spent consuming implies the opportunity cost of lower labor earnings.

Opportunity cost of time The (foregone) wage rate because time spent consuming could have been used to earn a higher labor income.

Full Income The sum of nonwage income, V, and *potential* wage income, wT, where w is the wage rate and T is time available for working and consumption. Full income reflects the fact that the economic or *opportunity* cost of time spent consuming is foregone wage income, had that same time been spent working.

Full price The sum of the money price and the opportunity cost of time required to consume a unit of a commodity. For good X, full price is equal to: $F_x = P_x + wt_x$, where P_X is the money price of X, w is the (foregone) wage rate, and t_x is the amount of time required to consume X efficiently.

Full price budget constraint The equation relating money income (nonwage income plus full wage income) to the money price and time cost of consuming each good. In a simple two-good case: $V + wT = F_Y Y + F_X X$, where T is time spent working or consuming, while F_Y and F_X are the full-prices of Y and X, respectively: $F_X = P_X + wt_x$.

Affordable market basket A market basket that is on or below the full income budget constraint; the consumer has both the money income and the available time to consume that combination of commodities.

Ratio of full prices Indicates that the opportunity cost of consuming one more unit of good X is the required sacrifice of good Y. Solving the full price budget constraint for Y, the ratio of full prices is the slope of that budget constraint: $Y = \dfrac{V + wT}{F_Y} - \dfrac{F_X}{F_Y} X.$

Minimizing full price The market provides a menu of time-intensive, low-price vs. timesaving, high-price stores. Based on individual wage rates, consumers attempt to minimize the full price of each good by searching stores until the trade-off between the value of time-savings equals the increase in market price.

Effects of a change in nonwage income When nonwage income increases, the full price budget constraint shifts parallel to its former position. Since the relative full prices of the goods do not change, a change in nonwage income will have a pure income effect on the choices of consumer goods.

Effects of a change in wage income When the wage increases, the full price budget constraint changes position and changes slope. More time-intensive goods increase in relative price while timesaving goods decrease in relative price. The income effect will tend to increase the consumption of all goods, but the substitution effect will increase the consumption of timesaving goods relative to time-intensive goods.

Maximizing utility The consumer allocates the full price budget constraint so that consumption occurs at the indifference curve tangent to that budget line. The consumer's marginal rate of substitution is equal to the ratio of full prices.

- ## PROBLEMS

---

1. It takes 1 hour to consume a unit of good X ($t_X = 1$) and 2 hours to consume a unit of good Y ($t_Y = 2$). The price of X (P_X) = \$10.00 and the price of Y (P_Y) = \$20.00. A consumer has nonwage income (V) of \$200 per week, and receives a wage rate (w) of \$10.00 per hour for up to 60 hours per week (i.e., available time = T = 60).

    a. Write the algebraic expression for this consumer's time constraint.

    _____

    b. Write the expression for this consumer's full income.

    _____

    c. Write the expression for the full price of X.

    _____

    d. Write the expression for the full price of Y.

    _____

    e. What is the maximum amount of X for this consumer?

    _____

f. What is the maximum amount of Y for this consumer?

_____

2. The indifference map for the consumer described in question #1 is plotted in **Chart 4-1**. Add the consumer's full price budget constraint and use it to answer the questions that follow.

Chart 4-1

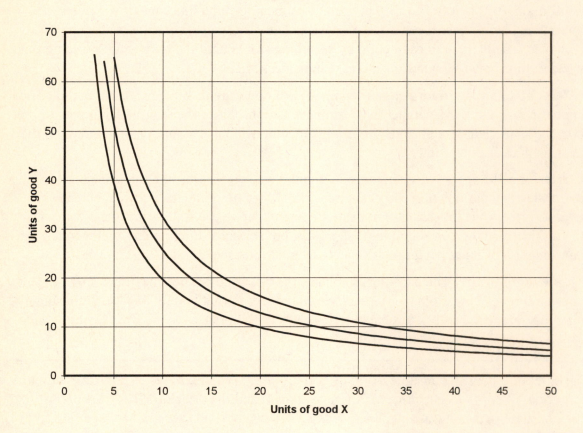

a. What is the slope of the full price budget constraint?

_____

a. How much X is consumed?

_____

b. How much Y is consumed?

_____

c. How much time is spent working?

_____

d. How much time is spent consuming X?

_____

e. How much time is spent consuming Y?

_____

3. Suppose that the consumer in problems 1 and 2 experiences an increase in nonwage income from $200 to $600 per week. Draw the new full price budget constraint in Chart 4-2 below and answer the following questions.

Chart 4-2

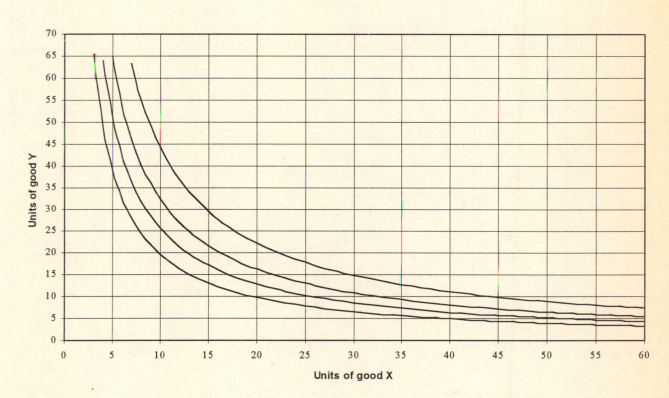

a. How much X is consumed?

_____

b. How much Y is consumed?

_____

c. How much time is spent working?

_____

d. How much time is spent consuming X?

_____

e. Did the slope of the full price budget change? Explain.

_____

_____

4. Suppose that the consumer form problem 1 and 2 experiences a wage increase from $10 to $20 per hour, while nonwage income remains at $600 per week. Draw the new full price budget constraint in **Chart 4-3** and answer the questions that follow.

Chart 4-3

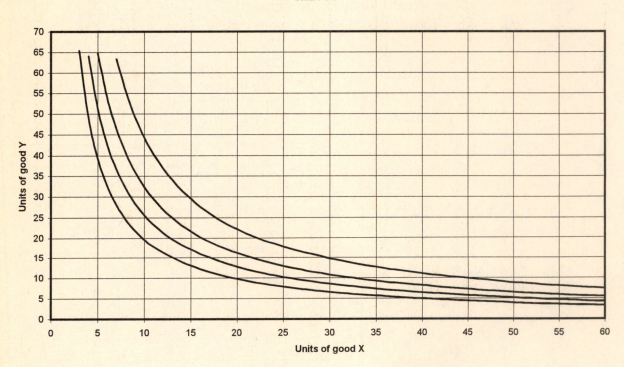

a. How much X is consumed?

_____

c. How much Y is consumed?

_____

d. How much time is spent working?

_____

e. How much time is spent consuming X?

_____

f. Did the slope of the full price budget change? Explain.

_____

_____

_____

4. While out shopping, the consumer discovers a new brand of good X, whose price is $15 but requires only 30 minutes to consume each unit. Will this new brand be attractive to the consumer? Briefly explain.

_____

_____

_____

5. On the same shopping trip, the consumer discovers a new brand of good Y, whose price is $25 and requires 45 minutes to consume each unit. Is this brand attractive to the consumer? Explain.

_____

_____

_____

• TRUE-FALSE QUESTIONS

For each of the following statements, indicate whether the statement is true (agrees with economic theory), is false (is contradicted by economic theory), or is uncertain (could be true or false; not enough information is given), and briefly explain your answer.

1. During the nineteenth century and the early part of the twentieth century, physicians typically made house calls. Today, patients almost always go to a physician's office for treatment. This change is probably due to changes in the tastes of patients.

_____

_____

_____

_____

2. Retailers who sell items at lower prices to customers with coupons than they do to customers without coupons are not maximizing profits.

_____

_____

_____

_____

3. An increase in a consumer's wage rate tends to increase the consumption of timesaving commodities.

_____

_____

_____

4. Higher-wage consumers tend to rent more video tapes than lower wage consumers.

_____

_____

_____

_____

5. An increase in nonwage income will tend to increase the total time a household spends in consumption.

_____

_____

_____

_____

• MULTIPLE CHOICE QUESTIONS

1. Full income is equal to:

    a. $wT_w + V$.

    b. $P_X + P_Y$.

    c. $wT + V$.

    d. $wt_X X + wt_Y Y$.

2. If good X takes 30 minutes to consume, $P_X = \$1.00$ and Fred's wage rate is $15/hour, then the full price of X for Fred is

    a. $1.00.   b. $7.50.   c. $8.50.   d. $16.00.

3. If good X takes 30 minutes to consume, $P_X = \$1.00$, Fred's wage rate is $15/hour, and Fred has nonwage income of $100 and 50 hours available, then the most of good X Fred could possibly consume (i.e., if consumption of Y is zero) is

    a. 50 units.

    b. 100 units.

    c. 11.76 units.

    d. 850 units.

4. If it takes 30 minutes to consume a unit of X ($t_X = 0.5$) and 1 hour to consume Y ($t_Y = 1$), while $P_X = \$1.00$ and $P_Y = \$2.00$, then

    a. X is less time-intensive per hour of expenditure than Y.

    b. Y is less time-intensive per hour of expenditure than X.

    c. X and Y are equally time-intensive per dollar expenditure.

d. we need to know the time available in order to reach a conclusion.

5. If $\dfrac{t_X}{P_X} > \dfrac{t_Y}{P_Y}$, a rise in non-wage income (V) will cause

    a. a fall in the full price of X relative to full price of Y.

    b. a rise in the full price of X relative to full price of Y.

    c. no change in the full price of X relative to full price of Y.

    d. one of the above, but we first need to know the wage rate.

6. If $\dfrac{t_X}{P_X} > \dfrac{t_Y}{P_Y}$, a rise in the wage rate (w), will cause

    a. a parallel and outward shift in the full price budget constraint line.

    b. a nonparallel and inward shift in the full price budget constraint line.

    c. a nonparallel and outward shift in the full price budget constraint line.

    d. something to occur but not enough information is given to answer this question.

7. As wage rates rise, we would expect wage earners spend a larger share of their budgets on

    a. golf games.

    b. automobiles.

    c. needlepoint kits.

    d. adult education classes.

8. If you are indifferent between paying an extra $5 for a shirt and driving 30 minutes to get the same shirt for $5 less, you value your own time at

    a. $5 per hour.

    b. $10 per hour.

    c. $15 per hour.

    d. whatever your own market wage is.

9. Suppose that the government raises social security taxes (a payroll tax on the first $65,400 of wages). This will tend to cause consumers to buy more:

   a. prewashed spinach salad.

   b. auto detailing.

   c. gardening tools.

   d. microwave brownie mix.

10. Using the theory developed in chapter 4, which of the following individuals is *least* likely to write snippy letters to the editor of the local paper?

    a. A kindergarten teacher.

    b. An unemployed miner.

    c. A 14-year-old.

    d. A retired air force colonel.

- # ANSWERS TO PROBLEMS, TRUE-FALSE, AND MULTIPLE-CHOICE QUESTIONS

Answers to Problems:

1. a. $2X + Y + T_w = 60$

   b. $V + wT = \$200 + \$10 \times 60 = \$800$

   c. $F_X = P_X + wt_X = \$10 + 1(\$10) = \$20$

   d. $F_Y = P_Y + wt_Y = \$20 + 2(\$10) = \$40$

   e. $X_{max} = \dfrac{V + wT}{F_X} = \dfrac{\$800}{20} = 40$

   f. $Y_{max} = \dfrac{V + wT}{F_Y} = \dfrac{\$800}{40} = 20$

2. a. Solving $F_X X + F_Y Y = 20X + 40Y = 800$ for Y, $Y = 20 - \frac{1}{2}X$, slope = -0.5.

   b. $X^* = 20$

   c. $Y^* = 10$

   d. $t_X = X(1) = 20$

   e. $t_Y = Y(2) = 20$

   f. $T_w = 60 - X(1) - Y(2) = 60 - 20 - 20 = 20$

Chart 4-1a

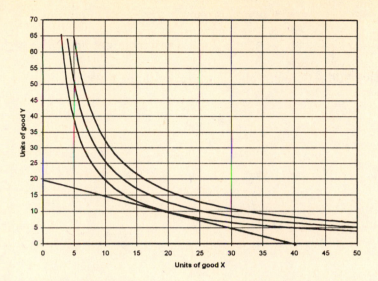

3. The new full budget constraint is a line between $Y_{max} = 30$ and $X_{max} = 60$, which is tangent at the point $X^* = 25$ and $Y^* = 12.5$.

Chart 4-2a

a. $X^* = 30$.

b. $Y^* = 15$.

c. $t_X = X(1) = 30$.

d. $t_X = Y(2) = 2(15) = 30$.

e. $T_w = T - t_X - t_Y = 60 - 30 - 30 = 0$.

f. The slope of the full price budget line *did not change* because this situation involved a change in nonlabor income only.

4. A. The Y intercept remains $Y_{max} = \dfrac{600+20(60)}{20+2(20)} = \dfrac{1800}{60} = 30$ and the X intercept remains

$Y_{max} = \dfrac{600+20(60)}{10+1(20)} = \dfrac{1800}{30} = 60$. That is, the full price budget line did not shift. So with the same full price budget constraint, the point of tangency remains at $X^* = 30, Y^* = 15$.

a. $X^* = 30$.

b. $Y^* = 15$.

c. $t_X = X(1) = 30$.

d. $t_X = Y(2) = 2(15) = 30$.

e. $T_w = T - t_X - t_Y = 60 - 30 - 30 = 0$.

f. The slope of the full price budget line did not change because $\dfrac{t_X}{P_X} = \dfrac{t_Y}{P_Y} = \dfrac{1}{10}$.

Since both goods have the same time intensity (1 hour of time per \$10 of expenditure), a change in the wage rate does not change the slope of the full price budget line.

Chart 4-3

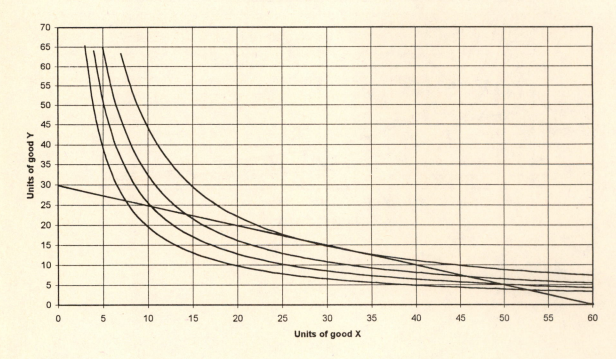

5. The full price of X decreases from $F_{X_0} = \$10 + 1(\$20) = \$30$ to $F_{X_1} = \$15 + \frac{1}{2}(\$20) = \$25$. Because the full price has declined, the new design will be attractive to the consumer.

5. The full price of X decreases from $F_{X_0} = \$10 + 1(\$20) = \$30$ to $F_{X_1} = \$15 + \frac{1}{2}(\$20) = \$25$. Because the full price has declined, the new design will be attractive to the consumer.

6. The full price of Y also decreases. The original full price was $F_{Y_0} = \$20 + 2(\$20) = \$60$. The new full price is $F_{Y_1} = \$25 + 0.75(\$20)$. Because the full price of Y has decreased, we expect the consumer to prefer the new design.

True-False Questions

1. *False*. The relative income of physicians has increased, making their time relatively more valuable than that of (most of) their patients. Therefore, it is economically efficient for the patients to travel rather than the physicians. There is no reason to expect that tastes are the explanation.

2. *False*. Customers who value their time more highly are less likely to clip coupons and are willing to pay higher prices. Differentiating between customers with and without coupons is one way that sellers can extract more consumer surplus.

3. *True*, other things remaining the same. As one's wage rate increases, the opportunity cost of consumption time increases, so we expect the higher wage consumer to purchase commodities that are less time-intensive.

4. *Uncertain, probably false*. Watching videotapes is a time-intensive, low price activity, so we would expect that lower-wage consumers will rent more such tapes. However, if the children in the household watch those tapes, and if entertaining one's children is a normal good, then the statement could be *true*.

5. *True*. With a parallel shift in the full price budget constraint, we expect consumers to buy more normal goods, which will require more time to consume.

Multiple Choice

1. c   2. c   3. b   4. c   5. c   6. d

7. b   (The other commodities are time-intensive since a newer automobile will tend to require less maintenance and may be driven faster).

8. b   (D might be the correct answer, but only if $w = \$10$).

9. c   (The opportunity cost of time has decreased.)

10. a   (A kindergarten teacher has the highest opportunity cost of time.)

Chapter 5

THE PRODUCTION FUNCTION AND COSTS OF THE FIRM

• LEARNING OBJECTIVES

After completing this chapter, you should be able to

1. Understand the firm's short-run production decision.

2. Explain the law of diminishing marginal product.

3. Understand the firm's long-run production decision.

4. Distinguish between increasing, constant, and decreasing returns to scale.

5. Find the cost-minimizing combination of factors to produce a given quantity using isocost and isoquants.

6. Explain the relationship between the slope of the long-run average cost curve and returns to scale.

7. Predict changes in the long-run total cost function if technology or factor prices change.

8. Draw a short-run total cost function when one factor is fixed.

9. Understand learning-by-doing: how the average cost curve may shift down with experience, as measured by the cumulative amount of a good produced in the past.

• CHAPTER OVERVIEW

The Production Function

The **production function** describes the maximum quantity that can be produced with each combination of factors of production, *given the state of technology*. For simplicity, we relate the rate of output, q, to the combination of two factors, L, labor, and K, capital. Mathematically, the production function takes a form like $q = f(L, K)$.

Economists find it convenient to distinguish between the **long run**, the planning horizon over which all factors are variable, and the **short run**, the actual production period when some factors of production are fixed. If we assume that L is the variable factor and that K is fixed at some level, K_0, we attribute all variation in output to the variation in the labor input only, $q = f(L, K_0)$. We specify this variant of the production function as the **total product function**. The graph of the total product curve is shown in **Figure 5-1**. We define the **average product** of labor as output divided by the amount of variable input: $\frac{C_0}{w_0} L_0$. We measure the average product as the slope of the ray drawn to the point of interest on the total product curve. Note that in **Figure 5-1**, one ray intersects the total product curve at about $q = 2$ and $q = 8$, while another ray touches the curve at one point, $q = 4$. That point of tangency identifies the maximum average product.

Total Product of Labor

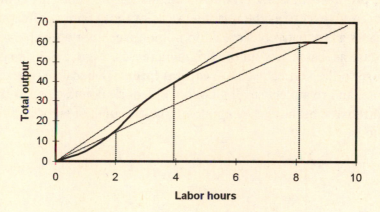

Figure 5-1

The slope of the total product curve is **marginal product of labor**, defined as the change in output divided by the change in the (labor) input: $MP_L = \dfrac{\Delta q}{\Delta L}$. **Figure 5-2** shows the marginal and average products of labor corresponding to the total product curve in Figure 5-1. In Figure 5-2, note that for $L > 2$, the marginal product of labor is declining. This reflects the **law of diminishing returns**, which states that eventually the marginal product of the variable factor (in this case, labor) must decrease as more of that factor is used. The law of diminishing returns always occurs because the services of the fixed factor are spread thinner and thinner. This means that marginal product can increase only initially, when the amount of variable factor is small. Over this range, $MP_L > AP_L$, causing AP_L to increase. Once falling MP_L becomes less than AP_L, average product must fall as well.

Average and Marginal Products of Labor

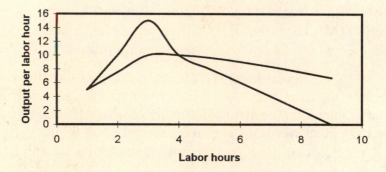

Figure 5-2

Isoquants and Factor Substitution

Over the long run, all factors are variable. Economists depict the relation between two inputs and the rate of output using **isoquants**, curves showing combinations of labor and capital that produce the same rate of output. Isoquants look very much like indifference curves. Indeed, profit-maximizing producers are indifferent about the combination of labor and capital used, except as the relative prices of those factors affect the firm's costs. Note that isoquants are negatively sloped, do not intersect, are bowed in toward the origin, and increase as distance from the origin increases. **Figure 5-3** depicts an isoquant map. Points close to the vertical axis are **capital intensive** because they employ large amounts of capital and relatively small amounts of labor. Points close to the horizontal axis are **labor intensive** because they employ large amounts of labor and relatively small amounts of capital.

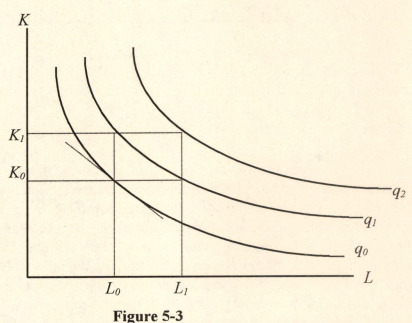

Figure 5-3

In Figure 5-3 we see that the firm can produce output q_1 with combination (L_0, K_1): . The firm could also produce q_1 with L_1 units of labor and K_0 units of capital. Moving along the isoquant involves substituting labor for capital. The **marginal rate of substitution (MRTS)** is the slope of the isoquant and indicates the amount of capital that is released when labor increases and output remains constant:

$$MRTS = \frac{\Delta K}{\Delta L} = -\frac{MP_L}{MP_K}.$$ **Diminishing MRTS** occurs because, as the production process

becomes more labor intensive, the marginal product of labor falls and the marginal product of labor increases. In other words, as capital is reduced by equal increments, it takes successively larger increases of labor to keep output constant.

Returns to Scale

Returns to scale describe the percentage change in output that results from changing all inputs by the same proportion. Returns to scale can be measured mathematically by the formula, $\lambda^b q = f(\lambda L, \lambda K)$, where λ is some positive constant representing the proportional change in all inputs. If $b = 1$, the production function exhibits **constant returns to scale.** For instance, if one typist on one computer can type 10 pages in an hour, we would expect that two typists, on two computers, could type 20 pages in an hour. If $b > 1$, the production function exhibits increasing returns to scale; **increasing returns to scale** usually reflect gains from specialization. **Decreasing returns to scale** ($b < 1$) typically occur when management or coordination snags prevent output from increasing proportionately to all inputs.

The Optimal Combinations of Inputs

The process by which management identifies the best combination of factor services for producing a specified rate of output is by finding the point of tangency between an **isocost line** and an isoquant. An isoquant line is obtained by solving the firm's cost equation, $C = wL + rK$, for one of the inputs, typically capital: $K = \dfrac{C}{r} - \dfrac{w}{r}L$. In this equation, r is the rental rate for capital services, w is the wage rate, and C is the firm's costs. The distinction between efficient and inefficient combinations of input services can be seen by plotting the isoquant map and the isocost lines on the same set of capital and labor axes.

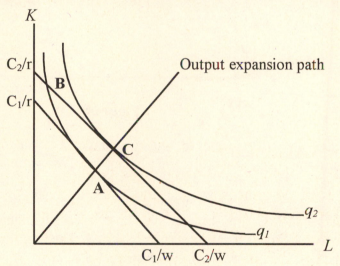

Figure 5-4

In **Figure 5-4**, point **B** indicates that output q_1 (the label on the isoquant) can be produced for cost level C_2, the label on the isocost line. This combination of input services is not efficient because it is possible to (1) increase the rate of output, holding input costs constant, or (2) decrease costs, holding output constant. Note that point **A** shows that the minimum cost of producing output q_1 is cost C_1. Point **C** indicates that q_2 is the maximum rate of output associated with cost level C_2. Point **B** is *not* efficient because the isoquant and isocost lines intersect. Point **A** and point **C** are efficient because the isoquant and isocost lines are tangent. An efficient allocation of resources requires that the last dollar spent on each input generates the same increase in output: $\dfrac{w}{MP_L} = \dfrac{r}{MP_K}$. When resources are allocated efficiently, it costs the same to increase output by increasing labor or by increasing capital.

Long-Run Total and Average Cost Functions

The **expansion path** is the line connecting all points of tangency between the isoquant and isocost lines. Plotting the output from each isoquant on the horizontal axis and the cost from the isocost line on the vertical axis yields the **long-run total cost function.** In **Figure 5-5**, the long-run total cost function first increases at a decreasing rate (indicating increasing returns to scale), then increases at an increasing rate (reflecting decreasing returns to scale).

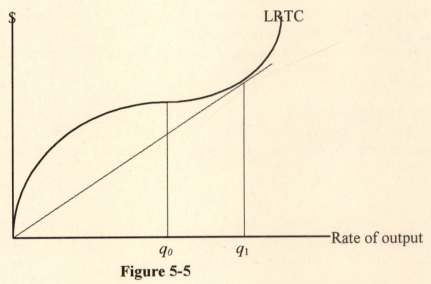

Figure 5-5

Long-run average cost is equal to long-run total cost divided by quantity. When there are increasing returns to scale ($q < q_1$ in Figure 5-5), long-run average cost decreases as output increases. When there are decreasing returns to scale ($q > q_1$ in Figure 5-5), long-run average cost increases with output. Long-run average cost reaches its minimum where LRAC = LRMC; long-run marginal cost reaches its minimum when the long-run total cost curve switches from convex to concave. The long-run average cost and long-run marginal cost curves are plotted in **Figure 5-6**.

Page 73

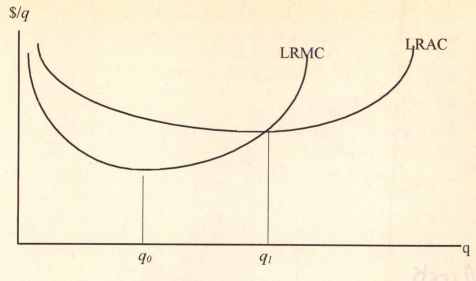

Figure 5-6

The **short-run cost function** shows the lowest total cost of producing each quantity when one factor is fixed. Total short-run cost equals the sum of **fixed cost** (the cost of the fixed input) and **variable cost** (the cost of the variable input). The total short-run cost is obtained by relating the cost from each isocost line with the rate of output associated with the **short-run expansion path.** This expansion path is the horizontal line generated by the fixed amount of capital. This expansion path will cross one point of tangency between an isoquant and an isocost line, implying that the short-run total cost curve will touch the long-run total cost curve at one point, shown as q^* in **Figure 5-7**. For rates of output below this tangency point, short-run total cost exceeds long-run total cost due to the high fixed cost. For rates of output above q^*, short-run total cost exceeds long-run total cost due to diminishing returns to the fixed factor. Any time the firm's rate of output deviates from the isoquant for which the fixed amount of capital is optimal, costs will be higher than would be the case were both inputs variable.

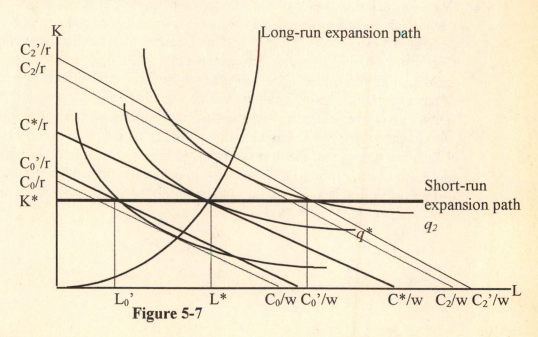

Figure 5-7

Figure 5-8 shows short-run total cost is everywhere above long-run total cost, except at that rate of output, q^*, where the firm is using the cost-minimizing combination of labor and capital. Note that, while the LRTC curve starts at the origin, SRTC begins at a positive fixed cost. Below q^*, short-run total cost exceeds long-run total cost because more capital is being used than would minimize cost. At q^*, LRTC = SRTC, since the firm is employing the optimal quantity of labor and capital to produce that rate of output. Above q^*, SRTC > LRTC because diminishing returns to the variable factor of production cause SRTC to rise faster than LRTC.

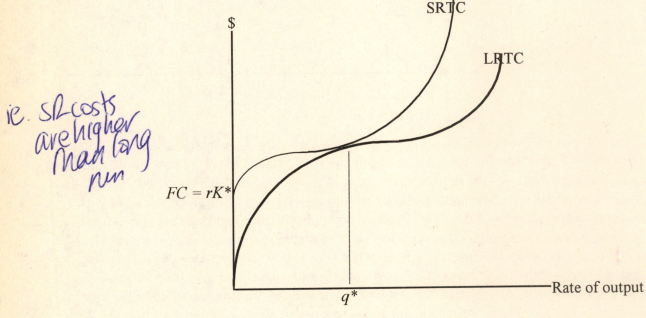

ie. SR costs are higher than long run

Figure 5-8

Shifts in the Long-Run Total Cost Function

We have seen that the long-run total cost function is a menu of production scale options when all factors of production are variable. Since the long-run total cost function is generated by the tangencies between the isoquant map (technology), and the isocost line (factor prices), it follows that changes in either technology or factor prices will change the long-run output/cost relation. In **Figure 5-9** we trace the effects of a change in the price of labor, with technology and the price of capital remaining constant. At wage rate w_0 and rental rate r_0, the firm minimizes the cost of producing q_0 units of output by hiring L_0 workers and installing K_0 capital units (point **A**). A decrease in the wage rate to w_1 rotates the isocost line so that the firm can now produce q_1 units of output with L_1 units of labor and K_1 at cost C_1 (point **B**). The long-run expansion path shifts from 0A to 0B, so that output q_0, as well as output q_0, would be produced with a more labor-intensive input mix.

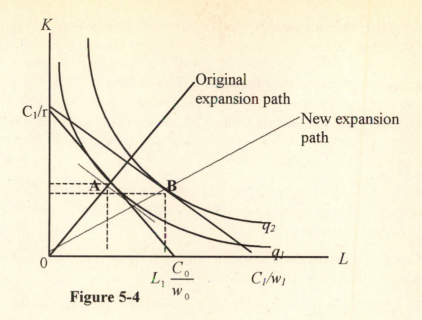

Figure 5-4

Learning-by-Doing

Another event that would modify the shape of the long-run total cost curve would be a change in technology, which could affect the shape or the spacing of the isoquants, and hence the shape of the long-run total cost curve. Typically, such a technological advance would be caused by forces outside the firm, say, basic research and development in the capital goods industry or a breakthrough at a research university. One type of technological advance can arise from forces inside the firm. As a firm or industry has greater experience with a technology, workers and managers learn to use that technology more efficiently. Professor Pashigian illustrates how **learning-by-doing** has reduced the average costs of production in the semiconductor industry and spurred Indianapolis racers to achieve faster average speeds.

• KEY TERMS

Production function The mathematical function of the form $q = f(L, K)$ which yields the maximum rate of input for each combination of factor services.

Factors of production Those inputs that generate output.

- **Labor** Human time and effort devoted to the production of a good or service.

- **Capital** The services of a commodity that is used to produce other commodities.

Long run A time horizon over which all factors of production are variable.

Short run A time period during which at least one factor, typically capital, is fixed.

Short-run production function The relation between the rate of output and the variable factor of production, typically labor.

Total product of labor A way of looking at the short-run production function whereby all variations in output are attributed to variations in labor.

Average and marginal products Relations between output per worker and the amount of labor used.

- **Average product of labor** The ratio of total output to labor: $AP_L = \dfrac{q}{L}$.

- **Marginal product of labor** The change in output divided by the change in labor: $MP_L = \dfrac{\Delta q}{\Delta L}$.

Law of diminishing returns The tendency for the marginal product of the variable factor of production to decrease as more of that factor is used, the other factor of production remaining constant.

Long-run production function The relation between input services and the rate of output when all factors of production are variable.

Isoquant The line or function that shows the minimum amount of capital for each amount of labor required to produce a given rate of output. Isoquants are negatively sloped, are bowed in toward the origin, do not intersect, and increase in magnitude with distance from the origin.

Marginal rate of technical substitution The slope of an isoquant line, indicating the amount of capital that can be released when labor is increased by one unit. The marginal rate of technical substitution equals minus one times the ratio of the marginal products of those inputs: $MRTS_{KL} = \dfrac{\Delta K}{\Delta L} = -\dfrac{MP_L}{MP_K}$.

Price of a factor The payment or opportunity cost resulting from using a factor's services for one time period. The price of labor is the wage rate (w); the price of capital is the rental rate (r).

Isocost function The amount of capital that can be hired given the quantity of labor and total cost. The isocost is obtained by solving the equation for the cost of inputs for capital: $C_0 = wL + rK \rightarrow K = \dfrac{C_0}{r} - \dfrac{w}{r}L$

Minimizing the cost of producing a given output The optimal combination of inputs is identified where the isoquant is tangent to the lowest possible isocost line, so that the marginal rate of technical substitution equals the factor price ratio: $-\dfrac{MP_L}{MP_K} = -\dfrac{w}{r}$.

Slope of the isocost line is the ratio of the factor prices: $\dfrac{\Delta K}{\Delta L}\bigg|_{C=constant} = -\dfrac{w}{r}$.

Slope of the isoquant The marginal rate of technical substitution: $MRTS_{KL} = \dfrac{\Delta K}{\Delta L}\bigg|_{q=constant} = -\dfrac{MP_L}{MP_K}$.

Expansion path The location of tangencies between isoquants (rates of output) and isocost lines which provides information for graphing the firm's *long-run total cost function*.

Long-run total cost function The function showing the minimum cost of producing each rate of output when all factors of production are variable.

Short- run total cost function The function showing the cost of producing each rate of output when at least one factor of production is fixed.

Shifts in the long-run total cost function Changes in long-run total cost that occur when factor prices change, or when technology changes which in turn, change the position of the firm's expansion path.

Learning-by- the doing Reductions in long-run total cost that occur because of experience within the firm or within industry. Learning-by-doing typically is a function of the cumulative production of a good or service.

• PROBLEMS

1. **Table 5-1** contains selected information about production in the short run, with labor as the variable factor.

   a. Compute the marginal and average products for each amount of labor input. (Note, as an approximation, marginal product is attributed to the greater labor input.)

   Table 5-1

Labor	Output	Average Product	Marginal Product
0	0		
1	20	_____	_____
2	35	_____	_____
3	45	_____	_____
4	48	_____	_____
5	50	_____	_____

   b. Given that r = price of capital = \$1, and w = price of labor = \$2, and $K = 10$, compute the costs of production in **Table 5-2.**

Table 5-2

Labor	Output	Variable Cost	Fixed Cost	Total Cost	Average Total Cost	Average Variable Cost	Average Fixed Cost	Marginal Cost
0	0	___	___	___				
1	20	___	___	___	___	___	___	___
2	35	___	___	___	___	___	___	___
3	45	___	___	___	___	___	___	___
4	48	___	___	___	___	___	___	___
5	50	___	___	___	___	___	___	___

2. Suppose that the production function has the form $q = L^{0.5} K^{0.5}$.

   a. Fill in the entries in **Table 5-3.**

Table 5-3
Labor Usage

		0	1	2	3	4	5
	0	0	0	___	___	___	___
Capital	1	0	1	___	___	___	___
Usage	2	___	___	___	___	___	___
	3	___	___	___	___	___	___
	4	___	___	___	___	___	___
	5	___	___	___	___	___	___

   b. Circle three combinations of labor and capital that produce 2 units of output.

   c. Does this production function exhibit diminishing returns to labor? Explain.

_____

_____

_____

   d. Does this production function exhibit increasing, decreasing or constant returns to scale? Explain.

_____

_____

_____

3. If we solve the production function in question #2 for capital, we get the equation of the isoquant for 2 units of output as: $K = \dfrac{4}{L}$. Compute the amount of capital required to produce 2 units of output for each level of labor in **Table 5-4**. Also, compute $MRTS_{KL}$ for each combination of inputs.

Table 5-4

Labor (L)	Capital (K)	ΔL	ΔK	MRTS
1				
2		____	____	____
3		____	____	____
4		____	____	____
5		____	____	____
6		____	____	____
7		____	____	____
8		____	____	____
9		____	____	____
10		____	____	____

4. If w = $4 and r = $4, compute the total cost of inputs for each point on the isoquant q = 2 in **Table 5-5**. Identify the cost minimizing combination of inputs.

Table 5-5

Labor (L)	Capital (K)	wL	rK	TC
1	____	____	____	____
2	____	____	____	____
3	____	____	____	____
4	____	____	____	____
5	____	____	____	____
6	____	____	____	____
7	____	____	____	____
8	____	____	____	____
9	____	____	____	____
10	____	____	____	____

5. **Chart 5-1** contains isoquants for q = 100 and q = 200 units of output. You are given that w = $10 and r = $10. Answer the questions that follow the chart.

Chart 5-1

a. What is the best combination of L and K if the firm desires to produce output = 25?

_____

b. What is the minimum cost of producing output = 25?

_____

c. What is the best combination of L and K for producing output = 50?

_____

d. What is the minimum cost of producing output = 50?

_____

e. Based on your answers to parts a through d, what will be the shape of the long-run total cost curve? Explain.

_____

_____

_____

_____

• TRUE-FALSE QUESTIONS

For each of the following statements, indicate whether the statement is true (agrees with economic theory), false (is contradicted by economic theory), or uncertain (could be true or false; not enough information is given), and briefly explain your answer.

1. Isoquants reflect relative rates of output; that is, numbers associated with isoquants reflect ordinal relationships only.

_____

_____

_____

_____

2. Efficient use of inputs requires producing the maximum rate of output at the minimum possible cost.

_____

_____

_____

_____

3. Diminishing average product of labor implies diminishing marginal product of labor.

_____

_____

_____

_____

4. A firm produces widgets, paying $5 per hour for capital and $10 per hour for labor. The plant manager finds she can replace two units of labor for each additional unit of capital employed. The firm is minimizing the cost of producing widgets.

_____

_____

_____

_____

5. Learning-by-doing implies that MP_L increases as the rate of output increases.

_____

_____

_____

_____

• MULTIPLE-CHOICE QUESTIONS

1. Suppose that a particular production function is given by the expression $q = 5KL$, where q = quantity, K = capital, and L = labor. If the firm employs 2 units of capital and 4 units of labor, then the quantity produced will be

   a. 5.

   b. 10.

   c. 40.

   d. impossible to tell without additional information.

2. In the short run, a firm increases its labor input from 10 to 11 workers, and quantity increases from 500 to 560 units. Which of the following statements is correct?

   a. The average product of the 11th worker is 50.

   b. The marginal product of the 11th worker is 50.

   c. The average product of the 11th worker is 60.

   d. The marginal product of the 11th worker is 60.

3. If the slope of a line from the origin to a point on the total product function exceeds the slope of the total product function at that point, then

   a. marginal product exceeds average product.

   b. marginal product is less than average product.

   c. marginal product equals average product.

   d. One of the above may be true, but it is impossible to tell without additional information.

4. Suppose a farmer doubles the usage of all inputs, and the quantity produced less than doubles. This is a case of

   a. increasing returns to scale.

   b. decreasing returns to scale.

   c. constant returns to scale.

   d. diminishing returns.

5. If Jane averages 1.1 points per shot and Hillary averages 1.3 points per shot, to increase the team's scoring the coach should

   a. get Jane to shoot more and Hillary to shoot less.

   b. get Hillary to shoot more and Jane to shoot less.

   c. discourage any change in either player's shooting.

   d. obtain additional information before making any changes.

6. Suppose that the marginal product of capital is 5 and the marginal product of labor is 10. Then the marginal rate of substitution of capital to labor (MRTS$_{KL}$) equals

    a. −0.5.

    b. −2.0.

    c. −5.0.

    d. −10.0.

7. Suppose that the wage (w) = $5.00 and the price of capital (r) = $15.00. Then at the cost-minimizing input combination, the marginal rate of technical substitution of capital to labor (MRTS$_{KL}$) equals

    a. −$0.33.

    b. −$3.00.

    c. −1/3.

    d. −3.

8. In an industry that experiences increasing returns to scale and constant factor prices, as the rate of output increases, long-run average cost will

    a. increase.

    b. decrease.

    c. remain constant.

    d. first decrease, then increase.

9. If the price of capital falls while the price of labor remains constant

    a. the firm will select a more capital-intensive technique.

    b. the cost of producing a particular quantity will fall.

    c. the expansion path will shift.

    d. all the above will occur.

10. If an industry experiences cost savings from learning-by-doing

    a. individual firms will experience declining long-run average costs at all rates of output.

    b. individual firms' long-run average cost curves will shift downward over time.

    c. the industry will tend to be dominated by one large producer.

    d. individual firms will experience increasing returns to scale.

• ANSWERS TO PROBLEMS, TRUE-FALSE, AND MULTIPLE CHOICE QUESTIONS

Answers to problems

1. a.

Table 5-1a

Labor	Output	Average Product	Marginal Product
0	0		
1	20	20	20
2	35	17.5	15
3	45	15	10
4	48	12	3
5	50	10	2

b.

Table 5-2a

Labor	Output	Variable Cost	Fixed Cost	Total Cost	Average Total Cost	Average Variable Cost	Average Fixed Cost	Marginal Cost
0	0	$0.00	$10.00	$10.00				
1	20	$2.00	$10.00	$12.00	$0.60	$0.10	$0.50	$0.10
2	35	$4.00	$10.00	$14.00	$0.40	$0.11	$0.29	$0.13
3	45	$6.00	$10.00	$16.00	$0.36	$0.13	$0.22	$0.20
4	48	$8.00	$10.00	$18.00	$0.38	$0.17	$0.21	$0.67
5	50	$10.00	$10.00	$20.00	$0.40	$0.20	$0.20	$1.00

2. a.

Table 5-3a

		Labor Usage					
		0	1	2	3	4	5
	0	0	0	0	0	0	0
Capital	1	0	1.00	1.41	1.73	2.00	2.24
Usage	2	0	1.41	2.00	2.45	2.83	3.16
	3	0	1.73	2.45	3.00	3.46	3.87
	4	0	2.00	2.83	3.46	4.00	4.47
	5	0	2.24	3.16	3.87	4.47	5.00

b. Two units of output can be produced with 1 unit of labor and 4 units of capital, 2 units of labor and 2 units of capital, or 4 units of labor and 1 unit of capital.

c. This production function *does* exhibit diminishing returns to labor, because for any row (i.e., holding capital constant), output increases at a decreasing rate as labor increases.

d. The production function exhibits *constant returns to scale*. When L = 1 and K = 1, q = 1. Doubling all inputs doubles output (when L = 2, and K = 2, q = 2).

3.

Table 5-4a

Labor (L)	Capital (K)	ΔK	ΔL	MRTS
1	4.00			
2	2.00	-2.00	1	-2.00
3	1.33	-0.67	1	-0.67
4	1.00	-0.33	1	-0.33
5	0.80	-0.20	1	-0.20
6	0.67	-0.13	1	-0.13
7	0.57	-0.10	1	-0.10
8	0.50	-0.07	1	-0.07
9	0.44	-0.06	1	-0.06
10	0.40	-0.04	1	-0.04

4.

Table 5-5a

Labor (L)	Capital (K)	wL	rK	TC
1	4.00	$4.00	$16.00	$20.00
2	2.00	$8.00	$8.00	$16.00
3	1.33	$12.00	$5.33	$17.33
4	1.00	$16.00	$4.00	$20.00
5	0.80	$20.00	$3.20	$23.20
6	0.67	$24.00	$2.67	$26.67
7	0.57	$28.00	$2.29	$30.29
8	0.50	$32.00	$2.00	$34.00
9	0.44	$36.00	$1.78	$37.78
10	0.40	$40.00	$1.60	$41.60

5.

5.

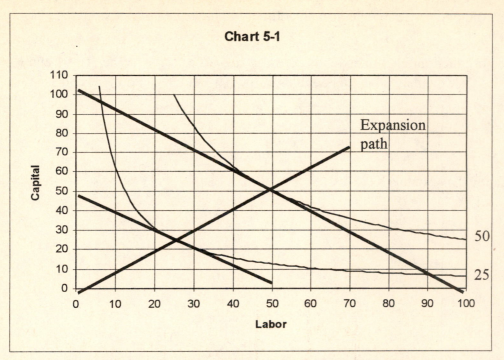

Chart 5-1

a. The optimal combination to produce 25 units of output is $L = 25$ and $K = 25$.

b. The minimum cost of producing 25 units of output is $10(25) + $10(25) = $500.

c. The optimal combination to produce 50 units of output is $L = 50$ and $K = 50$.

d. The minimum cost of producing 25 units of output is $10(50) + $10(50) = $1000.

e. The production function exhibits constant returns to scale, implying that the long-run total cost curve will be a straight line through the origin, with slope $1, that is LRTC $= 1 \times Q$.

Answers to True-False Questions.

1. *False*. Unlike indifference curves, whose labels do reflect only an ordinal ranking, the labels on isoquants represent actual rates of output and hence do not reflect only ordinal relationships.

2. *False*. Efficient use of inputs requires producing a *given* rate of output at minimum cost, *or* producing the maximum rate of output for a *given* cost.

3. *True*. Average product of labor can fall only if $MP_L < AP_L$. Since marginal product must eventually decrease with variable factor use, if average product of labor is falling, it has already passed its peak, meaning that marginal product of labor has also passed its peak and must be declining also.

4. *False*. In this case we have $\dfrac{MP_K}{MP_L} > \dfrac{r}{w}$. The firm can reduce costs or increase output by substituting capital for labor until: $\dfrac{MP_K}{MP_L} = \dfrac{r}{w}$, that is, until $MP_K = \frac{1}{2} MP_L$.

5. *False*. Learning-by-doing implies that the long-run total cost curve will shift downward as the total historical output increases. After the LRTC curve has shifted, the firm will continue to experience diminishing returns to fixed factors in the short run.

Answers to Multiple-Choice Questions

1. c

2. d

3. b

4. b

5. d (We do not know the marginal products of the two players.)

6. b

7. d ($MRTS_{KL}$ is measured in physical units, not dollars.)

8. b

9. d

10. b

Chapter 6
THE COST FUNCTIONS OF THE FIRM

• LEARNING OBJECTIVES

After completing this chapter, you should be able to

1. Explain the characteristic shapes of short-run cost curves.

2. Select the optimal distribution of output among plants by equating the marginal cost in each plant.

3. Explain the relationship between the shape of the long-run average cost function and the number of firms in the industry.

• CHAPTER OVERVIEW

Explicit and Opportunity Costs

To economists, all costs are opportunity costs. When a firm hires factors of production, the **explicit** or cash payments it makes to owners must cover the opportunity costs of transferring resources from alternative use. When a firm uses resources that belong to its owner(s), no cash payments are typically made, but **opportunity costs** occur just the same. As will be shown in subsequent chapters, economists must deduct both explicit costs and opportunity costs before judging whether resources are used efficiently.

Short-Run Costs

In Chapter 5 Professor Pashigian introduces the short run as a period during which factors of production are fixed: The firm has a specific supply of factor services on hand and cannot expand the use of that factor beyond its available level. It follows that the cost of those services is also fixed. If a firm has a lease for land or capital services, it must pay the same rent regardless of how much of that factor is actually used. The fixed cost is also a **sunk** cost if it cannot be recovered (e.g., by selling equipment or transferring a lease).

Variable costs are those costs that do change with the rate of output. The **variable cost function** relates the minimum variable cost to each possible rate of output in the short run. The **short-run total cost function** equals the sum of fixed cost and variable cost function. Fixed cost represents the intercept of the short-run total cost function. **Marginal cost** is the slope of the variable cost function and is also the slope of the short-run total cost function. **Figure 6-1** shows a short-run total cost function. Note that when output is zero, short-run total cost is positive. The average cost can be obtained as the slope of a ray from the origin to each point on the curve. The minimum average cost occurs at the tangent point. In Figure 6-1, minimum average variable cost occurs at q_0 and average total cost occurs at point q_1.

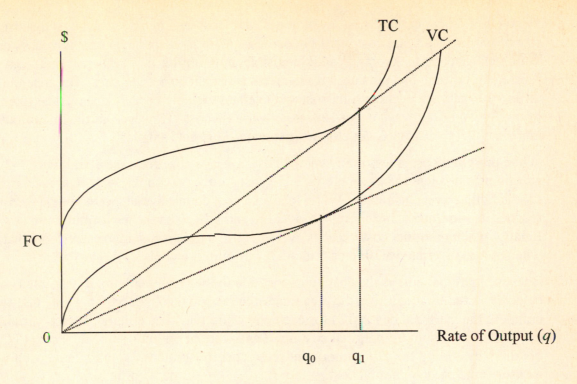

Figure 6-1

The **short-run average cost function** is obtained by dividing short-run total cost by the rate of output. Given TC = FC + VC, it follows that ATC = AFC + AVC; average total cost is the sum of **average fixed cost** and **average variable cost**. Because fixed cost is a constant, average fixed cost always decreases as output increases. Variable cost changes with output; the change in variable cost is **marginal cost**. Marginal cost is also the change in short-run total cost.

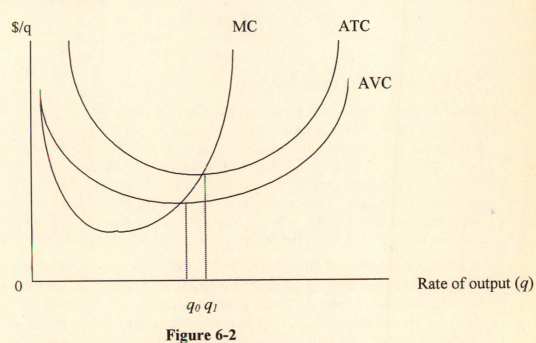

Figure 6-2

Figure 6-2 plots marginal cost, average variable cost, and average total cost against the rate of output. Marginal cost initially decreases, then increases as output increases due to diminishing returns. Average variable cost declines until it intersects marginal cost. Average total cost also falls until it intersects marginal cost, then rises. Because the difference between average total cost and average variable cost equals average fixed cost, average total cost always exceeds average variable cost. However, as the rate of output increases, ATC and AVC get closer together as AFC gets smaller.

When marginal cost is less than average cost, average cost decreases. In Figure 6-2, marginal cost is less than average variable cost from $q = 0$ until $q = q_0$; average variable cost is falling over this range. When marginal cost equals average cost, average cost reaches its minimum. In Figure 6-2, average variable cost reaches its minimum at q_0. Finally, when marginal cost exceeds average cost, average cost increases. Note that, when $q > q_0$, average variable cost increases as output increases.

Because marginal cost is the change in cost due to the change in output, variable cost can be constructed by measuring the area under the marginal cost curve. In **Table 6.1**, we compute the marginal cost (MC) for each rate of output. The column labeled variable cost (VC) is the sum of marginal cost up to each rate of output. Since total cost (TC) is obtained by adding the same amount of fixed cost to variable cost, marginal cost also measures the *change* in total cost.

Table 6.1

Output	MC	VC	TC
0			$200
1	$21	$21	$221
2	$14	$35	$235
3	$9	$9	$244
4	$6	$15	$250
5	$5	$5	$255
6	$6	$11	$261
7	$9	$9	$270
8	$14	$23	$284

Sunk Costs and Variable Costs

When making a decision, a person or firm should compare the change in outcomes with the action taken. **Sunk costs** are historic costs that cannot be changed by any action one might take. An important rule in economics is *opportunity costs matter; sunk costs do not matter*. Ignoring this rule is known as the **fixed cost fallacy**. Those who lost money but who continued to gamble trying to recover past losses have largely financed the casinos in Las Vegas. Money that the house has already won is a sunk cost to the gambler. Financial survival requires forward-looking wagers: Does the expected gain (the money in the pot times the probability of winning) exceed the size of the wager?

In making short-run decisions, fixed costs should be ignored because modifying the rate of output–even by reducing output to zero–cannot change them. It is a fallacy to allocate production among two plants based on fixed costs. A firm operating two plants should compare the *variable costs* of each plant when allocating output among them. Always producing in the plant with the lower fixed costs will eventually cause the *marginal cost* in that plant to exceed the marginal costs in the other plant. Moving output from the former to the latter plant will reduce the firm's *variable cost*, which is the only cost relevant to short run decisions.

Long run costs

Before a firm begins operations, management it makes a long-run decision: what size plant should we invest in? The long run cost curve traces out the minimum cost of producing each rate of output. In developing the theory of cost minimization in chapter 5, we assumed that the firm could find the tangency point between the isoquant and its associated isocost line. In **Figure 6-3** we plot the rate of output for a firm experiencing constant returns to scale and constant factor prices. Note that the long-run average costs and long-run marginal costs are both constant and equal to each other. Figure 6-3 depicts two short-run average cost functions and the associated short-run marginal cost functions. To produce q_1 units of output, management hires the optimal quantity of labor and capital. Hence, the minimum short-run average cost along SAC_1 occurs at output. Once this plant is in place, management can change the rate of output only by varying the variable input (labor). For rates of output less than q_1, $SAC_1 > LRAC$, since the firm is employing more capital (whose cost is fixed) and less labor (whose cost is variable) than are implied by the long-run average cost function. Below q_1, $SMC_1 < LRMC$, because costs cannot fall as far. If output is cut to zero, costs would be zero in the long run, but fall only to fixed cost (the cost of capital) in the short-run. Above q_1, $SMC_1 > LRMC$ and $SAC_1 > LRAC$, due to diminishing returns.

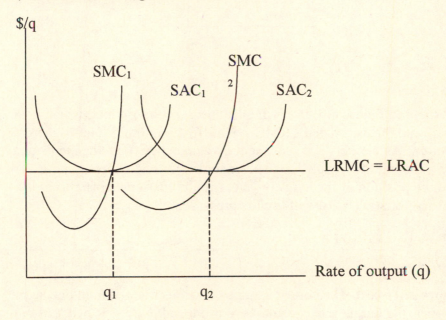

Figure 6-3

Had management elected to build a larger plant (e.g., hired the optimal quantity of labor and capital to produce q_2), then the firm would incur larger fixed costs and lower variable costs to produce output up to q_2. Again, we note that SAC_2 is tangent to LRAC at output q_2. Producing less than q_2 causes SAC_2 to rise due to high overhead. Producing more than q_2 causes SAC to rise due to diminishing returns.

Learning-by-Doing

Learning-by-doing occurs when experience with a production process increases the efficiency of input use. Typically, learning-by-doing is a cumulative process, whereby the long-run average cost and long-run marginal cost curves shift downward over time as workers and management gain experience with a new product or new process. The important thing to remember is that learning-by-doing does not affect the *shape* of these long-run cost functions. Learning-by-doing affects the position of these curves. We map out this pattern in **Figure 6-4.**

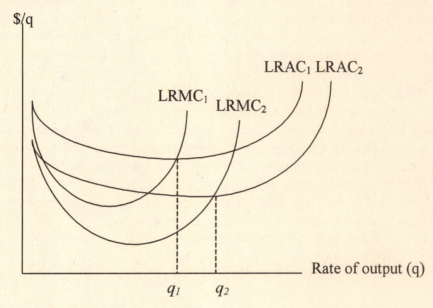

Figure 6-4

According to Figure 6-4, the firm introduces a new product, which it can produce with $LRAC_1$ and the associated $LRMC_1$. Note that minimum long-run average cost occurs at output q_1. As workers and management gain experience, the long-run average cost shifts downward and to the right, so that economies of scale now occur until output q_2. But while the position of the long-run average and marginal cost curves did shift downward, the characteristic U-shape of each is preserved.

• KEY TERMS

Explicit cost   A payment made to the owner of a factor of production, typically in cash.

Opportunity cost   The cost of using a factor of production in one activity instead of another is the output that it could have produced in its next best alternative use. Examples of opportunity cost include forgone wage income, interest returns on funds invested in inventory, or rent on warehouse space by people running their own businesses.

Fixed factor   A factor of production that cannot be increased in the short run, that typically generates a fixed cost.

Variable factor   A factor of production that can be increased or decreased with the rate of output. The costs associated with variable factors are *variable costs*.

Short run A period of time over which some costs and their associated input services are fixed. The short run is characterized by positive (fixed) costs when output is zero, and by increasing marginal costs due to diminishing returns to variable factors of production.

Long run   A time horizon over which all factors of production can be varied. Firms face long-run decisions when they start up and when contracts associated with fixed inputs expire and can be renegotiated.

Fixed cost The cost of inputs hired under contract. Whether or not the firm uses these input services, the costs of those services must be paid.

Variable cost   A cost associated with using a variable factor of production. Variable cost is zero when the rate of output is zero, and variable cost increases as the rate of output increases.

Short-run marginal cost The change in cost due to the change in the rate of output, during a period over which at least one factor of production is fixed. Marginal cost equals the ratio of each variable factor's price to its marginal product. If labor is the only variable factor: $MC = \dfrac{\Delta C}{\Delta q} = \dfrac{w}{MP_L}$.

Short-run average cost   The ratio of short-run total cost to output, over a period during which at least one input is fixed: $SRATC = \dfrac{SRTC}{q} = \dfrac{FC + VC}{q} = AFC + AVC$.

Long-run average cost. The ratio of long-run total cost to output, over a time horizon when all factor services are variable: $LRAC = \dfrac{LRTC}{q}$.

Equating the marginal cost in all plants The idea that a firm wishing to minimize the cost of production, should allocate its output among different plants so that the short-run marginal cost is identical for all plants.

Internal economies of scale The phenomenon whereby long-run total costs increase with output at a decreasing rate, causing long-run average costs to decline. When internal economies of scale occur over all rates of output, a natural monopoly will tend to develop in the industry.

Internal diseconomies of scale The phenomenon by which long-run total cost increase with output at an increasing rate, causing long-run average costs to increase. When internal diseconomies of scale occur over all rates of output, the industry tends to have many small-sized firms.

Long-run marginal cost The cost of increasing the (planned) rate of output by one unit when all factors of production are variable. Long-run marginal cost equals the common ratio of the price of each factor to its marginal product, identified by the point of tangency between each isoquant and the associated isocost lines. When labor and capital are the only factors, $LRMC = \dfrac{DC}{Dq} = \dfrac{w}{MP_L} = \dfrac{r}{MP_K}$.

• PROBLEMS

1. **Table 6-2** provides information on marginal costs in two plants, which are the only plants operated by the same firm. Use this information to answer the questions that follow.

Table 6-2

Quantity	Plant 1 MC ($)	Plant 2 MC ($)
1	0.50	1.00
2	0.75	1.25
3	1.00	1.50
4	1.25	1.75
5	1.50	2.00
6	1.75	2.25
7	2.00	2.50
8	2.25	2.75
9	2.50	3.00
10	2.75	3.25

a. What is the variable cost of producing 5 units in plant 1?

_____

b. If the firm wishes to produce 6 units, how should the output be allocated between the two plants?

_____

c. What is the marginal cost of the 6th unit of output?

_____

d. What is the variable cost of producing 6 units of output?

_____

e. What would happen if the firm tried to produce six units of output in one plant and no output in the other?

_____

_____

2. There are only four possible plant sizes in industry Y. The SRAC data are given in the table on the next page.

a. Fill in the LRAC in **Table 6-3.**

Table 6-3

Quantity	SRAC1	SRAC2	SRAC3	SRAC4	LRAC
1	1	2	3	4	_____
2	0.5	1	2	3	_____
3	1	0.5	1	2	_____
4	2	1	0.5	1	_____
5	3	2	1	0.5	_____
6	4	3	2	1	_____
7	5	4	3	2	_____
8	6	5	4	3	_____

b. Plot the SRAC curves in **Chart 6-1** below and then identify LRAC with a darker line.

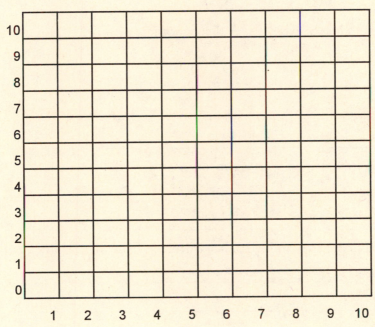

Cost per unit

Quantity

c. Does this industry have an optimal plant size? Explain.

_____

_____

3. **Table 6-4** below provides data on the long-run average costs of three industries.

Table 6-4

Quantity	Industry 1	Industry 2	Industry 3
100	5	10	10
200	5	12	9
300	5	14	8
400	5	16	7
500	5	18	6
600	5	20	5
700	5	22	4

a. Which industry experiences economies of scale? _____

b. Which industry experiences constant returns to scale? _____

c. Which industry experiences diseconomies of scale? _____

d. Which industry will have many small firms? _____
   Explain: _____

   _____

e. Which industry will have one large firm? _____
   Explain: _____

   _____

f. Which is the only industry that will have firms of varying sizes? _____
   Explain: _____

   _____

• TRUE-FALSE QUESTIONS

For each of the following statements, indicate whether the statement is true (agrees with economic theory), false (is contradicted by economic theory), or uncertain (could be true or false; not enough information is given), and briefly explain your answer.

1. When allocating output among different plants, production should always occur in the plant with the lowest average total cost.

   _____

   _____

   _____

   _____

2. A firm that experiences constant returns to scale and constant factor prices will encounter a constant long-run average cost.

   _____

   _____

   _____

   _____

3. An industry characterized by decreasing long-run marginal cost across all rates of output will tend to be dominated by one producer.

   _____

   _____

   _____

   _____

4. If long-run marginal cost equals long-run average cost, then long-run average cost is minimized.

   _____

   _____

   _____

   _____

5. Because average fixed cost always decreases with output, firms should attempt to produce as much output as possible to minimize average total cost.

_____

_____

_____

_____

• MULTIPLE-CHOICE QUESTIONS

1. Fred quit his $35,000-a-year job as a teacher to open his own sandwich shop. He pays $15,000 per year in rent, $12,000 per year for one employee, and $10,000 per year for supplies. Fred's explicit costs equal

   a. $15,000.

   b. $27,000.

   c. $37,000.

   d. $62,000.

2. Jill's light bill is $100 per month, she pays $150 per month on a loan for her barber chair, and she quit her job as a barber, which was paying her $2,000 per month. Her fixed cost of doing business is now

   a. $0.

   b. $100.

   c. $250.

   d. $2,250.

3. Jill can get another barber job at $2,000 per month. She can sell the barber chair and pay off the loan. Her sunk cost of doing business is

   a. $0.

   b. $100.

   c. $250.

   d. $2,250.

4. Your team is ahead 120 to 80, and the game is really boring. If you choose to walk out before the final whistle, you would be ignoring

   a. marginal cost.

   b. variable cost.

   c. sunk cost.

   d. total cost.

5. If the total cost of producing 100 units is $5,000 and the fixed cost equals $1,000, average variable cost is

   a. $40.

   b. $50.

   c. $4,000.

   d. $5,000.

6. If, at the current rate of output, short-run marginal cost = $15.00 and short-run average cost = $10.00, then

   a. short-run average cost is constant.

   b. short-run average cost is falling.

   c. short-run average cost is rising.

   d. One of the above may be true, but it is impossible to tell without additional information.

7. When $q = 1$, MC = $10, and when $q = 2$, MC = $8. The average variable cost for producing two units of output is:

   a. $8.

   b. $10.

   c. $9.

   d. $18.

8. Suppose that a firm operates two plants and plans to increase the rate of output. In the short run, the marginal cost in plant 2 is twice as much as the marginal cost of producing the same quantity in plant 1. To minimize the cost of producing an additional 60 units of output, the firm should

   a. produce all additional units in plant 1.

   b. produce all additional units in plant 2.

   c. divide the output between the two plants to equate the marginal cost.

   d. divide the output between the two plants to equate the average cost.

9. Suppose that long-run average cost is minimized at an output of 100,000 units. The firm is currently operating a plant designed to produce 100,000 units. Which of the following statements about the firm's cost functions are true when it is actually producing 100,000 units?

   a. LRAC = SRAC.

   b. LRMC = SRMC.

   c. SRAC = SRMC.

   d. All of the above are true.

10. The long-run average total cost function consists of:

   a. the set of plant capacities that generates the lowest short-run average cost of producing each quantity.

   b. the set of plant capacities that generates the lowest short-run average variable cost of producing each quantity.

   c. the set of plant capacities that generates the lowest short-run average fixed costs of producing each quantity.

   d. all the above.

• ANSWERS TO PROBLEMS, TRUE-FALSE QUESTIONS, AND MULTIPLE-CHOICE QUESTIONS

• Answers to problems

1. a. $VC = \$0.50 + 0.75 + 1.00 + 1.25 + 1.50 + 1.75 = \$6.75$.

   b. Produce 4 units in plant 1 and 2 units in plant 2.

   c. $MC = \$1.25$.

   d. $VC = \$0.50 + 0.75 + 1.00 + 1.00 + 1.25 + 1.25 = \$5.75$.

   e. If the firm had tried to produce all six units of output in plant 1 and no output in plant 2, variable costs would have been \$1.00 higher than if output had been divided between the two plants. If the firm had tried to produce all six units of output in plant 2 and no output in plant 1, variable costs would have been \$4.00 higher than if output had been divided between the two plants.

2. a.   **Table 6-1a**

Quantity	LRAC
1	1
2	0.5
3	0.5
4	0.5
5	0.5
6	1
7	2
8	3

   b. **Chart 6-1a** shows the relation between LRAC and the SRAC curves.

   c. The industry does not have an optimal plant size because the minimum long-run average cost occurs in the range between 2 and 5 units of output.

Chart 6-1a

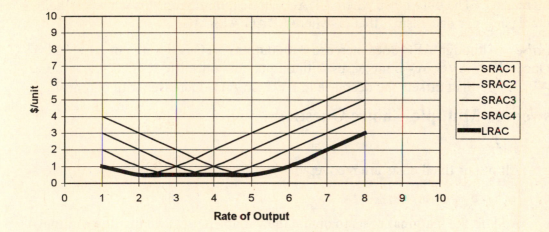

3. a. Industry 3 experiences economies of scale.

   b. Industry 1 experiences constant returns to scale.

   c. Industry 2 experiences decreasing returns to scale.

   d. Industry 2 will have many small firms, because firms producing less output would have lower average costs than firms producing more output. Hence, small firms would have a competitive advantage over large firms.

   e. Industry 3 will tend to have one large firm. When firms experience protracted economies of scale, natural monopoly tends to result.

   f. Industry 1 will tend to have firms of various sizes, since neither large firms nor small firms will tend to have a competitive advantage.

Answers to True-False Questions

1. *False.* When allocating output among different plants, production should be divided so that all plants have the same *marginal* cost.

2. *True.* A firm that experiences constant returns to scale and constant factor prices experiences a long-run total cost function of the form $LRTC = cq$, where c is both long-run marginal cost and long-run average cost, both of which are constant.

3. *True.* If long-run marginal cost continues to fall as output increases, long-run average cost will be lower for larger producers, giving the largest firm in the market a competitive advantage. This situation is called *natural monopoly*.

4. *True.* If LRAC > LRMC, then LRAC is declining. If LRAC < LRMC, then LRAC is increasing. The only place where LRAC can be minimumized is when it is neither increasing nor decreasing, that is, where LRAC = LRMC.

5. *False.* Although AFC does increase with output, ATC is the sum of AFC and AVC. Once MC > AVC, AVC increases with output, and once MC > ATC, the increase in AVC more than offsets the decrease in AFC, so ATC increases with output.

Answers to Multiple-Choice Questions

1. c   2. d

3, a   (All of her fixed costs are recoverable.)

4. c   5. a   6. c

7. c   (Add up the marginal costs to obtain the variable cost; then divide by output.)

8. c   (If the firm were already minimizing cost, marginal cost would be equal in each plant. Equating marginal cost would imply producing 40 units in plant 1 and 20 units in plant 2.)

9. d   (When producing 100,000 units, LRMC = LRAC and SRMC = SRAC. Since LRTC = SRTC, answers a, b and c all follow logically.

10. a

Chapter 7

THE SUPPLY FUNCTIONS OF A COMPETITIVE FIRM

- ## LEARNING OBJECTIVES

After completing this chapter, you should be able to

1. Understand the market conditions under which a competitive firm operates.

2. Explain why the price-taking firm's demand curve is horizontal, and relate this assumption to the price elasticity of demand.

3. Demonstrate why marginal revenue equals price for the price taker.

4. Find the rate of output that maximizes the firm's profit in the short run.

5. Derive the firm's short-run supply curve from the marginal cost and average variable cost curves.

6. Find the profit-maximizing rate of output in the long run.

7. Derive the firm's long-run supply curve from its long-run marginal cost curve.

8. Explain why a profit-maximizing competitive firm completely exhausts all internal economies of scale.

- ## CHAPTER OVERVIEW

The Price-Taking Firm and Marginal Revenue

For a competitive firm, market supply and demand determine the price. That means that the firm is a **price taker**; the firm can produce as much or as little as its owner wants without changing market price. A firm that tries to charge a price above the market price will sell nothing; a firm that tries to sell below market price would be swamped with more orders than it could ever fill.

Total revenue for the firm is price times quantity: $R = P \times q$. Since price (P) is constant, regardless of units produced or sold, the total revenue function is plotted as straight line. **Marginal revenue** is the change in revenue with respect to quantity and is equal to market price: $\text{MR} = \dfrac{\Delta R}{\Delta q} = P$.

The **price elasticity of demand** facing the competitive firm is *infinitely elastic*. In general, the smaller the market share of a given firm, the more elastic the firm's demand function. Since the competitive firm's market share is infinitesimally small, the firm's demand curve is infinitely price-elastic. Further, the greater the number of substitutes for a product, the greater is the elasticity of demand for that product. In a competitive market, all firms produce a homogeneous product, which is a perfect substitute for every other firm's product. Thus each firm's demand curve is perfectly price-elastic.

Profit Maximization in the Short Run

In this chapter we assume that the owners of a competitive firm wish to maximize profit. Maximizing profit means maximizing the difference between total revenue and total (economic) cost. Since the market determines the firm's price, the only way the firm can change its revenue is by increasing or decreasing the amount of output it produces. In the short run, certain factor services and the associated costs of those services are fixed. The only way the firm can change its costs is by changing variable costs. Given the firm's short-run production function and the prices of variable inputs, the only way the firm can influence its variable costs is by changing its rate of output. In **Figure 7-1**, the firm's profit equals the distance between total revenue and total cost. At q_0 the firm breaks even for the first time; that is, revenue equals total cost. At q_2, total cost has again caught up with revenue. The profit-maximizing rate of output must occur somewhere between q_0 and q_2.

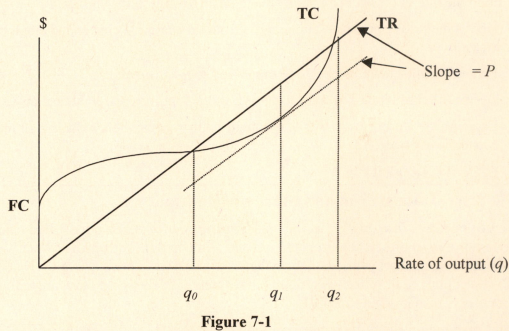

Figure 7-1

In Figure 7-1, the profit-maximizing rate of output occurs at q_1, where the total cost curve (**TC**) is parallel to the revenue curve, **TR**. Since the slope of **TC** = MC, and the slope of **R** is P, the profit-maximizing rate of output occurs where MC = P.

Figure 7-2 illustrates the same analysis using the marginal revenue (price) and marginal cost curves. Note how marginal cost first decreases with output as variable inputs become more specialized. We see that average variable cost also declines with output for awhile. Eventually, however, diminishing returns causes marginal cost to increase with output. Once marginal cost exceeds average variable cost, average variable cost increases also. The intersection between marginal cost and average variable cost identifies the **shutdown price**. If price falls below minimum average variable cost, the firm will incur smaller losses by producing nothing rather than trying to produce a positive amount.

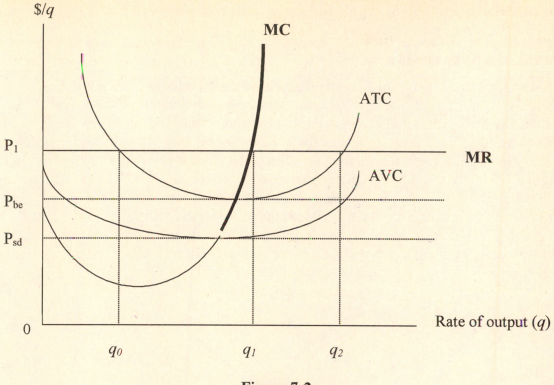

Figure 7-2

In Figure 7-2 we see the per unit costs and revenue derived from the total cost and total revenue functions plotted in Figure 7-1. Note that at price P_1 the firm beaks even where the horizontal marginal revenue line intersects the average total cost curve. At q_0, marginal revenue (price) exceeds marginal cost, so profit is still increasing as output increases. At q_2, marginal cost is so much greater than marginal revenue that it does not even show in the diagram; at q_2, profit is falling as output increases. Only at q_1, where marginal cost equals price, is output neither increasing nor decreasing. This, indeed, is the profit-maximizing rate of output.

In Figure 7-2, the break-even price occurs at the level where average total cost reaches its minimum. At prices greater than P_{be}, like $P = P_1$, the firm covers all costs–both explicit costs and opportunity costs–when it produces the profit-maximizing rate of output. For prices lower than P_{be}, like $P = P_{sd}$, the firm incurs economic losses when it produces the profit-maximizing rate of output. Between P_{be} and P_{sd}, the firm is better off producing where marginal cost equals price than it would be if it produced nothing. This is because, as long as price exceeds average variable cost, revenue is sufficient to cover variable costs, with something left over to apply to fixed costs. If the firm shut down, it would lose all its fixed costs. But if the price were less than P_{sd}, then revenue would be less than variable costs. In addition to losing all its fixed costs, the firm would lose the difference between variable costs and revenue. In such an event, the firm would minimize its losses by shutting down (setting output equal to zero) and losing only its fixed costs.

The firm's **short-run supply curve** is the portion of its marginal cost curve that lies above its average variable cost curve. In Figure 7-2, the short-run supply curve is the darkened portion of the marginal cost curve. Since marginal cost must exceed average variable cost, the short-run supply curve must be positively sloped. For the competitive firm, the **price elasticity of supply** equals the slope of its marginal cost curve times the ratio of price to quantity at that point.

Break-even Analysis

The most important decision an entrepreneur ever makes is whether or not to start a business. Unfortunately, before he or she starts operations, the would-be producer has little if any actual information about costs or revenue. Typically, an entrepreneur may be able to estimate fixed costs, total cost for a single rate of output (say, by asking a friend already in business), and the revenue function (since market price may be known). In **Figure 7-3**, Sally Jones has estimated that revenue will equal $R_1 = P_1q$ and that total cost will equal $TC = FC + bq$. In this case, $P_1 > b$, so there is some rate of output, q_1, where revenue is expected to exceed costs. Based on the strength of her revenue and cost *forecasts*, Sally may decide to go into business for herself. If her estimates are unrealistically optimistic, she will fail. If her forecasts are accurate or conservative, she will succeed.

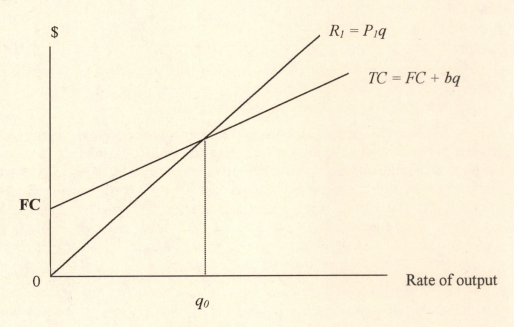

Figure 7-3

Once Sally opens her business she will have much better information than she did when she performed her breakeven analysis. Typically, her total cost curve will look more like the one in **Figure 7-1**, revealing that there are two rates of output where revenue and cost are equal. More important, though, once she is able to track the marginal cost of production, she will know precisely where marginal cost equals price. The moral is that entrepreneurs should always make their decisions based on the most reliable information available *at that time*. A crude break-even analysis launched Sally's successful career in business. But she should not ignore vital information from her own experience.

The Long-Run Supply Function of a Competitive Firm

In the long run, all of a firm's costs are variable. It follows that the long-run shutdown price for the firm is the minimum point on the firm's long-run average cost curve. If the price remained above the shut-down point for the firm to make investment decisions, the firm would attempt to expand output and capacity along its long-run marginal cost curve. It follows that the firm's long-run supply function is the portion of its long-run marginal cost curve that lies above its long-run average cost curve. This implies that the firm must **exhaust its internal economies of scale**, which cause its long-run average cost curve to decline with output, before it can reach a point on its long-run supply curve.

• KEY TERMS

Price-taking firm When price is determined by supply and demand in a competitive market, the individual rate of output does not effect that price. This causes the firm's marginal revenue to equal the market price.

Marginal revenue The change in revenue divided by the change in output. When a firm is a price taker, marginal revenue equals market price.

Price elasticity of demand for a competitive firm When a firm is a price taker, the price elasticity of demand for that firm is infinite. If it charges even a penny above the market price, it sells nothing. If it charges even a penny less than the market price, the quantity demanded would swamp its ability to produce.

Supply elasticity of a competitive firm The percentage change in quantity supplied divided by the percentage change in market price. For a competitive firm, the supply elasticity equals the slope of its marginal cost curve times the ratio of price to quantity at that point.

Setting marginal cost equal to price Producing that rate of output where marginal cost equals price (marginal revenue) maximizes profit, as long as price exceeds average variable cost.

Revenues cover variable cost If price is less than minimum average variable cost, the firm 's loss minimizing output is zero. The competitive firm shuts down if revenue does not cover variable cost.

Shutdown price The price identified by the minimum point on the average variable cost curve. For any price above the shutdown price, the firm should produce the rate of output where marginal cost equals price. For any price less than the shutdown price, the firm should produce zero output. If price equals the shutdown price, the firm will incur losses equal to fixed cost, whether it produces where marginal cost equals price, or shuts down.

Short-run supply function That portion of the short-run marginal cost function above the minimum average variable cost that identifies the rate of output that maximizes profit, predicting what the firm will produce.

Long-run supply function That portion of the long-run marginal cost function above the minimum long-run average cost that identifies the rate of output that maximizes profit, predicting what the firm will produce if the price persists at that level long enough for investment decisions to be made.

Exhaustion of economies of scale in the long run In order to be on its long-run supply function, the firm must be producing at least at the rate of output associated with its minimum long-run average cost curve. The only way this can happen is if the firm has exhausted all internal economies of scale.

Nonnegative profits in the long run Whenever price falls below the minimum point on its long-run average cost curve, the firm will leave the industry. Hence, profit cannot be negative for a profit-maximizing competitive firm in long-run equilibrium.

• PROBLEMS

1. Maria is trying to decide whether to quit her position as an associate with a law firm, that pays her $5,000 per month, and open her own practice. She figures it will cost her $3,000 a month to rent office space and pay a receptionist. It will cost her $250 per case in staff time for a legal assistant. Her experience with her current firm indicates that she could bill $1,000 per case.

   a. What are Maria's fixed costs? _____

   b. What is Maria's estimated marginal cost? _____

   c. Maria estimates that she could handle ten cases per month by herself and her staff. In **Chart 7-1**, plot her total cost line and her total revenue line.

Chart 7.1

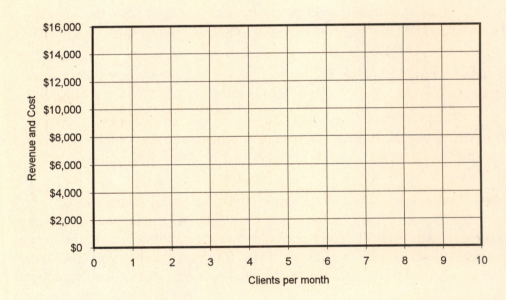

Clients per month

   d. According to your diagram in Chart 7-1, is it feasible for Maria to open her own law office? Briefly explain your answer.

   _____

   _____

e. Suppose she decided that she could charge $1,500 per case. Would this change your answer to part d? Briefly explain.

_____

_____

2. Below are the short-run total costs for the Aardvark Cab Company (the first cab company in the phone directory). The owner knows from experience that he gets 240 calls per day at an average fare of $10. He can either dispatch these calls to his own cabs or forward the calls to another cab company. Since each cab can handle 20 calls per day, he must decide how many cabs to keep on the road. More cabs mean more trips but higher maintenance costs. Use the information from **Table 7-1** to answer the questions that follow.

Table 7-1

Trips	Total Cost	Variable Cost	Average Total Cost	Average Var. Cost	Marginal Cost
0	$500	___	___	___	___
20	$680	___	___	___	___
40	$840	___	___	___	___
60	$980	___	___	___	___
80	$1,100	___	___	___	___
100	$1,200	___	___	___	___
120	$1,320	___	___	___	___
140	$1,460	___	___	___	___
160	$1,620	___	___	___	___
180	$1,800	___	___	___	___
200	$2,000	___	___	___	___
220	$2,220	___	___	___	___
240	$2,460	___	___	___	___

a. Fill in the missing spaces. Note that quantity (trips) increases by increments of 20 when you compute marginal and average variable costs.

b. What is the lowest fare required for the owner take calls instead of referring them to other companies (i.e., what is Aardvark's shut-down price)?

_____

c. If Aardvark were not already in business, would its owner be likely to enter, given cost and price conditions? Briefly explain.

_____

_____

d. How many trips per day should the company accept to maximize profit? Explain.

_____

_____

e. How much profit is the owner receiving every day?

_____

f. Based on your answer to part e, will the owner of the Aardvark Cab Company be able to make a capital gain by selling the company to another operator? Briefly explain.

_____

_____

3. Peter Piper sells Piper's Select Pickles. He has computed that the marginal cost of pickle-packing is MC $= 10 + 2q$, where q is the cases of pickles packed. His total costs are TC $= 200 + 10q + q^2$. Use this information to answer the questions that follow.

a. What are Peter's fixed costs of pickle-packing? _____

b. What is the equation for Peter's average variable cost? _____

_____

c. What is Peter's shutdown price? _____

d. If pickles sell for $30 a case, how many cases should Peter produce? _____

e. Is pickle packing profitable? Provide precise proof. _____

_____

• TRUE-FALSE QUESTIONS

For each of the following statements, indicate whether the statement is true (agrees with economic theory), false (is contradicted by economic theory), or uncertain (could be true or false; not enough information is given), and briefly explain your answer.

1. Once a firm has surpassed its break-even level of output, the more it produces the more profitable the business will be.

_____

_____

_____

_____

2. There are 1,000 firms producing a homogeneous product. The price elasticity of the market demand curve is $-\frac{1}{2}$. Therefore, any firm that raises its price can expect to increase its revenue.

_____

_____

_____

_____

3. A competitive firm's long-run supply curve tends to be more price-elastic than its short-run supply curve.

_____

_____

_____

_____

4. Whenever a firm's revenue cannot cover its fixed costs, the firm should shut down.

_____

_____

_____

_____

5. Whenever a firm's revenue cannot cover its variable costs, the firm should shut down.

_____

_____

_____

_____

• MULTIPLE CHOICE QUESTIONS

1. Which one of the following industries most closely approximates a competitive industry?

   a. Automobiles.

   b. Carbonated soft drinks.

   c. Milk.

   d. Personal computers.

2. If the slope of the total revenue function of a competitive firm is +10, then

   a. price = $10.

   b. marginal revenue = $10.

   c. total revenue = $10q$.

   d. all of the above.

3. For a competitive firm, the price elasticity of demand

    a. is the same as the price elasticity of the market demand curve.

    b. is less elastic than the price elasticity of the market demand curve.

    c. is the same as the supply elasticity.

    d. is infinitely elastic.

4. If a firm is not a price taker and its market share declines, we would expect its price elasticity of demand to

    a. become more price-elastic.

    b. become less price-elastic.

    c. remain the same.

    d. do one of the above, but it is impossible to tell without additional information.

5. If marginal cost = $5, marginal revenue = $8, total revenue = $1,000, total cost = $1,500, and fixed cost = $500, in the short run the firm should

    a. increase output.

    b. decrease output.

    c. leave output unchanged.

    d. shut down.

6. Break-even analysis is most appropriate for

    a. deciding what rate of output to produce.

    b. deciding whether to remain in business.

    c. deciding whether to enter an unfamiliar industry.

    d. all of the above.

7. One advantage of permitting the unrestricted importation of foreign goods into the country is that it

    a. raises price elasticity of demand for domestic producers and therefore raises prices.

    b. lowers price elasticity of demand for domestic producers and therefore raises prices.

    c. raises price elasticity of demand for domestic producers and therefore lowers prices.

    d. lowers price elasticity of demand for domestic producers and therefore lowers prices.

8. If average variable cost at the current quantity equals $4 and price equals $3, in the short-run the firm should

   a. increase output.

   b. decrease output.

   c. shut down.

   d. keep output at present levels.

9. If long-run average cost is minimized at q_1, where it equals $6, and price equals $7, the firm should

   a. produce at q_1.

   b. produce more than q_1.

   c. produce less than q_1.

   d. impossible to tell without additional information.

10. If we observe falling prices in a competitive industry in long-run equilibrium, likely explanations include

    a. falling factor prices.

    b. technological improvements.

    c. realization of internal economies of scale.

    d. (a) and (b).

    e. all of the above.

- ## ANSWERS TO PROBLEMS, TRUE-FALSE, AND MULTIPLE-CHOICE QUESTIONS

Answers to Problems

1. a. Maria's fixed costs are $8,000 per month.

   b. Marginal cost would be $250 per case.

c. Here is Maria's breakeven diagram.

Chart 7.1a

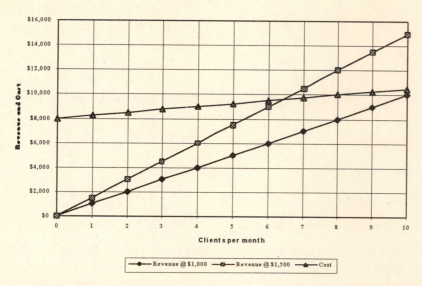

d. According to the diagram, Maria will not be able to break even with ten or fewer cases, so opening her own law office is not feasible.

e. At $1,500 per case, Maria could breakeven with slightly more than six cases per month, making opening her own law office economically feasible.

2. a. Table 7-1a provides the variable cost, average variable cost, and marginal cost data.

Table 7-1a

Trips	Total Cost	Variable Cost	Average Total Cost	Average Var Cost	Marginal Cost
0	$500	$0	na	na	na
20	$680	$180	$34.00	$9.00	$9.00
40	$840	$340	$21.00	$8.50	$8.00
60	$980	$480	$16.33	$8.00	$7.00
80	$1,100	$600	$13.75	$7.50	$6.00
100	$1,200	$700	$12.00	$7.00	$5.00
120	$1,320	$820	$11.00	$6.83	$6.00
140	$1,460	$960	$10.43	$6.86	$7.00
160	$1,620	$1,120	$10.13	$7.00	$8.00
180	$1,800	$1,300	$10.00	$7.22	$9.00
200	$2,000	$1,500	$10.00	$7.50	$10.00
220	$2,220	$1,720	$10.09	$7.82	$11.00
240	$2,460	$1,960	$10.25	$8.17	$12.00

b. The shutdown price is the minimum average variable cost, which is approximately $6.83.

c. Minimum average total cost is precisely $10.00. If these conditions had prevailed at the time of Aardvark's entry decision, the owner(s) would have been indifferent about entering this market or some other market, since all inputs would have earned a normal return.

d. To maximize profit, the firm should equate marginal cost to price, which occurs at 200 calls per day.

e. With 200 calls per day, total revenue would be $2,000, total cost would be $2,000, and economic profit would be zero.

f. The owner should not be able to obtain a capital gain by selling the company to another buyer, since an informed buyer could purchase the same resources on the market and receive zero economic profit.

3. a. Fixed costs equal $500.

b. Average variable cost is given by $AVC = \dfrac{10q + q^2}{q} = 10 + q$.

c. Minimum average variable cost occurs when output is zero and AVC = $10. Therefore, the shutdown price is $10.

d. If pickles sell for $30 per case, Peter determines the optimal number of pickles by equating marginal cost and price: $10 + 2q = 30 \rightarrow q^* = 10$, since $P > \$10$.

e. Profit = $30(10) - (200 + 10(10) + (10)^2 = \$300 - \$400 = -\$100$. No, pickle packing is not particularly profitable.

Answers to True-False Questions

1. *False*. Once a firm has passed its break-even point, profit will increase only up to that rate of output where marginal cost equals price. Producing so that $MC > P$ will cause profit to decline.

2. *False*. With 1,000 firms producing a homogeneous product, each firm is a price taker. Each firm faces a perfectly elastic demand curve, despite the fact that the market demand is price-inelastic at that price. Any firm that tried to raises its price unilaterally would sell zero output.

3. *True*. In the long run, firms can vary all their inputs, so that the long-run marginal cost curve is flatter than short-run marginal cost, implying a more price-elastic long-run supply curve.

4. *False*. When a firm's revenue cannot cover its *variable* costs the firm should shut down. If all variable costs are covered, revenue left over can be applied to fixed costs, and the firm is better off operating (producing a positive rate of output) than by shutting down.

5. *True*. See the answer to question 4.

Answers to Multiple-Choice Questions

1. c (Milk comes closest to being a homogeneous product.)

2. d

3. d

4. a

5. a (Price exceeds marginal cost, and revenue covers variable costs, so the firm will increase profits or decrease losses by expanding the rate of output.)

6. c (Break-even analysis is inappropriate for deciding the rate of output, since one should equate MC = P, and for determining whether to stay in business, since one should compare P and minimum AVC.)

7. c

8. c

9. b (Where average variable cost is minimized, MC = AVC = $6. Since MC = $6 at q_1 and P = $7, the firm should expand output.)

10. d (If a competitive industry is already in equilibrium, firms will already have exhausted internal economies of scale.)

Chapter 8

PRICE DETERMINATION IN A COMPETITIVE INDUSTRY

• LEARNING OBJECTIVES

After completing this chapter, you should be able to

1. Describe the long-run market equilibrium in a competitive industry.

2. Describe the short-run market equilibrium in a competitive industry.

3. Contrast the short-run and long-run competitive equilibria.

4. Derive the long-run market supply function for a constant cost industry.

5. Derive the long-run supply function for an increasing cost industry.

6. Contrast the impacts of an unexpected demand shift on a constant cost industry and an increasing cost industry.

7. Explain the role of economic rent in allocating scarce managerial resources.

8. Follow the process of cost-saving innovation in the short run and the long run.

9. Understand how licensing and other restrictions on the number of firms affect price, output, and the size of the firm.

10. Illustrate the effect of a per unit tax on market equilibrium price and output.

11. Explain how the price elasticity of demand affects the sharing of a tax between buyers and sellers.

12. Describe the welfare effects of a per unit tax.

• CHAPTER OVERVIEW

Competitive Equilibrium in Constant-Cost Industries

The short-run analysis of market competition assumes that the number of firms is fixed. In the long-run, the number of firms increases in response to positive economic profit and decreases if firms are experiencing economic losses.

Figure 8-1 illustrates the effect of an increase in market demand in the short run. The panel on the left depicts the unit-cost functions of a typical firm. At the initial equilibrium price of P_0, the firm is receiving zero economic profit, producing q_0 units of output. Note that $ATC = MC = P_0$ when the firm produces q_0. The panel on the right depicts the short-run market equilibrium. The market price is P_0 because that is where the market demand curve, D_0, intersects the short-run market supply curve, S_0. The market equilibrium quantity, Q_0, is the sum of the output of all the firms at that price. If there are n_0 firms in the industry, $Q_0 = n_0 q_0$.

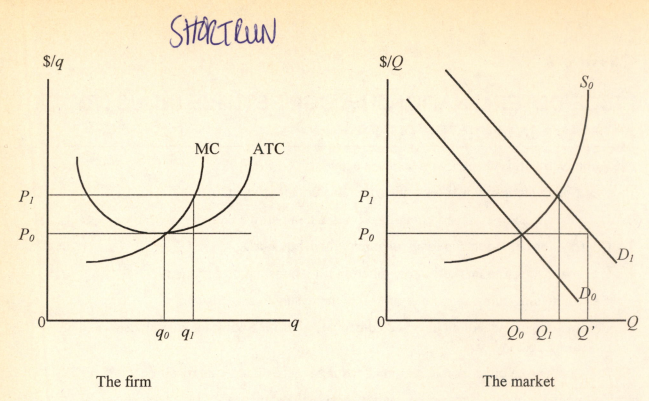

The firm   The market

Figure 8-1

The increase in market demand to D_1 upsets the equilibrium price. If the price remained at P_0, the quantity demanded, Q', would exceed the quantity supplied, which would remain at Q_0. The market price must increase until, at P_1, quantity demanded equals quantity supplied, Q_1. On the left-hand panel we see that the typical firm responds to the increase in the equilibrium price by increasing its rate of output. Indeed, $Q_1 = n_0 q_1$; the quantity supplied increases in the short run because each firm produces more output, not because the number of firms increases.

Figure 8-1 depicts a market in **long-run equilibrium** at price P_0 and quantity Q_0 because, at that price, the typical firm is receiving zero economic profit. Revenue is just sufficient to cover the sum of explicit and opportunity costs to produce output q_0 efficiently. When market demand increases, price must increase to encourage the n_0 firms in the industry to expand output, thus avoiding a shortage of the good. As a result of the increase in the market price, with the number of firms remaining constant, the incumbent firms receive positive economic profit. This profit (equal to $[P_1\text{-ATC}]q_1$), encourages entrepreneurs to enter this industry. Positive economic profit and the fixed number of firms mean that the short-run equilibrium at (P_1, Q_1) is not a long-run equilibrium.

Figure 8-2 continues the analysis of long-run equilibrium. In order to complete that analysis, we must determine how an increase in the number of firms affects the prices of factors of production. The simplest case is the **constant-cost industry**, in which entering firms have the same unit-cost functions as established firms. Because incumbent firms enjoy economic profits, new firms are attracted into that industry, causing the number of firms to increase. The increase in the number of firms causes a rightward shift in the short-run market supply curve, from S_0 to S_1. As supply increases, the short-run equilibrium price decreases until, at price P_0, both short-run and long-run competitive equilibria are again restored. Note that in the new long-run equilibrium the market quantity is Q', the quantity demanded when the demand curve originally shifted. Because economic profit encourages new firms to enter the market, two outcomes occur in a constant-cost industry: (1) The process of firm entry eventually eliminates economic profit. (2) The shift in the short-run supply curve eventually delivers to consumers the entire quantity demanded at the long-run equilibrium price. Because the price tends to return to P_0 when market demand increases or decreases, the **long-run supply function (LRS),** is a horizontal line at that price. Although each firm is now producing only q_0 units of output, industry output has increased because $Q' = n_1 q_0$.

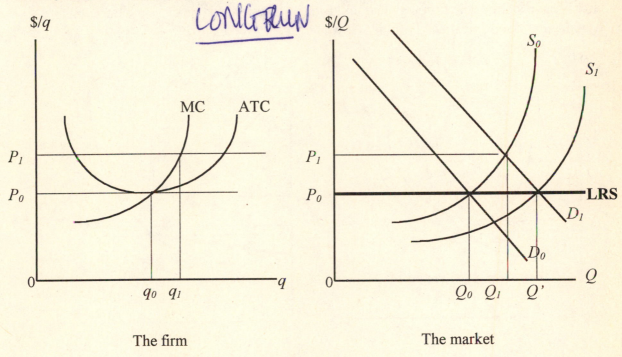

The firm   The market

Figure 8-2

The Increasing-Cost Industry

The increasing cost industry is an industry in which new firms have higher unit costs than did incumbent firms before entry started. As in the constant-cost case, the process of market entry occurs until the last firm to enter receives zero economic profit. In the constant cost case, the elimination of economic profit occurs wholly through the decrease in equilibrium price. In the increasing cost case, economic profits are squeezed between the decrease in the equilibrium price and the increase in the firm's unit-cost functions. This process is depicted in **Figure 8-3.**

Again, we start with a long-run equilibrium at price P_0 and quantity Q_0, where the representative firm is making zero economic profits producing quantity q_0, with $Q_0 = n_0 q_0$. An increase in demand increases the short-run equilibrium price to P_1 and the equilibrium quantity to $Q_1 = n_0 q_1$, with incumbent firms now earning positive economic profits. As new firms enter the market, the short-run supply curve again shifts to the right, reducing the equilibrium price. However, the average and marginal cost curves for the firm gradually increase due to two factors: **external diseconomies of scale** and **specialized factors of production**. External diseconomies of scale mean that as factor use increases the industry demand for inputs tends to increase the price of those inputs. External diseconomies of scale increase unit costs of both established and entering firms. As we will see below, specialized factors of production mean that entering firms have higher unit costs than established firms do. Specialized factors of production lead to **economic rent.** Eventually, when the supply curve shifts to S_1, the market price has fallen to P_2, equal to the minimum long-run average cost for the entering firm. Depending on how its cost curves have shifted, the firm may end up producing more, less, or the same output as it produced at the original equilibrium. However, we know that $Q' = n_1q_2 > Q_1$.

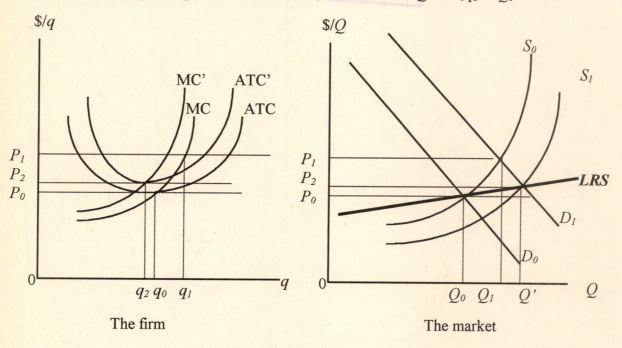

The firm   The market

Figure 8-3

Long-run vs. Short-run Price Elasticity of Supply

The **price elasticity of supply** measures the percentage change in quantity supplied due to a 1 percent increase in the market price, following a change in demand. In the short run, the changes in price and quantity follow the short-run market supply curve. The short-run supply curve is positively sloped because of diminishing returns to variable factors. The long-run price elasticity of supply reflects the adjustment of incumbent firms to the minimum point on each long-run average cost curve and the change in the number of firms due to economic profits or losses. In the case of a constant-cost industry, the long-run supply function is infinitely elastic, since long-run equilibrium price is constant. With an increasing cost industry, the price elasticity of supply will be less than infinite, but, because the number of firms can change, the long-run price elasticity will always be greater than the short-run supply elasticity. In the limiting case, when the number of firms is fixed by licensing or some other artificial restriction, the long run market supply curve will follow the individual firm's long-run marginal cost curves, which are more elastic than the short-run marginal cost curves.

Economic Rent

In an increasing cost industry, owners of superior or specialized factors of production can receive *economic rent* as the industry expands. Suppose that the firm in **Figure 8-3** is able to retain its lower marginal and average total cost curves, while entering firms experience higher costs. It would appear that the incumbent firm would continue to receive economic profit after the new long-run equilibrium price occurred at P_2. However, the cost advantage enjoyed by the incumbent firm would be tied to one or more factors of production. For instance, the advantage may come from a favorable location: Established firms may have lower transportation costs than entering firms. Or the owner-entrepreneur may be especially skilled in controlling costs or motivating workers. In either case, the owner of the land or the manager would receive bids from entering firms to transfer that resource to them. Having offers to lease the land or manage another firm increases the opportunity cost of using that resource in the original firm.

Economic rent is the payment to the owner of a factor in excess of the minimum necessary for the factor's services to be supplied. In our example, economic rent would equal the rent another firm would pay for the location minus the rent necessary to keep that land in the industry in question. Alternatively, if the entrepreneur could earn $100,000 managing someone else's firm, and is willing to work in her own firm for $50,000 per year, any income over $50,000 would offset the $100,000 opportunity cost of being her own boss. Economic profits are always a short-run phenomenon. In the long run, all economic profits are either eliminated through market entry, or they become economic rent.

The long-run industry supply curve will also have a positive slope if entrepreneurs differ in their managerial ability. As the price of the product rises, entering firms will tend to have less efficient managers than established firms. Entry will stop when entering firms cannot achieve positive economic profit, although established firms may continue to have revenue exceeding economic costs when the firm produces where price equals long-run marginal cost. Again, however, those economic profits turn into economic rent. Established managers receive job offers from entrepreneurs who recognize their superior talent. Instead of receiving, say, $50,000 in revenue over economic costs, the established managers now find they have job offers for $50,000 in excess of what they are taking as wages from their current firm. Presto! The invisible hand changes economic profit into economic rent.

Barriers to entry may prevent the short-run supply curve from shifting to the right if the number of firms is artificially held constant. For instance, the number of taxicabs in a city may be limited to the number of *medallions* that the Taxi Authority has issued. Companies that have taxi medallions will continue to receive revenue in excess of costs in the long run because the number of medallions does not increase as quickly as demand. This is clearly a factor in Las Vegas, which has a rapid increase in tourism, but a very slow increase in medallions.

If barriers to entry entail transferable licenses, then the economic profit will become economic rent. Suppose that by having a taxi medallion, a taxi company receives revenue of $5,000 in excess of its economic costs. Further, suppose that the market rate of interest is 10 percent. It follows that the value of the taxi medallion will equal approximately $50,000, because one would have to invest $50,000 in the market to receive an annual income of $5,000 if the market rate of interest remained at 10 percent. The $5,000 of excess revenue over explicit costs is no longer economic profit; it is a normal return on a scarce productive asset.

Per Unit Taxes and Market Equilibrium

If the government imposes a **per unit tax** on the product of a competitive industry, the marginal cost of selling an additional unit will be equal to the pretax marginal cost plus the per unit tax. The long-run average cost of the firm will be the pretax long-run average cost plus the per unit tax. Long-run average cost will reach a minimum at the same rate of output with the tax as it would without the tax. The rise in average total cost at that rate of output will equal the pretax minimum average cost plus the per unit tax.

In the short run, the per unit tax will be shared between the buyer and the seller according to the relative elasticity of demand and supply. In the long run, all of the per unit tax will be paid by the buyer if the good is produced in a constant-cost industry, because firms will exit until the after-tax price is restored. However, price may not rise to equal the tax in an increasing-cost industry because some of the tax will be paid out of pretax economic rent.

A per-unit tax will impose an excess burden. In a constant-cost industry, the excess burden will equal the reduced consumer surplus caused by the reduction in quantity demanded at the higher price. In an increasing-cost industry, the excess burden will be shared by buyers (lower consumer surplus), and sellers (lower economic rent).

• KEY TERMS

Long-run industry equilibrium The combination of price and output that exists when each firm is receiving zero economic profit, producing at the minimum point on its long-run average cost curve.

Constant-cost industry An industry in which the number of firms can increase or decrease without changing the position of the marginal firm's average total cost curve. In a constant cost industry, the long-run supply curve will be a horizontal line at the level of minimum long run average cost for the efficient firm.

Short-run industry supply function The curve or function obtained by the sum of the quantity supplied by each firm in an industry at each price. The short-run industry supply function is the horizontal sum of the short-run marginal cost curve (above average variable cost) for each firm in the industry.

Short-run industry equilibrium That quantity and price combination identified by the point of intersection between the industry demand and industry supply curves.

Horizontal industry supply function The long-run supply function for a constant cost industry when firms are free to enter or leave the industry.

Role of profits and losses Economic profits by incumbent firms signal to new firms that they can receive more than the opportunity cost of inputs. Economic profits encourage new firms to enter faster than old firms exit, causing a net increase in the number of firms and a rightward shift in the short-run industry supply curve. Economic losses play the opposite role. When there are economic losses, established firms leave the industry faster than new firms enter, so that the number of firms decreases and the industry supply curve shifts to the left, increasing equilibrium price and reducing equilibrium quantity until the marginal firm receives zero economic profits.

Adjustment of an industry to a shift in market demand When a market in long-run competitive equilibrium experiences an increase in market demand, the short-run equilibrium price will increase, causing incumbent firms to experience positive economic profit. The existence of positive economic profit causes the number of firms to rise, so that the industry supply curve shifts to the right. As a result, price falls (and cost may rise), unit price equals minimum long-run average cost, and long-run equilibrium is restored. A decrease in demand works in the opposite direction, reducing price, causing economic losses, until enough firms leave the market so that short-run supply shifts to the left and price rises until price equals minimum average cost again.

Increasing-cost industry An industry in which factor prices increase as the number of firms increase. As a result, as the industry expands, long-run equilibrium price also increases, which causes the long-run supply curve to be positively sloped.

External pecuniary economies If expansion in the number of firms causes the cost curves of firms to shift downward, then as demand increases, long-run equilibrium price will decrease. This will cause the long-run supply curve to have the appearance of a negative slope.

Economic rent Payments for the services of a factor of production in excess of what would be required for those services to be supplied. If barriers to entry or specialized factors prevent the elimination of economic profit, that economic profit will become economic rent in the long run.

Differences in managerial ability One factor that can cause economic rent. As an industry expands, firms with superior managers will receive economic profit, while new firms with average managers will receive zero economic profit. As the new firms bid for the services of the superior managers, the salaries of those managers will rise. Superior managers who own their firms will no longer receive positive economic profit because the opportunity cost of running their own companies will rise to absorb that economic profit.

Switching to a new technology The advantages in a new technology depend on the average total cost under the new technology compared to the average variable cost of an established technology. For this reason, established firms may not immediately switch to the new technology but may wait until old equipment has to be replaced, so that the average total cost of the new technology is less than the average variable cost of the old technology.

Changing the shape of the supply function through licensing and entry barriers
Barriers to entry, such as licensing, which prevent the number of firms from increasing. This causes the market supply curve to follow the short-run supply curve rather than the more elastic long-run supply curve that would result through firm entry.

Placing a per unit tax on a competitive industry A tax represents an increase in the cost of selling a commodity. The effect of the tax is to increase the equilibrium price. In the short run, the equilibrium price will be shared between the buyers and the sellers according to the elasticity of demand and supply. In the long run, all the per-unit tax will be paid by the buyer.

Maximizing the sum of consumer and producer surplus A phenomenon that occurs under competitive conditions, where price is determined by the free operation of supply and demand, and where firms are free to enter and exit. Any market interference that increases consumer surplus (i.e., by restricting price) will further reduce producer surplus. Any impediment to entry that increases producer surplus will further reduce consumer surplus.

• PROBLEMS

1. This problem examines the effects of entry and exit on equilibrium price and quantity in a constant-cost industry. We are given that LRAC is minimized when quantity = 10 units. Short-run marginal cost is given by $MC = 10 + q$. (Note that ATC = 20 when $q = 10$.)

    a. Setting MC = p and solving for q, compute the equation for the firm's short-run supply function.

    b. If 1,000 identical firms are in the market, what is the formula for the industry supply function?

    c. Market demand is given by the expression $Q_d = 40,000 - 1,000\,P$. What is the industry equilibrium price?

d. What is the industry equilibrium output?

_____

e. How much output will an individual firm produce at this equilibrium price?

_____

f. How much economic profit/loss does this firm experience?

_____

2. a. If the industry in question 1 is a constant cost industry, what is the long-run equilibrium price?

_____

b. Describe the long-run supply curve for this industry.

_____

c. What is the quantity demanded at the long-run equilibrium price?

_____

d. How many firms have to enter or exit for long-run competitive equilibrium to be established?

_____

3. Continuing with the industry in questions 1 and 2, suppose the market again reached long-run equilibrium, and then demand increased to $Q_d = 55,000 - 1,000\,P$.

a. What is the new short-run equilibrium price?

_____

b. How much economic profit is the typical firm now receiving in the short-run?

_____

c. What is the quantity demanded at the long-run equilibrium price?

_____

d. How many firms must enter or exit before long-run equilibrium price is reestablished?

_____

4. Suppose that Peter P. is such an excellent manager that long-run average cost achieves a minimum value of $18 when $q = 10$ because his MC = 8 + q. All other firms continue to experience a minimum LRAC of $20 when $q = 10$.

a. What will be the value of long-run equilibrium price?

_____

b. How much will Peter's economic profit be in the short run?

_____

c. How much will new firms offer Peter P. to manage their firms?

_____

d. What is Peter P.'s economic rent?

_____

5. Continue your analysis of the same industry. Suppose that the government decides to impose a $2 per unit tax on the commodity in this industry.

a. If the industry is in long-run equilibrium according to your answer to question 3, what will be the value of the *short-run* equilibrium price and quantity?

_____

b. How much of the tax will the average buyer pay?

_____

c. How much of the tax will the average seller pay?

_____

d. What will be the long-run equilibrium price with the $2 per unit tax?

_____

e. How much of the tax will the buyers pay?

_____

f. How much of the tax will the sellers pay?

_____

• TRUE-FALSE QUESTIONS

For each of the following statements, indicate whether the statement is true (agrees with economic theory), false (is contradicted by economic theory), or uncertain (could be true or false; not enough information is given), and briefly explain your answer.

1. In a constant-cost industry, shifts in the demand curve have no effect on *short-run* equilibrium price or quantity.

_____

_____

_____

_____

2. In an increasing-cost industry, the long-run equilibrium price tends to increase when the demand curve shifts to the right.

    _____

    _____

    _____

3. When barriers to entry take the form of a transferable license (the number of firms are fixed, but the right to sell can itself be sold), established firms will receive economic profit in long-run equilibrium.

    _____

    _____

    _____

4. A per unit tax, imposed on a commodity produced in a constant-cost competitive industry, will be shared between the buyer and the seller in the short run, but will be borne wholly by the buyer in the long run.

    _____

    _____

    _____

5. A per unit tax, imposed on a commodity produced in an increasing-cost competitive industry, will be shared between the buyer and the seller in the short run, but will be borne wholly by the buyer in the long run.

    _____

    _____

    _____

• MULTIPLE-CHOICE QUESTIONS

1. If a market experiences an increase in demand for the product, in the short run
    a. price rises, quantity sold is unchanged, and the number of firms in unchanged.
    b. price rises, quantity sold increases, and the number of firms is unchanged.
    c. price rises, quantity sold increases, and the number of firms increases.
    d. price is unchanged, quantity sold increases, and the number of firms increases.

2. If a constant-cost industry experiences an increase in demand, after long-run equilibrium is reestablished

    a. price rises, quantity sold is unchanged, and the number of firms in unchanged.

    b. price rises, quantity sold increases, and the number of firms is unchanged.

    c. price rises, quantity sold increases, and the number of firms increases.

    d. price is unchanged, quantity sold increases, and the number of firms increases.

3. If an increasing-cost industry experiences an increase in demand, after long-run equilibrium is reestablished

    a. price rises, quantity sold is unchanged, and the number of firms in unchanged.

    b. price rises, quantity sold increases, and the number of firms is unchanged.

    c. price rises, quantity sold increases, and the number of firms increases.

    d. price is unchanged, quantity sold increases, and the number of firms increases.

4. In order for an industry to be a constant-cost industry, it is necessary that

    a. all firms have identical cost curves.

    b. factor prices remain constant in response to industry expansion.

    c. there be neither pecuniary economies nor diseconomies.

    d. all of the above be true.

5. If a market is initially in long-run equilibrium and then experiences a decrease in demand, firms incur economic losses in the short-run because price is less than

    a. marginal cost.

    b. average cost.

    c. variable cost.

    d. total cost.

6. The effect of *external pecuniary diseconomies of scale* is to cause the long-run industry supply curve to have a

    a. positive slope.

    b. negative slope.

    c. slope of zero.

    d. U-shape (first a negative slope, then a positive slope).

7. Cyrano earns $500,000 per year as a pinup model. If modeling were not so lucrataive, he would use his CPA qualifications and earn $60,000 per year. Cyrano's economic rent is

a. zero.

b. $60,000.

c. $440,000.

d. $500,000.

8. If a per unit tax of $5.00 is imposed on a product produced in a constant-cost industry, then the *short-run* equilibrium price of the product will increase by

a. exactly $5.00.

b. by less than $5.00.

c. by more than $5.00.

d. some amount, but it is impossible to tell without additional information.

9. If a per unit tax of $5.00 is imposed on a product produced in a constant cost industry, then the *long-run* equilibrium price of the product will increase by

a. exactly $5.00.

b. less than $5.00.

c. more than $5.00.

d. some amount, but it is impossible to tell without additional information.

10. In the long run, economic rents and active markets for scarce managerial talents will

a. ensure that entrants are at a cost disadvantage relative to established firms.

b. result in a constant-cost industry.

c. ensure that economic profits continue in the long run.

d. cause economic profit to become zero.

- ## ANSWERS TO PROBLEMS, TRUE-FALSE AND MULTIPLE-CHOICE QUESTIONS

Answers to Problems

1. a. $MC = p$ implies $10 + q = p$ or $q_s = p - 10$.

   b. $Q_s = 1,000(q_s) = 1,000(p - 10) = 1,000p - 10,000$, or $Q_s = -10,000 + 1,000p$.

   c. $Q_d = Q_s$ implies $40,000 - 1,000p = -10,000 + 1,000p$

   $$50,000 = 2,000p, \text{ implying } p = \frac{50,000}{2,000} = \$25.$$

d. $Q_s = 1,000(25) - 10,000 = 15,000$ and $Q_d = 40,000 - 1,000(25) = 15,000$.

e. $q_s = -10 + 25 = 15$ units.

f. Revenue $= 25(15) = \$375$. TC $= 200$ at $q = 10$. TC at $15 = 200 + 11 + 12 + 13 + 14 + 15 = 265$, so economic profit $= \$375 - 265 = \$110$.

2. a. In a constant cost industry, the long-run equilibrium price equals the minimum long run average cost, which in this case, is $20.

b. The long-run supply curve is a horizontal line at $P = \$20$.

c. At the long-run equilibrium price, quantity demanded $= 40,000 - 1,000(20) = 20,000$.

d. Since each firm will produce 10 units in long-run equilibrium, there would be $\dfrac{20,000}{10} = 2,000$ firms in long-run equilibrium, given the position of the demand curve.

3. a. The new industry supply curve is $Q_s = -20,000 + 2,000P$. Setting the quantity supplied equal to quantity demanded,

$$-20,000 + 2,000P = 55,000 - 1,000P$$

$$3,000P = 75,000 \rightarrow P = \frac{75,000}{3,000} = \$25$$

b. When $P = \$25$, the typical firm produces 15 units of output, as shown in question 1. It follows that economic profit $= \$110$.

c. At the long-run equilibrium price of $20, $Q_d = 55,000 - 1,000(20) = 35,000$.

d. With each firm producing 10 units of output, restoring long-run equilibrium price will require 3,500 firms.

4. a. If one firm achieves a lower cost due to superior management, the long-run equilibrium price will remain at $20.

b. At $P = \$20$, Peter will produce 12 units of output, his costs will be $180 + 19 + 20 = \$219$. Revenue $= \$240$, so economic profit $= \$21$.

c. New firms will offer Peter up to $21 above the going rate to manage their firms.

d. Assuming that Peter was paying himself his opportunity cost, his economic rent is now $21 per period.

5. a. If the industry is in long-run equilibrium with 3,500 firms, each firm's supply curve becomes $q_s = -10 + (P-2)$, so that industry supply equals $Q_s = 3,500(-12+P) = -42,000 + 3,500P$. The equilibrium price will be given by the equality between quantity demanded and quantity supplied

$$-42,000 + 3,500P = 55,000 - 1,000P$$

$$4,500P = 97,000 \rightarrow P = \frac{97,000}{4,500} = \$21.56$$

$$Q_S = -42,000 + 3500(21.56) = 33,444$$

$$Q_d = 55,000 - 1,000(21.56) = 33,444$$

b. The average buyer pays $21.56 - $20.00 = $1.56 of the tax.

c. The average seller pays $22.00 - 21.56 = $0.44 of the tax.

d. Since this is a constant-cost industry, the long-run equilibrium price is $22.

e. The buyers will pay the full tax.

f. The sellers will pay none of the tax.

Answers to True-False Questions

1. *False.* In a constant-cost industry, the *short-run* supply curve is positively sloped. An increase in demand will increase the short-run equilibrium price and quantity. Market entry will increase market supply, eventually returning the *long-run* equilibrium price to its original level.

2. *True.* In an increasing-cost industry, the long-run supply curve is positively sloped, so that an increase in demand will increase long-run equilibrium price and quantity.

3. *False.* Suppose that licensed firms receive $5,000 per year in economic profit due to a transferable entry barrier (license). If the market rate of interest is 10 percent, would-be entrants will pay up to $50,000 for the license. So, by not selling the license, the established firms are foregoing interest income of $5,000. Hence, the $5,000 is now matched by an opportunity cost and is no longer economic profit.

4. *True.* In a constant cost industry, the short-run supply curve is positively sloped. So a per-unit tax will shift the supply curve upward by the amount of the tax, resulting in an increase in the equilibrium price *less than the tax*. This implies that the tax is shared between buyers and sellers. However, in the long run, firms will exit until they receive zero economic profit, which implies that the long-run equilibrium price must increase by the full amount of the tax.

5. *False.* An increasing-cost industry implies that inframarginal firms are receiving economic rent. So, when the per unit tax results in lower profit in the short-run, some established firms lose economic rent. This means that the price does not increase by the full amount of the tax. Sellers in both the short run and the long run absorb some of the tax.

Answers to Multiple-Choice Questions

1. b
2. d
3. c
4. d
5. b
6. a (As firms enter, factor prices increase.)
7. c
8. b (Some of the tax is absorbed by sellers.)
9. a
10. d

Chapter 9
Pricing Under Monopoly

• LEARNING OBJECTIVES

After completing this chapter, you should be able to

1. Explain the market conditions necessary to produce a monopolist.

2. Describe the profit-maximizing output and price decisions of a monopolist.

3. Demonstrate why consumer surplus and producer surplus are smaller under a monopoly than under competitive market conditions.

4. Illustrate how barriers to entry in the long run imply greater long-run profits than short-run profits for a monopoly seller.

5. Demonstrate the effects of a decrease in marginal cost on the quantity, price, and profits for a monopolist.

6. Contrast the effects of a lump sum tax to a per unit tax on a monopolist's output, price, and profits.

7. Understand the dilemma faced by a monopoly seller of a durable good unless output is restricted to the monopoly output.

• CHAPTER OVERVIEW

Definition of Monopoly

The word *monopoly* literally means "one seller." This chapter focuses on monopolists that are the sole producers of a good or service. The next chapter will discuss *cartels*, which are combinations of producers who collude to charge a monopoly price.

Typically, monopolies can emerge for three reasons. **Patents** give patent holders the exclusive right to specific products or production processes for seventeen years. **Internal economies of scale** give one large producer substantial cost advantages over smaller rivals. These cost advantages often lead to a **natural monopoly.** Monopolies may also emerge from **franchises** that give one firm an exclusive right to sell in a particular area.

As a practical matter, a monopoly product must have no close substitutes. If there are very close substitutes for a firm's product, that firm is not a monopolist. It may be a *competitive* firm, if there are many substitutes, or an *oligopoly* firm, if there are a few close substitutes.

Demand and Marginal Revenue

A monopolist confronts a negatively sloped market demand curve for its product. The monopolist can therefore control the price of its product by selecting a rate of output. The **inverse demand curve** is the function that relates the market-clearing price of a monopolist's product to the quantity produced. Suppose that there is one movie theater in a small college town and that the quantity of tickets demanded is given by the equation, $Q_d = 500 - 50P$, where P is the ticket price charged to all patrons. Solving the demand curve for P, we get $P = \dfrac{500 - Q}{50} = \$10 - .02Q$. Since revenue is given by

$R = P \times Q = (10 - .02Q)Q = 10Q - .02Q^2$, average revenue is equal to price:

$AR = \dfrac{10Q - .02Q^2}{Q} = 10 - .02Q$. Another name for the inverse demand function is the **average revenue function.**

In our example, if the theater owner wishes to close the theater for a day, he merely sets the ticket price at \$10 or higher, so that the quantity demanded equals zero. To sell one ticket, the price must be set at $P = \$9.98$. To sell a second ticket, the price must be cut by 2 cents to: $P = \$9.96$. In order to sell the second ticket, the theater owner had to reduce the price on *both* tickets to \$9.96. Revenue increased from \$9.98 to \$19.92, or by \$9.94. The **marginal revenue** is the change in revenue divided by the change in quantity sold; it is equal to the price minus the output sold times the price reduction necessary to sell one more unit: $\text{MR} = \dfrac{\Delta(P \times Q)}{\Delta Q} = P + Q \times \dfrac{\Delta P}{\Delta Q}$.

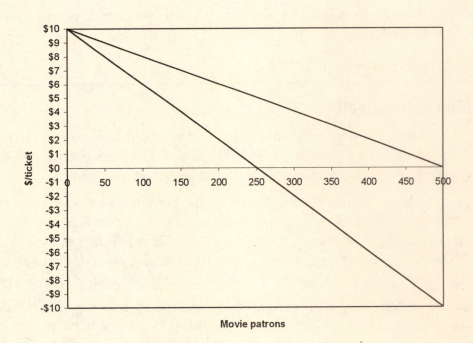

Figure 9-1

Figure 9-1 shows the relation between output, price, and marginal revenue for a movie theater confronting a linear market demand curve. Note that both average revenue and marginal revenue have the same intercept, but the slope of the marginal revenue line is twice the slope of the average revenue line.

If the monopolist has an empty theater (because the ticket price was set at $10), total revenue will be zero. Once the price is below $10, ticket revenue will be positive. The marginal revenue function starts at the same price as does the average revenue function. If the monopolist wants 500 people in his theater, the ticket price must be set at $0; again, total revenue will be zero. What happens is that revenue grows as patrons increase from 0 to 250; revenue then declines if the number of patrons increase from 250 to 500. Revenue will be maximized when ticket sales are 250, which corresponds to a ticket price of $5.

Table 9-1 presents the data used to generate Figure 9-1. The first column is the number of movie patrons and the second column is the price required to attract the last patron, i.e., $P = \$10 - .02Q$. The third column is total revenue, $R = P \times Q$. The fourth column is the point-price elasticity of demand, given by $E = \dfrac{\Delta Q / Q}{\Delta P / P} = -50 \times \dfrac{P}{Q}$. Note that marginal revenue is positive when demand is price elastic, marginal revenue is negative when demand is price inelastic, and marginal revenue is zero when demand is unit price elastic. A profit-maximizing monopolist would never intentionally set output where the demand curve was price inelastic, since this would cause marginal revenue to become negative.

Movie Patrons (Q)	Ticket Price (P)	Total Revenue (P x Q)	Marginal Revenue	Point - Price Elasticity
0	$10	$0	$10	- infinity
50	$9	$450	$8	-9.00
100	$8	$800	$6	-4.00
150	$7	$1,050	$4	-2.33
200	$6	$1,200	$2	-1.50
250	$5	$1,250	$0	-1.00
300	$4	$1,200	-$2	-0.67
350	$3	$1,050	-$4	-0.43
400	$2	$800	-$6	-0.25
450	$1	$450	-$8	-0.11
500	$0	$0	-$10	0.00

Table 9-1

Because marginal revenue is the change in revenue due to the last unit produced, total revenue can be measured by adding the area under the marginal revenue curve. In our example, marginal revenue between zero and 250 movie patrons forms a triangle with height $10 and width 250 units. The area under this triangle is $\frac{1}{2}(250 \times 10) = \$1,250$, which is precisely the total revenue shown in Table 9-1.

Setting the Profit Maximizing Rate of Output

A monopoly firm is like a competitive firm in that profit is maximized at that rate of output where marginal cost equals marginal revenue, as long as price exceeds average variable cost. Unlike the price taker, for whom MR = P, MR < P for the **price maker.** Because marginal revenue is less than price, the monopolist must first set the rate of output where MC = MR and then consult the average revenue curve to determine the market price.

Returning to our movie theater example, it is reasonable to assume that the cost of showing a movie to one more patron is zero. Suppose that the movie theater seats 500 patrons and the operator wishes to maximize the number of patrons attending each show. Table 9-1 indicates that the market-clearing price is $0, which implies total revenue of $0. The theater operator would be better off (financially) raising the ticket price as long as the point-price elasticity is greater than -1 (that is, as long as $0 < E < -1$). Note that when $P = 5, only 250 tickets would be sold, and revenue would be maximized at $1,250 per showing. This revenue-maximizing price occurs precisely where the marginal revenue equals 0, which corresponds to a point price elasticity of -1.

Because the monopolist would lose revenue if the demand for the product were price inelastic, the relevant range for marginal revenue is only between 0 and 250 units. The fact that the owner of the theater could seat more than 250 patrons is irrelevant, since revenue would be lower if $Q > 250$ than it would be when $Q = 250$.

Short-Run Profit Maximization

Table 9-2 presents the more usual case of a monopolist who incurs a positive marginal cost for each unit of output. For simplicity, we will assume that the marginal cost is a constant $5 and that the inverse demand function is given by $P = $15 - .02Q$. When the inverse demand function is linear, the marginal revenue function has twice the slope: $MR = $15 - .04Q$. Note that the rate of output extends only to 375 units, since that is the rate of output where $E = -1$, so that MR = 0. We assume that the firm has a fixed cost of $500, so that total cost is $C = $500 + $5Q$.

Output	Price	Total Revenue	Marginal Revenue	Price Elasticity	Marginal Cost	Total Cost	Profit
(Q)	(P)	(P x Q)	(MR)	(E)	(MC)	(TC)	(π)
0	$15.00	$0.00	$15	- infinity	$5	$500	-$500.00
25	$14.50	$362.50	$14	-29.00	$5	$625	-$262.50
50	$14.00	$700.00	$13	-14.00	$5	$750	-$50.00
75	$13.50	$1,012.50	$12	-9.00	$5	$875	$137.50
100	$13.00	$1,300.00	$11	-6.50	$5	$1,000	$300.00
125	$12.50	$1,562.50	$10	-5.00	$5	$1,125	$437.50
150	$12.00	$1,800.00	$9	-4.00	$5	$1,250	$550.00
175	$11.50	$2,012.50	$8	-3.29	$5	$1,375	$637.50
200	$11.00	$2,200.00	$7	-2.75	$5	$1,500	$700.00
225	$10.50	$2,362.50	$6	-2.33	$5	$1,625	$737.50
250	$10.00	$2,500.00	$5	-2.00	$5	$1,750	$750.00
275	$9.50	$2,612.50	$4	-1.73	$5	$1,875	$737.50
300	$9.00	$2,700.00	$3	-1.50	$5	$2,000	$700.00
325	$8.50	$2,762.50	$2	-1.31	$5	$2,125	$637.50

Table 9-2

At zero output, profit equals negative fixed cost, $\pi = -500$, where π = economic profit. To sell 25 units, price must fall from $15 to $14.50. The marginal revenue of the 25th unit is only $14.50 because $0.02 must be cut on each of the first 25 units to sell the 25th. At $Q = 25$, profit has risen (losses have fallen) from -$500 to -$262.50. The monopolist is gaining $14.50 revenue for the 25th unit, which only costs $5 to produce. Clearly the monopolist does not wish to stop at this point. Indeed, the monopolist would continue to produce until MC = MR, when the rate of output is 250 units. Once the profit-maximizing rate of output has been identified, the monopolist sets the price according to the average revenue (inverse demand) curve.

Figure 9-2 depicts the monopolist's output and price decision graphically. The first step is to identify Q_M, where $MC = MR$. The second step is to identify P_M as the market-clearing price for Q_m. The third step is to compare the monopoly price with the average variable cost. If $P_M < \text{AVC}(Q_M)$, then the monopolist, like the competitive producer, should shut down operations. As long as $P_M > \text{AVC}(Q_M)$, the monopolist is better off producing than shutting down, even if economic profits are negative. Finally, if $P_M > \text{ATC}(Q_M)$, then the monopolist earns positive economic profit. However, unlike the competitive producer, the monopoly producer need not worry about the entry of competitors eliminating economic profit, if legal or natural barriers to entry persist in the long run.

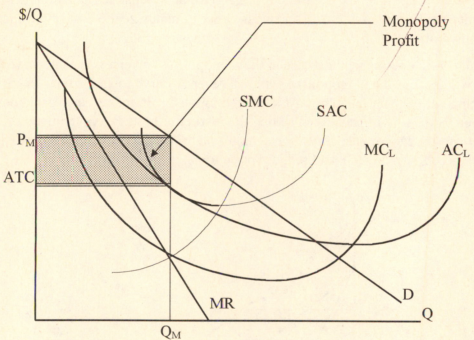

Figure 9-2

Figure 9-2 shows that the monopolist is operating in both short-run and long-run equilibrium. The long-run equilibrium price is identified by the intersection of the long-run marginal cost curve, MC_L, and the marginal revenue curve, MR. Unlike the case with the competitive firm, the long-run marginal cost curve need not be increasing at the profit-maximizing rate of output; all that is required is that MR be decreasing faster than MC at output Q_M. The ideal plant size for producing output Q_M is identified by the intersection of SMC with MC_L, which in turn implies that the short-run average cost curve is tangent to the long-run average total cost curve at Q_M.

The relation between price and marginal revenue implies two related consequences of monopoly pricing. First, the price elasticity of demand at Q_M determines the optimal markup of marginal cost. Given $MR = P(1 + \frac{1}{E})$, where E = point price elasticity of

demand, MR = MC implies that $\frac{P}{MC} = \left(1 + \frac{1}{E}\right) = \frac{E+1}{E}$, so that, $P = MC\left(\frac{E}{E+1}\right)$. The

more elastic the demand for the monopolist's good or service, the smaller will be the mark-up of price over marginal cost. The second implication is that since $E < 0$, the only way that markup pricing leads to a positive price is if $E + 1$ is also negative, which means the demand for the monopolist's product must be price-elastic.

Short-Run vs. Long-Run Responses to Changes in Demand

The distinction between short-run and long-run responses to demand changes can apply to the monopoly firm as well as the competitive firm. Under market competition, the number of firms adjusts in the long run in response to positive or negative economic profits caused by demand changes. If a monopoly market is to remain a monopoly, barriers to entry must persist in the long run. The adjustment of a monopoly to changes in market demand rely on changes in the monopolist's plant size in order to minimize the cost of producing the monopoly output.

In **Figure 9-3**, a permanent increase in the monopolist's (inverse) demand curve from D_0 to D_1 would cause the monopolist's marginal revenue curve to shift from MR_0 to MR_1. Operating with a plant given by SAC_0, the monopolist responds by increasing output to Q', where $SMC_0 = MR_1$, and then setting the market price at P'. Given time for adjustment, the monopolist constructs a larger plant, yielding SAC_1, then expands output to Q_1, where $LRMC = MR_1$, and reduces price to P_1.

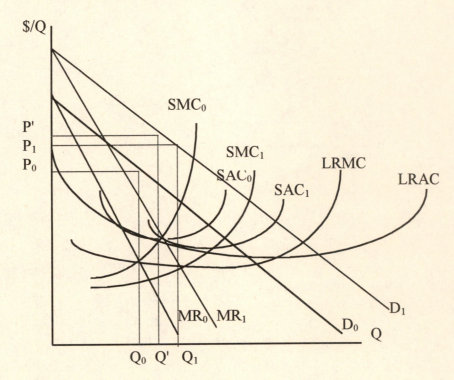

Figure 9-3

Page 139

Adoption of a Cost-Reducing Innovation

In Chapter 7 we saw how a competitive firm would adopt a cost-reducing technology when the average total cost of the new technology became less than the average variable cost of the old technology. In Chapter 9, Professor Pashigian shows that the monopoly producer has essentially the same incentive. In **Figure 9-4** the monopolist is producing output Q_0 and charging price P_0 and is in long-run equilibrium. A technological breakthrough shifts the long-run marginal cost curve downward from MC_{L0} to MC_{L1}. In order to take advantage of the new technology, a new plan must be constructed. Initially, the monopolist may find that the new technology is not cost effective because the average cost of the new technology exceeds the average variable cost of the old technology. But, as the old plant ages, the AVC curve approaches the ATC curve until the average variable cost of the old plant exceeds the average total cost of the new plant. At that point, it pays the monopolist to switch to the new technology. As a result, long-run marginal cost shifts downward, and the optimal rate of output increases from Q_0 to Q_1. In order to sell the additional output, the price must be reduced from P_0 to P_1.

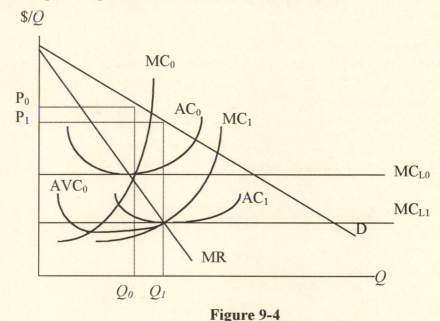

Figure 9-4

Competing to Be a Monopolist

Although a monopolist has no competitors within a market, would-be monopolists often have rivals for the right to become a monopolist. Such is the case when a local government awards a cable-TV franchise. If the government auctions off the right to become a monopolist, the maximum amount an applicant would bid equals potential monopoly profit per period. For instance, if potential monopoly profit were $1 million per year, and the applicant could otherwise invest funds at a 10 percent rate, the most that applicant would bid would be $10 million. If successful, the $10 million price of the franchise becomes a sunk cost, and average total costs rise to absorb the cost of the franchise itself. The successful bidder ends up receiving a normal return on its investment, but the franchisee must charge a monopoly price to generate that return.

In **Figure 9-5**, a franchise monopolist would want to produce quantity Q_M and charge price P_M in order to obtain the economic profit given by the shaded area $(P_M - AC_L)Q_M$. If the franchise price were equal to these potential profits, the long-run average cost curve would shift to $AC_{L'}$, providing a normal return on the complete investment (including the franchise price) as long as the winner continued to produce the monopoly output and charged the monopoly price. However, if the government awarded the franchise to the operator willing to charge the lowest price, the successful bidder would agree to provide service level Q^* and charge price P^*. The moral of the story is that a government that wishes to serve the interests of its citizen-consumers should not seek to transfer monopoly profit from the franchisee to itself. That government will serve its constituents best if it encourages a price as close as possible to the competitive ideal.

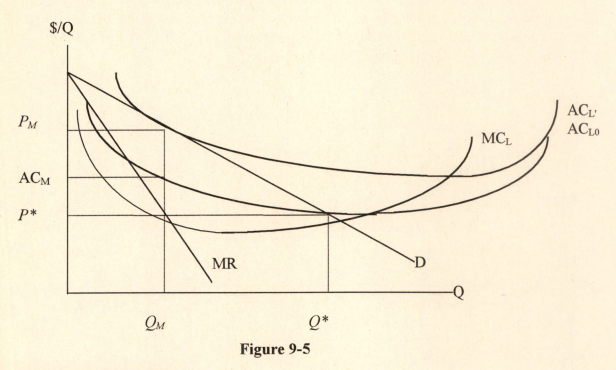

Figure 9-5

The Tyranny of Durability

We learn in this chapter that the ability of the monopolist to obtain and keep a positive economic profit depends on its ability to create and perpetuate an artificial scarcity of its product. Under competitive conditions, market entry guarantees that price falls to the minimum point on the long-run average cost curve so that long-run profits are zero. Professor Pashigian deals with the intriguing case of a monopolist selling a durable commodity, like land, whose total quantity exceeds the level that would maximize revenue. In **Figure 9-6**, the inelastic supply of land is a vertical line at Q^*, which exceeds output Q_M where MR = 0. The monopolist has an incentive to sell the Q_M parcels at price P_M. However, this leads to a surplus of $Q^* - Q_M$. If this surplus were dumped on the market, the price of the units already sold would also fall to P^*. Unless the monopolist can reassure buyers that the parcels will remain scarce, the most an informed buyer would bid would be P^*. Hence, the monopolist has an incentive to "retire" parcels $Q^* - Q_M$ from the real estate market by converting those parcels into parks or some other nonresidential use.

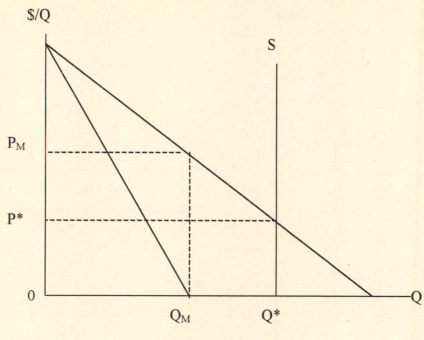

Figure 9-6

Social Objection to Monopoly and Taxing the Monopolist

Because monopolies are profitable, governments often see monopoly profit as undesirable in itself rather than as a symptom of the real problem—that monopoly creates an artificial scarcity, causing a misallocation of resources. **Figure 9-7** shows the deadweight loss associated with a monopoly. Under competitive conditions, an industry confronting a horizontal long-run supply curve would lead to price P_c and quantity Q_c, maximizing consumer surplus, the triangle AP_cB. Facing the same cost conditions, a monopoly would restrict output to Q_M, where $MR = MC_L = S_L$. This shrinks consumer surplus to AP_MC. Part of the lost consumer surplus is converted into monopoly profit; but part of the former consumer surplus is a deadweight loss, since output $Q_c - Q_M$ is not produced and resources are ultimately allocated to the production of commodities consumers desire less than this one. It is because of this deadweight loss of consumer surplus that most economists find monopoly undesirable.

There are three potential remedies to monopoly distortions of resource allocation: taxation, regulation, and antitrust law. From an economic perspective, taxation is the least-desirable option because it does nothing to alleviate the artificial scarcity generated by monopoly and may make the situation worse. A per unit tax would shift the marginal cost curve to $MC_L, + t$ which would cause output to fall from Q_M to Q_M', further reducing consumer surplus. If the profit must be taxed, a lump-sum tax, equal to monopoly profit, would keep the profit maximizing output at Q_M and the price at P_M, leaving the consumer surplus at the same post-monopoly level.

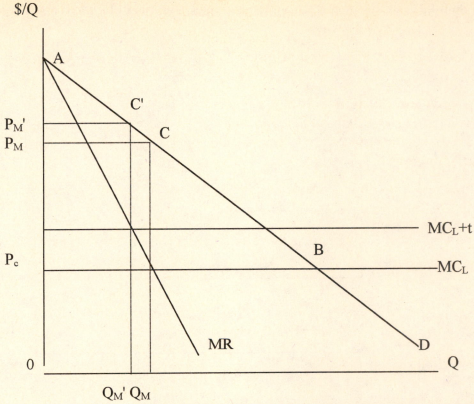

Figure 9-7

Efficient regulation would set the price at P_c -- the price that would prevail in the long run if the market were competitive. Faced with a ceiling price of P_c, the monopolist would face a constant marginal revenue function, just as a price taker would. Profit maximization would now require producing output Q_c, maximizing consumer surplus. The problem with regulation is the difficulty of determining what P_c is, particularly since the monopoly has an incentive to overstate costs in order to obtain a higher rate. Antitrust seeks to prevent monopoly from occurring in the first place by discouraging contracts, combinations, and conspiracies in restraint of trade, and by prohibiting mergers that would have an adverse impact on competition. Like regulation, anti-trust law can be costly to enforce, particularly when firms seeking to monopolize the market will attempt to make their behavior appear reasonable.

• KEY TERMS

Pure monopoly   A market with only one seller with no close substitutes, so that the market demand curve is the demand curve for the seller's product.

Barriers to entry Restrictions on the entry of additional sellers into the market. Barriers to entry may stem from internal economies of scale, or from government restrictions like licenses, franchises, or patents.

Close vs. distant substitutes Since a monopoly sets price in the elastic region of the demand curve, price increases will reduce expenditure on the monopolist's product. All other goods behave like substitutes for the monopolist's product. However, none of the other commodities are such close substitutes that the monopolist must react to changes in the price charged by other firms.

Price making The ability to set the market price for a good or service by deciding how much to produce.

Inverse demand function Solving the market demand function so that price is a function of output. The inverse demand function indicates the market clearing price for each rate of output a monopoly produces. The inverse demand function is also known as the **average revenue function.**

Total revenue function Price times quantity. Given an average revenue function of the form $P = a - bQ$, total revenue is simply $P \times Q = (a - bQ)Q = aQ - bQ^2$.

Marginal revenue function The function giving the change in revenue at each rate of output: $\text{MR} = \dfrac{\Delta R}{\Delta Q} = P + Q\dfrac{\Delta P}{\Delta Q} = a - bQ - bQ = a - 2bQ$.

Price elasticity and markup over cost Marginal revenue equals price times $(1 + 1/E)$, where $E =$ the point-price elasticity of demand. Setting $MR = MC$, we obtain the optimal markup over marginal cost: $\text{MR} = P\left(1 + \dfrac{1}{E}\right) = \text{MC} \rightarrow P = \text{MC}\left(\dfrac{E}{E+1}\right)$.

The social objection to monopoly   Because $P > \text{MR}$ for a monopolist, the monopolist sets output below the level where $\text{MC} = P$, which is the economic optimum. In restricting output, the monopolist creates a deadweight loss, so that the loss of consumer surplus due to monopoly exceeds the monopolist's profit.

Deadweight loss The loss in consumer surplus due to monopoly that does not show up as monopoly profit.

Antitrust policy   The use of legislative and judicial authority to prohibit or regulate behavior designed to reduce output to charge a monopoly price. The first antitrust law is the **Sherman Antitrust Act**. Passed in 1890, this law prohibits combinations, conspiracies and contracts in restraint of trade.

Price regulation The use of government authority to impose ceiling prices on prices charged by natural and franchise monopolies. Ideally, regulators set the price at or near where the market would set the price. In practice, prices are set to guarantee the monopoly a normal profit, thereby giving the firm an incentive to incur wasteful costs to obtain a price increase closer to the monopoly price.

Adjustment to an increase in demand When the demand curve confronting a monopolist shifts to the right, the firm will increase output only if marginal revenue now exceeds marginal cost at the previous profit-maximizing rate of output. If the demand increase causes the demand to become less price-elastic, the firm might respond by increasing price but decreasing output.

Adoption of a cost-reducing innovation Like a competitive firm, a monopoly would adopt a cost-saving innovation only if the average total cost under the new technology were less than the average variable cost under the old technology.

Competing to be a monopolist The process of would-be monopolists bidding up to the expected monopoly profit in order to win the competition to be a monopolist. In this case, the winner of the competition would receive only a normal profit on its entire outlay (including the cost of acquiring the monopoly power). Nevertheless, the firm would charge a monopoly price as the only way of making its "investment" pay off.

Selling a monopoly In selling a franchise to a monopoly supplier, the government will typically serve its constituent-customers better by extracting the promise that output will be sold a the lowest sustainable price (where AC_L intersects market demand) than by bidding away monopoly profit.

Per unit tax A tax that increases marginal cost causing the monopoly to cut output and raise price, further distorting the misallocation of resources and increasing the deadweight loss caused by the monopoly.

Lump sum tax A tax that increases only fixed costs and not marginal cost. A lump sum tax can be used to confiscate monopoly profits without worsening the misallocation of resources. However, a lump sum tax, by itself, would not improve the allocation of resources.

The tyranny of durability If the quantity that a monopolist has to sell exceeds the monopoly profit-maximizing price, then informed buyers will refuse to pay any more than the market clearing price, since that would be the long-run equilibrium price if all the available quantity were placed on the market. This causes monopolies to signal to buyers that the excess quantity will not be placed on the market. In the case of real estate, such assurances can take the form of donations of land for public parks, schools, or churches.

Infinitely durable goods Commodities, like land or mineral deposits, that essentially last forever.

• PROBLEMS

1. **Table 9-3** provides information about the demand conditions facing a monopolist. Complete the table and plot the demand curve and marginal revenue curve in **Chart 9-1**. Note, $\Delta Q / \Delta P = -5$. Compute point-price elasticity in the last column.

Price	Quantity	Total Revenue	Marginal Revenue	Price Elasticity
$20	0	_____	_____	_____
$19	10	_____	_____	_____
$18	20	_____	_____	_____
$17	30	_____	_____	_____
$16	40	_____	_____	_____
$15	50	_____	_____	_____
$14	60	_____	_____	_____
$13	70	_____	_____	_____
$12	80	_____	_____	_____
$11	90	_____	_____	_____
$10	100	_____	_____	_____

Chart 9-1

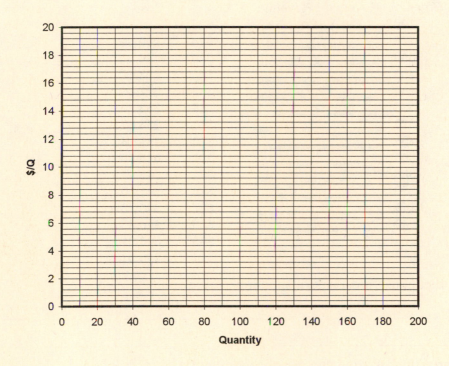

a. Suppose that long-run marginal cost is constant at $2 per unit. Plot the marginal cost in Chart 9-1.

b. What is the profit-maximizing rate of output?

c. What is the profit-maximizing price?

_____

d. Is the profit-maximizing price consistent with the optimal markup? Explain.

_____
_____

e. What is the total revenue at the profit-maximizing rate of output?

_____

f. If the monopolist faces a fixed cost of $500, what is the monopolist's economic profit?

_____

2. Suppose that a cable TV company computes the following market demand and cost characteristics for a new residential subdivision. Complete **Table 9-3** and answer the questions that follow:

Table 9-4

Number of Homes	Price ($/month)	Total Revenue	Marginal Revenue	Marginal Cost	Average Cost	Profit
0	$100			$28		
500	$95	_____	_____	$24	$260.00	_____
1,000	$90	_____	_____	$20	$140.00	_____
1,500	$85	_____	_____	$16	$98.67	_____
2,000	$80	_____	_____	$12	$77.00	_____
2,500	$75	_____	_____	$8	$63.20	_____
3,000	$70	_____	_____	$12	$54.67	_____
3,500	$65	_____	_____	$16	$49.14	_____
4,000	$60	_____	_____	$20	$45.50	_____
4,500	$55	_____	_____	$24	$43.11	_____
5,000	$50	_____	_____	$28	$41.60	_____
5,500	$45	_____	_____	$32	$40.73	_____
6,000	$40	_____	_____	$36	$40.33	_____
6,500	$35	_____	_____	$40	$40.31	_____
7,000	$30	_____	_____	$44	$40.57	_____

a. Does this market constitute a natural monopoly? Explain.

_____
_____

b. What is the profit-maximizing number of subscribers?

_____

c. What is the monthly price that will create the profit maximizing number of subscribers?

_____

d. What is the monthly profit the firm would realize at the profit-maximizing rate of output?

_____

e. What is the most the company should bid for a contract to serve this subdivision?

_____

f. What is the lowest price the company could charge and still receive a competitive return?

_____

_____

g. Which approach to selling the monopoly–auctioning the franchise or setting a maximum price–would best serve the residents of the housing development? Explain.

_____

_____

_____

3. In **Chart 9-2**, MC_L is the monopolist's marginal cost curve. Alternatively, if this industry were competitive, S_L would represent the long-run supply curve of the industry. Using the data in the chart, answer the questions that follow.

Chart 9-2

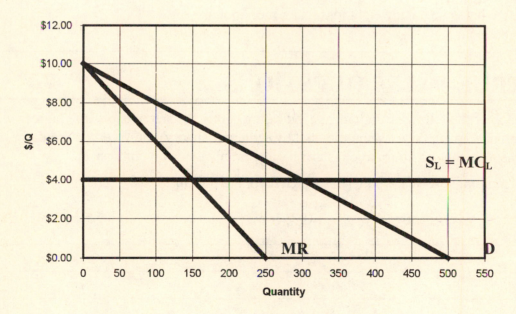

a. What would be the long-run equilibrium price and quantity under competitive market conditions?

_____

b. What would be the consumer surplus under competitive conditions?

_____

c. What rate of output and price would maximize revenue for the monopolist?

_____

d. What rate of output and price would maximize profit for the monopolist?

_____

e. How do you explain the discrepancy between your answers for parts c and d?

_____

_____

_____

f. If the monopolist constructs the optimally sized plant to produce the profit-maximizing rate of output, what will be the monopolist's profits?

_____

g. What is the consumer surplus under the monopoly profit-maximizing output and price combination?

_____

h. What is the deadweight loss under monopoly?

_____

● TRUE-FALSE QUESTIONS

For each of the following statements, indicate whether the statement is true (agrees with economic theory), false (is contradicted by economic theory), or uncertain (could be true or false; not enough information is given), and briefly explain your answer.

1. A monopoly sells a product for which there are no substitutes.

_____

_____

_____

_____

2. Monopolies always make positive economic profits in both the short run and the long run.

_____

_____

_____

_____

3. If price exceeds marginal cost at the current rate of output, a monopoly is not producing enough output.

_____

_____

_____

_____

4. While typically generating excess burdens when imposed on a competitive market, ceiling prices may reduce the excess burden when imposed on a monopoly.

_____

_____

_____

_____

5. The tyranny of durability means that monopolies must convince buyers that they will never sell more than the monopoly profit-maximizing quantity.

_____

_____

_____

_____

● MULTIPLE CHOICE QUESTIONS

1. Which one of the following must exist for a pure monopoly to prevail in the long run?

   a. existence of close substitutes

   b. barriers to entry

   c. infinite price elasticity of demand

   d. all of the above

2. If, in the short run, a monopolist is producing at a point where marginal revenue is equal to $5.00 and marginal cost is equal to $6.00, the monopolist should

   a. leave the rate of output unchanged.

   b. increase the rate of output.

   c. decrease the rate of output.

   d. do one of the above, but it is impossible to tell without additional information.

3. If, in the short run, a monopolist is producing at a point where price is equal to $6.00 and marginal cost is equal to $5.00, the monopolist should

   a. leave the rate of output unchanged.

   b. increase the rate of output.

   c. decrease the rate of output.

   d. do one of the above, but it is impossible to tell without additional information.

4. Suppose that price falls from $12.50 to $10.00 and quantity sold increases from 4 to 5 units, then the marginal revenue of the 5th unit is

   a. $12.50.

   b. $10.00.

   c. $5.00.

   d. $0.00.

5. If quantity sold falls from 4,000 to 3,000 units and total revenue increases, then the price elasticity of demand at 4,000 units must have been

   a. inelastic.

   b. elastic.

   c. unitary elastic.

   d. zero.

6. If, at the rate of output where MR = MC, P_M < AVC, the monopolist should

   a. shut down if MC is increasing.

   b. shut down if MC is falling at a slower rate than MR.

   c. expand output if MC is falling at a faster rate than MR.

   d. take any of the above actions; each would be appropriate.

7. If the government wished to force a monopolist to provide the same output as a competitive industry would, the government should

   a. levy a lump sum tax.

   b. levy a per unit tax.

   c. impose a price floor.

   d. impose a price ceiling.

8. Which of these events would occur if a competitive industry were transformed into a monopoly?

   a. Price would fall, output would rise, and consumer surplus would increase.

   b. Price would fall, output would fall, and consumer surplus would fall.

   c. Price would rise, output would rise, and consumer surplus would rise.

   d. Price would rise, output would fall, and consumer surplus would fall.

9. Following a cost-saving innovation, a competitive industry will experience increased profits in the short run and _____ profits in the long run. A monopolist will experience increased profits in the short run and _____ profits in the long run, as long as demand does not change.

   a. zero, increased

   b. zero, zero

   c. decreased, zero

   d. increased, increased

10. Which of the following ways of awarding a cable franchise will maximize the number of subscribers to the service?

    a. Award to company with most efficient management

    b. Open the award to competitive bidding

    c. Award to company that will charge the lowest monthly fee

    d. Award to company with newest technology

• ANSWERS TO PROBLEMS, TRUE-FALSE, AND MULTIPLE-CHOICE QUESTIONS

Answers to Problems

1. The completed table should look like this

Price	Quantity	Total Revenue	Marginal Revenue	Price Elasticity
$20	0	$0	$20	
$19	10	$190	$18	-19.00
$18	20	$360	$16	-9.00
$17	30	$510	$14	-5.67
$16	40	$640	$12	-4.00
$15	50	$750	$10	-3.00
$14	60	$840	$8	-2.33
$13	70	$910	$6	-1.86
$12	80	$960	$4	-1.50
$11	90	$990	$2	-1.22
$10	100	$1,000	$0	-1.00

a. The plot of price, marginal revenue, and marginal cost should look like this

Chart 9-1a

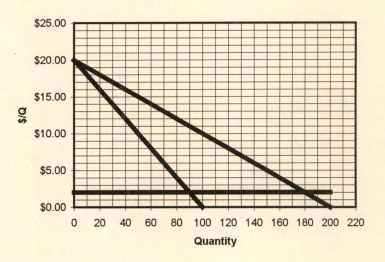

b. $Q_M = 90$

c. $P_M = \$20 - .1(90) = \$11.00$.

d. The profit-maximizing price is consistent with the optimal markup. When $Q = 90$,

$$E = -1.22, \quad P = MC\left(\frac{E}{E+1}\right) = 2\left(\frac{-1.22}{-0.22}\right) = 2(5.5) = \$11$$

e. $R = \$11(90) = \$990$.

f. $\pi = R - (FC+VC) = \$990 - (500 + 2(90)) = \$990 - 680 = \$310.$

2.

Table 9-4a

Number of Homes	Price ($/month)	Total Revenue	Marginal Revenue	Marginal Cost	Average Cost	Profit
0	$100	$0	$100	$28		-$102,000
500	$95	$47,500	$90	$24	$256.00	-$80,500
1,000	$90	$90,000	$80	$20	$138.00	-$48,000
1,500	$85	$127,500	$70	$16	$97.33	-$18,500
2,000	$80	$160,000	$60	$12	$76.00	$8,000
2,500	$75	$187,500	$50	$8	$62.40	$31,500
3,000	$70	$210,000	$40	$12	$54.00	$48,000
3,500	$65	$227,500	$30	$16	$48.57	$57,500
4,000	$60	$240,000	$20	$20	$45.00	$60,000
4,500	$55	$247,500	$10	$24	$42.67	$55,500
5,000	$50	$250,000	$0	$28	$41.20	$44,000
5,500	$45	$247,500	-$10	$32	$40.36	$25,500
6,000	$40	$240,000	-$20	$36	$40.00	$0
6,500	$35	$227,500	-$30	$40	$40.00	-$32,500
7,000	$30	$210,000	-$40	$44	$40.29	-$72,000

a. This firm does constitute a natural monopoly, since average cost is still declining when it intersects the market demand curve at approximately 6,000 homes.

b. Marginal revenue and marginal cost are both $20 at $Q = 4,000$, which is the profit-maximizing rate of output.

c. The market-clearing price when $Q = 4,000$ is $60, which is the profit-maximizing (monopoly) price.

d. When $Q_M = 4,000$, $R = \$240,000$; $C = 4,000(45) = \$180,000$, so $\pi_M = \$60,000$.

e. Since the $60,000 is an economic profit (a return over the opportunity costs of inputs), the firm should bid a maximum of $60,000.

f. The lowest price the firm could charge and still receive a competitive return is $40 per month, since this is the price where the average total cost curve intersects the market demand curve.

g. Having the firm agree to supply cable service at $40,000 per month would generate a consumer surplus of $\frac{1}{2}(100 - 40)6,000 = \$180,000$. With the monopoly price, consumer surplus would be $\frac{1}{2}(100 - 60)4,000 = \$80,000$. Even adding the $60,000 payment to the monopoly consumer surplus (under the assumption that the payment for the monopoly franchise would reduce taxation by a like amount), consumer-taxpayers would be better off if the break-even price were charged.

3. a. The long-run competitive equilibrium price is $4, and quantity is 300.

b. Under long-run competitive equilibrium, consumer surplus would be $\frac{1}{2}(10 - 4)300 = \$900.$

c. Revenue would be maximized where $MR = 0$, that is, when $Q = 250$, $P = \$5$.

d. $Q_M = 150$, $P_M = \$7$.

e. When $Q = 250$, MR = 0 while MC = \$4, so this is *not* the profit maximizing rate of output. Profits increase as output decreases until, at $Q = 150$, MR = MC = \$4.

f. At the optimally sized plant to produce 150 units of output, AC = \$4, so
$\pi = (7 - 4)150 = \$450$.

g. Consumer surplus = $\frac{1}{2}(10 - 7)150 = \$225$.

h. Deadweight loss = Consumer surplus under competition - (monopoly profit + consumer surplus under monopoly) = \$900 - (450+225) = \$225.

Answers to True-False Questions

1. *False.* A monopoly sells a product for which there are no *close* substitutes. We know that monopolies set price in the elastic region of the demand curve where the composite good acts as a substitute good for the monopoly-sold good. Although all other goods taken together behave as substitutes for the monopoly good, these will be different goods for different consumers, so there is no *close* substitute.

2. *False.* One way of being a monopoly is being the only firm in an industry that ought not have any firm (i.e., price is less than average variable cost for all rates of output). Such a firm would shut down, not making a profit in either the long run or the short run. And if monopoly price is greater than average variable cost but less than average total cost, the monopoly will make negative economic profit in the short run but shut down in the long run. Finally, if a firm buys a monopoly franchise at a price that returns only zero economic profit, the firm will not make monopoly profits in either the short run or the long run.

3. *Uncertain.* If marginal revenue = marginal cost, price will exceed marginal cost, and the monopoly will have no incentive to increase output. Therefore, the statement might be true. However, if marginal revenue exceeds marginal cost so that the firm does have an incentive to increase output, price will also exceed marginal cost. So the statement might be true. We need to know the relation between price and marginal revenue before we can determine whether the statement is true or false.

4. *True.* Ceiling prices generate excess burdens when they are placed below the competitive equilibrium price, since consumer price increases by less than the producer surplus decreases. However, a ceiling price under monopoly conditions forces marginal revenue to equal price up to the point where the ceiling price intersects the demand curve. This causes the monopoly to increase output while decreasing price, which in turn increases consumer surplus by more than producer surplus decreases.

5. *True.* With a durable good, buyers are concerned over the potential resale price. If they expect the future price to be lower because the monopolist "dumps" the excess quantity, they will postpone their purchase to take advantage of the bargain. Therefore, the seller must dispose of all the quantity at the same time, permanently taking the "surplus" off the market lest buyers refuse to pay more than the market clearing price for the entire quantity available.

Answers to multiple choice questions.

1. b

2. c

3. d (We must know the relation between marginal revenue and marginal cost before we can answer the question.)

4. d

5. a

6. d

7. d

8. d

9. a

10. c

Chapter 10

PRICING UNDER OLIGOPOLY AND MONOPOLISTIC COMPETITION

• LEARNING OBJECTIVES

After completing this chapter, you should be able to

1. Understand how an industry with many firms can form a cartel to achieve monopoly profits for the group.

2. Understand why cartels are unstable due to the incentives to cheat by members of the group.

3. Distinguish between cooperative and noncooperative solutions to the duopoly problem.

4. Derive the Cournot solution to the duopoly problem, and contrast the equilibrium price and quantity with the monopoly solution.

5. Derive the equilibrium output and price under the Bertrand model of duopoly, and explain why this model predicts that the competitive outcome emerges in any model with more than one seller.

6. Explain the meaning of a Nash, equilibrium and apply this concept to the Cournot and Bertrand models of oligopoly.

7. Relate the predictions of the Bertrand and Cournot models of oligopoly to the assumptions about the demand functions facing each type of firm.

8. Explain why a policy of meeting a rival's price raises price.

9. Describe the events in the electrical manufacturer's conspiracy and the lessons of this case for the success of a pricing conspiracy.

10. Explain how repeated games and sequential games give rise to Nash equilibria.

11. List the assumptions of the monopolistic competition model of profit maximization among producers of differentiated products. Contrast the short-run and long-run equilibria under monopolistic competition.

• CHAPTER OVERVIEW

Cartels

A **cartel** is a market with two or more producers who limit output to achieve monopoly profits. **Figure 10-1** shows a perfectly functioning cartel. Like a monopoly, the cartel's profit-maximizing rate of output occurs at Q_M, where marginal revenue equals marginal cost. The market-clearing price for Q_M is P_M along the market demand curve. Output would be divided among the producers so that the marginal cost in each plant equals the marginal revenue for the group. Each cartel-members profit is the difference between the monopoly price and its average cost at that price.

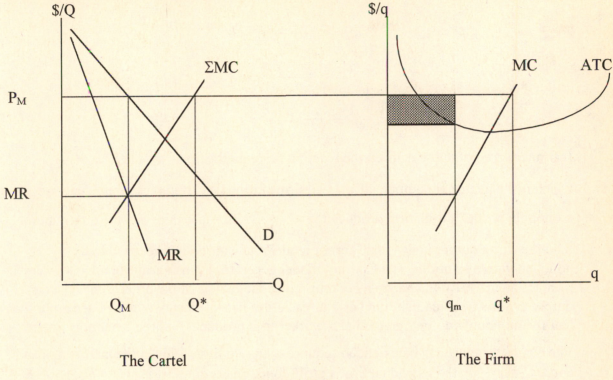

The Cartel   The Firm

Figure 10-1

The reason why there is no perfect cartel follows from the incentive that individual firms have to cheat. In Figure 10-1, the firm faces a quota of q_M, which yields a share of monopoly profits shown by the shaded area. However, the firm's owner would like to produce q^*, where its marginal cost equals P_M. But if all firms cheat, total output rises to Q^* and the market-clearing price falls below the monopoly price. This series of events came to pass in the OPEC oil cartel in the early 1980s.

Oligopoly

A market with a few sellers is called an **oligopoly**. Because there are few sellers, the dominant feature of oligopoly is **rivalry**, as each firm tries to anticipate the response of its rivals before it takes action. The simplest form of oligopoly is **duopoly**, a market with two sellers. If the two sellers cooperate, they could produce the monopoly output and share the monopoly profit between them. But because duopolists would have an incentive to cheat, a series of **noncooperative** outcomes may emerge.

The **Cournot model** is one of the more famous noncooperative models. Because there are two firms, the price of the product depends on the quantity produced by both firms. The simplest model assumes that the duopolists produce identical products, so consumers buy only from the firm charging the lowest price. Price is a linear function of the output of both firms, $P = a - bQ$, where $Q = Q_1 + Q_2$. For each firm, marginal cost is a constant, c. If each firm takes the other's output as given, then $MR_i = a - bQ_j - 2bQ_i$, where i refers to the firm in question and j is the rival. Equating $MR_I = c$ for each firm and solving for Q_I yields a reaction function for each firm:

$$q_1 = \frac{a - c - bq_2}{2b}$$

$$q_2 = \frac{a - c - bq_1}{2b}$$

$$q_1^* = q_2^* = \frac{a - c}{3b}$$

If firm 2 were not in the market, the reaction function for firm 1 would be $q_1 = \frac{a - c}{2b}$, which is the monopoly output. If the two firms formed a cartel, they could generate monopoly profits if each firm produced $q_i = \frac{a - c}{4b}$. Because duopolists produce more than the cartel output under the Cournot model, the Cournot model produces a noncooperative solution. The Cournot model generates a **Nash equilibrium**, whereby no firm has an incentive to change its output, given the output of the other firm. The cartel output is not a Nash equilibrium because each firm has an incentive to produce more than half the monopoly output, given that the other firm produces half the monopoly output.

The Cournot model can be extended to more than two firms. Given the market demand curve $P = a - bQ$, the individual firm's profit function becomes $\pi(q_i) = (a - bnq)q_i - cq_i$, where n is the number of firms (the firm has n-1 rivals) and q is the average output of all firms. Professor Pashigian shows that the firm's profit-maximizing output is

$$q_i = \frac{1}{n+1} \times \frac{a - c}{b}$$

The resulting price is $P = \frac{a}{n+1} + \frac{n}{n+1}c$. As the number of firms gets larger, the Cournot price approaches marginal cost.

The Bertrand Model

The **Bertrand model** assumes that consumers purchase only from the firm announcing the lowest price. Professor Pashigian uses the example of firms that announce their prices by printing catalogs – there are substantial costs of changing a price once announced. In this model, each firm has an incentive to undercut its rival, announcing a price as close to marginal cost as possible. The only **Nash equilibrium** is when each firm is charging a price equal to marginal cost, so that market output is the quantity demanded when $P = c$, that is $Q = \frac{a - c}{b}$.

The Cournot model predicts that price approaches marginal cost as the number of rivals increases. The Bertrand model predicts that equilibrium price reaches marginal cost when the second firm enters the market. Because these models have such strikingly different predictions, economists have investigated actual markets to see which model is the better predictor. Professor Pashigian points out that in the study of retail tire prices, the difference between monopoly and duopoly prices is not significant. As the number of rivals increases, prices decline toward the competitive level, but not continuously. Investigations of auction markets show that as the number of bidders increases, the price paid by buyers increases until, with seven to eight bidders, prices approximate competitive prices. Empirical evidence seems to support the Cournot model over the Bertrand model.

Facilitating and Preventing Collusion

Collusion is like any other economic activity: Participants adopt cooperative strategies when they perceive that the benefits of cooperation exceed the benefits of cheating. The practice of **meeting competition** facilitates collusion because each seller knows that if it undercuts the price of its rival, its price will be matched. Any benefit from cheating on a cooperative strategy would be short-lived. Buyers can prevent conspiracy by sellers in a number of ways: (a) by announcing winning bids; (b) by creating confusion by always awarding the contract to the same firm, when faced with identical bids; (c) by offering longer contracts to raise the value of cheating. Firms trying to detect cheating by members of the industry group will find it easier if (a) the number of buyers is large, (b) customers are generally loyal, and (c) price information is readily available.

Game Theory

Game theory is the study of strategic interaction among a small number of agents. A game is a situation of mutual interdependence among agents. In **noncooperative games** a firm maximizes its profit given the strategy of a rival. If the firm's profit-maximizing strategy does not depend on the strategy of a rival, the firm has a **dominant strategy.** A **prisoner's dilemma** occurs when the dominant strategies of two agents lead to an outcome that is not in the best interest of either agent. If only one agent has a dominant strategy, the other agent will assume that its rival will adopt that dominant strategy and will select its strategy contingent on the strategy of the rival.

In a **sequential game,** the **first mover** can obtain a substantial advantage by anticipating the reaction of rivals. To analyze a sequential game, economists use a **game tree** to show where the payoffs grow out of the branches formed by different sequential decisions. When an incumbent appears to have a **dominant strategy** that does not punish a rival for market entry, the incumbent may have to make a **commitment** to make the deterrent strategy credible. One example of a credible commitment was the opening of the movie *Independence Day* on July 2, 1996, which pre-empted the opening of other major motion pictures that summer.

Monopolistic Competition

Monopolistic competition is a hybrid market structure that incorporates some of the aspects of monopoly (firms face negatively sloped demand curves) and competition (there is free entry of new firms). **Figure 10-2** contrasts the short-run and long-run equilibrium price and quantity outcomes for monopolistic competition. The panel on the left shows that the short-run output and price decision for the monopolistic competitor is identical to the decision of the monopolist: Set output where marginal cost equals marginal revenue, and then set output according to the demand curve. Like any firm, the monopolistic competitive firm will shut down if price is less than average variable cost and will receive economic profit if price exceeds average total cost. The firm in the left panel Figure 10-2 is receiving positive economic profit.

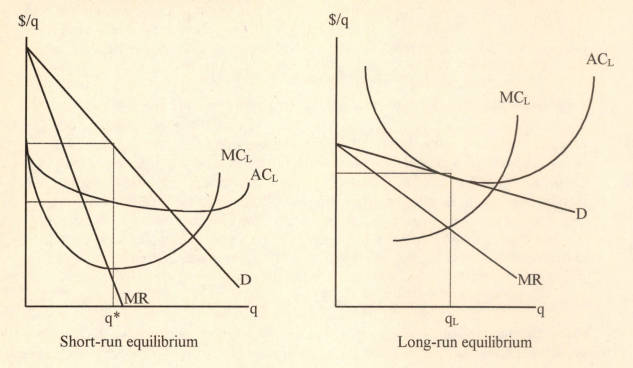

Figure 10-2

In the long run, firms will enter a monopolistically competitive industry in much the same way as they would enter a perfectly competitive industry. By itself, product differentiation neither guarantees profit nor creates barriers to entry. As firms enter, the demand curve for an incumbent firm shifts in toward the origin. It the firm does nothing, the demand curve shifts until it becomes tangent to the average cost curve at the profit-maximizing price-quantity combination. Although incumbent firms may seek to resist entry by changing product design or by advertising more aggressively, these activities tend to increase average cost, which again leads to zero-profit equilibrium in the long run. The lesson is that, with free (or nearly free) entry in the long run, the zero-profit long-run equilibrium will prevail whether there is product differentiation (monopolistic competition) or not (perfect competition).

• KEY TERMS

Cartel A contract, conspiracy, or combination of more than one producer, coordinating their output and price decisions to achieve monopoly profit.

Cooperative behavior Actions designed to achieve maximum value for a group. Team members may cooperate to win a game. Firms in an industry may cooperate to achieve cartel profits.

Concentration ratio A measure of the competitiveness of a market, computed as the ratio of the sales of the four largest firms in an industry to the total sales in the industry.

Propensity to cheat The temptation to break a cooperative agreement when individual agents can achieve more by breaking the agreement as long as other agents keep the agreement.

Prisoner's dilemma A game-theory situation in which all agents have a propensity to cheat, so that the outcome of the cheating makes each player worse off than they would have been had they all kept the agreement.

Self-enforcing agreement An agreement that is kept because it is in the interest of all parties to do so.

Oligopoly A market with a few sellers characterized by an awareness of rivalry.

Duopoly A market with two sellers.

Cournot model A theory of duopoly in which each firm takes the other's output as given. The equilibrium outcome is determined where the two firm's reaction functions intersect.

Noncooperative behavior The opposite of cooperative behavior, wherein each agent attempts to achieve its best outcome, without regard to how that behavior affects the other members of the group. The Cournot and Bertrand models of duopoly are examples of noncooperative behavior.

Nash equilibrium in quantities and prices A combination of output and prices whereby no seller has an incentive to change its behavior, given the behavior of the other sellers.

Reaction function A mathematical relation that gives one firm's output based on the output of the other firm(s).

Bertrand model A model of duopoly behavior in which the firm charging the lowest price makes all the sales for the market. The equilibrium outcome has all firms charging the lowest sustainable price, typically a price equal to long-run marginal cost.

Effect of the number of competitors on price Under the Cournot model, as the number of competitors increases, price approaches marginal cost. Under the Bertrand model, price equals marginal cost with the addition of the second seller to the market. Empirical evidence seems to support the predictions of the Cournot model.

Meeting competition The practice of a seller announcing that it will match the price charged by any rival. Ironically, this practice tends to stifle price competition.

Game theory A branch of mathematics and economics that analyzes situations with a small number of agents in a setting wherein strategy may result in cooperative or noncooperative behavior.

The cost of detecting price cutting The major determinant of whether price cutting by one rival will result in price cutting by all firms in an oligopolistic industry.

Dominant strategy A strategy that is optimal regardless of the behavior of one's opponent.

Repeated games Games that are "played" on a regular basis, that allow for learning, punishment, and rewards to modify behavior.

Punishment strategy A strategy meant to deter cheating by threatening behavior that would harm all players in a noncooperative game.

Credible commitment The announcement of a strategy that would appear to be suboptimal as a way of modifying behavior. A credible commitment typically involves self-imposed sunk costs, which make it difficult to back off from an announced strategy.

Monopolistic competition A market with differentiated products that are close substitutes. Firms maximize profit in the short run by setting output where marginal cost equals marginal revenue. In the long run, market entry results in zero economic profit, much as in perfect competition.

• PROBLEMS

1. Assume that there are 100 firms in a market, each with a marginal cost given by MC = $10 + 0.1q$. The market demand curve is $Q = 40,000 - 1,000P$. Use this information to answer the questions that follow.

   a. If each firm acts as a price taker, determine the expression for the profit maximizing output. (Hint: Set MC = P and solve for q.)

   _____

   b. If the firms behave as price takers, what is the market supply equation?

   _____

   c. Compute the competitive equilibrium price and quantity for the industry.

   _____

   d. If the firms form a cartel, what is the equation for marginal revenue? (Hint:
   $MR = P - Q \times \dfrac{\Delta P}{\Delta Q}$.)

   _____

   e. If the 100 firms form a cartel, what would be the monopoly profit-maximizing output and price?

   _____

   f. What would be the quota assigned to each firm to support the cartel output and price?

   _____

   g. If an individual firms believed it could cheat on its production quota, what output would maximize the firms' profit, assuming that all other firms produced their quotas?

   _____

h. What happens to the market price if all firms "cheat" the way the firm does in part g?

_____

2. Assume that there is a monopoly firm producing with a constant marginal cost given by $MC = 10$. The inverse demand curve is given by $P = 200 - .01Q$. Use this information to answer the questions that follow.

a. What is the marginal revenue equation for this monopolist?

_____

b. What is the profit-maximizing output and price for this monopolist?

_____

c. If a second firm enters the market producing the same product with the same long-run marginal cost, what is the residual (inverse) demand curve confronting the second firm?

_____

d. What is the profit-maximizing output and price for the second firm, assuming that the first firm continues to operate as a monopolist?

_____

e. Derive the reaction function of the former monopoly firm. Is the monopoly output a Nash equilibrium? Explain your answer.

_____

_____

_____

f. What is the Cournot equilibrium in this example?

_____

_____

g. Is the Cournot equilibrium a Nash equilibrium? Explain.

_____

_____

_____

3. Suppose that the firms in question 2 announce their prices by printing catalogs and believe that it is impossible to change price once the catalogs are printed.

   a. If the duopoly is currently at a Cournot equilibrium, does either firm have an incentive to cut the price the next year? Explain.

   _____

   _____

   _____

   b. Given your answer to part b of this question, what type of market model would best describe the pricing behavior of the duopolists?

   _____

   _____

   _____

   c. What is the long-run equilibrium price under this scenario?

   _____

   _____

   _____

   d. If firm 1 announced a policy of "meeting the competition," would your answer to part c change? Explain.

   _____

   _____

   _____

4. Mom's Pizza Parlor is one of 100 pizza restaurants in town. Mom's Pizza faces an inverse demand curve for pizza given by $P = \$10 + .5\overline{p} - .01q$, where P is the price of Mom's Pizza, $\overline{p}$ is the average price of pizza for her competitors, and q is the number of pizzas Mom sells per day.

   a. If the average price of a pizza is $10, what is the inverse demand equation for Mom's Pizza?

   _____

   b. What is the marginal revenue function for Mom's Pizza?

   _____

   c. If Mom's marginal cost is a constant $4 per pizza, what is her profit-maximizing output and price?

   _____

d. If Mom has fixed costs of $1,000 per day, what will Mom's daily economic profit be?

_____

e. Based on your answer to part d, will the number of pizza parlors tend to increase or decrease over time? Explain.

_____

_____

_____

• TRUE-FALSE QUESTIONS

For each of the following statements, indicate whether the statement is true (agrees with economic theory), false (is contradicted by economic theory), or uncertain (could be true or false; not enough information is given), and briefly explain your answer.

1. When a group of firms conspire to produce a monopoly output and charge a monopoly price, the resulting price and quantity combination is a Nash equilibrium.

_____

_____

_____

_____

2. If the residual demand curve confronting a duopolist lies everywhere below its long-run average cost curve, the market is a natural monopoly.

_____

_____

_____

_____

3. A noncooperative output and price combination is more likely to emerge in a one-time game than in a repeated game.

_____

_____

_____

_____

4. Short-run profit-maximizing behavior under monopolistic competition is consistent with markup pricing.

    _____

    _____

    _____

    _____

5. Because long-run equilibrium price under monopolistic competition is higher than minimum long-run average cost, monopolistically competitive firms are inefficient.

    _____

    _____

    _____

    _____

• MULTIPLE-CHOICE QUESTIONS

1. If a cartel is organized in a former competitive market, we would expect

    a. price to increase and output to decrease.

    b. output to increase and price to decrease.

    c. both output and price to increase.

    d. both output and price to decrease.

2. According to the Cournot model, the entry of a second firm into a former monopoly market will cause

    a. both output and price to increase.

    b. both output and price to decrease.

    c. output to decrease and price to increase.

    d. output to increase and price to decrease.

3. The Cournot model predicts that in a duopoly with both firms having identical costs, each firm will produce

    a. half the competitive output.

    b. half the monopoly output.

    c. two-thirds of the monopoly output.

    d. two-thirds of the competitive output.

$$q_i = \frac{1}{(n+1)} \frac{a-c}{b}$$

$$\frac{1}{2+1} \frac{a-c}{b}$$

4. The Bertrand model predicts that in a duopoly with both firms having identical and constant long-run marginal costs, each firm will produce

   a. ½ the monopoly output.

   b. ½ the competitive output.

   c. 2/3 the monopoly output.

   d. 2/3 the competitive output.

5. In the Bertrand model, if firm 1 announces a price of $5.50 and firm 2 announces a price of $5.00 for good A;

   a. firms 1 and 2 split the market equally.

   b. firms 1 and 2 split the market in proportion to the price differential.

   c. firm 1 supplies the entire market.

   d. firm 2 supplies the entire market.

6. When firms tell consumers that they will "meet the competitor's price," the result is

   a. monopoly prices.

   b. competitive prices.

   c. prices higher than competition but lower than monopoly.

   d. prices higher than monopoly.

7. The chance of detecting price cutting will be lower

   a. the larger the number of buyers.

   b. the larger the turnover of customers.

   c. the more price information that is available.

   d. all of the above.

8. In the payoff matrix below, the first entry in each cell represents the payoff to firm 1 and the second entry represents the payoff to firm 2. What is firm 1's dominant strategy?

		Firm 2's Strategy	
		A	B
Firm 1's	A	12/10	20/-10
Strategy	B	10/20	0/0

   a. A.

   b. B.

   c. It depends on what firm 2 decides to do.

   d. Firm 1 does not have a dominant strategy.

9. In the short run, the monopolistically competitive firm sets output where

   a. marginal cost equals marginal revenue.

   b. marginal cost equals price.

   c. average cost equals price.

   d. marginal cost equals average cost.

10. In the long run, the monopolistically competitive firm sets output where

   a. marginal cost equals marginal revenue.

   b. price equals marginal cost times the optimal markup.

   c. average cost equals price.

   d. all the above.

• ANSWERS TO PROBLEMS, TRUE-FALSE, AND MULTIPLE-CHOICE QUESTIONS

Answers to Problems

1. a. $MC = P \rightarrow 10 + .1q = P \rightarrow q_s = -100 + 10P$

    b. $Q_s = 100q_s = 100(-100 + 10P) = -10,000 + 1,000P$

    c. Set quantity supplied equal to quantity demanded and solve for P_e and Q_e

    $$Q_s = Q_d \rightarrow -10,000 + 1,000P = 40,000 - 1,000P$$

    $$2,000P = 50,000;\ P_e = \frac{50,000}{2,000} = \$25$$

    $$Q_e = -10,000 + 1000(25) = 40,000 - 1,000(25) = 15,000$$

    d. If the firms form a cartel, $MR = 40 - .001Q - .001Q = \$40 - .002Q$.

    e. Output would be allocated among the firms so that $MC = 10 + .001Q$ (each firm produces 1 percent of the output)

    $$MR = MC \rightarrow 40 - .002Q = 10 + .001Q$$

    $$.003Q = 30,\ Q_M = \frac{30}{.003} = 10,000;\ P_M = 40 - .001(10,000) = \$30$$

    f. Each firm would produce 1 percent of output, so $q_i = 0.01(10,000) = 100$.

    g. The firm would like to produce where its marginal cost equals the monopoly price

    $$q^* = -100 + 10(30) = -100 + 300 = 200\,.$$

    h. If all firms "cheat" on the cartel agreement, $Q_s = 100(200) = 20,000$, creating a surplus of 10,000 units at the cartel price. The price would fall to \$20, since

$40 - .001(20,000) = \$20$, which is below the competitive price of \$25. The cartel would be destroyed.

2. a. $MR = 200 - .01Q - .01Q = 200 - .02Q$

    b.   Setting marginal revenue equal to marginal cost, we solve for Q_M and P_M:

    $$MR = MC \rightarrow 200 - .02Q = 10$$

    $$.02Q = 190; \; Q_M = \frac{190}{.02} = 9,500$$

    $$P_M = 200 - .01(9,500) = \$105$$

    c.   The second firm will take the monopoly price as the intercept of its residual demand curve $P_R = 105 - .01Q$.

    d.   Set the entrant's residual marginal revenue function equal to marginal cost, and solve for quantity (Q_2) and the new price

    $$MR_r = 105 - .02Q_2 = 10 \rightarrow .02Q_2 = 95$$

    $$Q_2 = \frac{95}{.02} = 4,750, \; P_2 = \$47.50$$

    e.   The reaction function of the former monopoly firm (firm 1) is obtained by subtracting $.01Q_2$ from MR_1, setting MR_1 equal to MC_1 and solving for Q_1

    $$MR_1 = 200 - .01Q_2 - .02Q_1 = 10$$
    $$.02Q_1 = 190 - .01Q_2 \rightarrow Q_1 = 9,500 - .5Q_2$$
    $$When\, Q_2 = 4,750, Q_1 = 9,500 - .5(4,750) = 7,125$$

    The monopoly output and price is not a Nash equilibrium because firm 2 produces a positive output, though the monopolist assumed firm 2's output would be zero, and firm 1 reduces its rate of output when the second firm enters.

    f.   The second firm's reaction function would be $Q_2 = 9,500 - .5Q_1$. Solving the two reaction functions simultaneously:

    $$\begin{array}{ccc} Q_1 + .5Q_2 = 9,500 & Q_1 + .5Q_2 = 9,500 & Q_1 = Q_2 = 6,333 \\ .5Q_1 + Q_2 = 9,500 & 2Q_1 + Q_2 = 19,000 & P = 200 - .01(12,667) = 73.33 \end{array}$$

    g.   By definition, the Cournot solution is a Nash equilibrium because neither firm has an incentive to change its output, given the output of the other:

    $$Q_1 = 9,500 - .5Q_2 = 9,500 - .5(6,333) = 6,333$$
    $$Q_2 = 9,500 - .5Q_1 = 9,500 - .5(6,333) = 6,333$$

3. Under the Cournot equilibrium, each firm has (gross) economic profits of 462,309 - 10(6,333) = \$398,979.

    a.   By cutting price to, say, \$70, firm 2 could sell 13,000 units

    ($Q_d = \dfrac{200 - 70}{.01} = 13,000$), which would generate revenue of \$910,000 and costs of \$130,000, yielding profits of \$780,000. This would lead firm 1 to cut the price to, say \$60, and so forth, until price equals \$10 and profit for each firm is 0.

   b. The Bertrand model describes this kind of behavior.

   c. The long-run equilibrium price under the Bertrand model would be $P = MC_L = \$10$.

   d. If firm 2 anticipated that any price cut would be matched by firm 1, then it would understand that it would always have half the market at any price. Since the Cournot equilibrium is a Nash equilibrium when each firm has half the market, firm 2 would have no incentive to undercut the price. The Cournot equilibrium would prevail in the long run.

4. a. $P = 10 + .5(10) - .01q = 15 - .01q$

   b. $MR = 15 - .01q - .01q = 15 - .02q$

   c. $MR = MC \rightarrow 15 - .02q = 4, .02q = 11 \quad q^* = \dfrac{11}{.02} = 550, \quad P^* = 15 - .01(550) = \$9.50$

   d. $\pi = 9.50(550) - \$1,000 - 4(550) = 5,225 - 3200 = 2,025$

   e. Because Mom is making positive economic profits, we would expect the number of pizza parlors to increase until economic profit became zero.

True-False Questions

1. *False*. Because members of a cartel have an incentive to cheat – that is, produce more than their output quota, the cartel profit-maximizing output and price is **not** a Nash equilibrium

2. *True*. If the residual demand curve confronting a duopolist was everywhere below its long-run average cost curve, the second firm would have no incentive to enter the market, and leaving but one firm in the market: a natural monopoly.

3. *True*. In a one-time game, cheating may not be detected and it will be difficult for the rival to retaliate. However, in a repeated game, both players have a greater opportunity to learn and retaliate, making non-cooperative outcomes less likely.

4. *True*. The monopolistically competitive firm sets output where marginal cost equals marginal revenue, then sets the price according to its inverse demand curve. Given that $MR = P\left(1 + \dfrac{1}{E}\right) = MC \rightarrow P = MC\left(\dfrac{E}{E + 1}\right)$, which is an optimal markup policy.

5. *Uncertain*. While it is true that price for a differentiated product is greater than the minimum point on the long-run average cost curve, it is also true that the consumer is willing to pay a premium for the variety monopolistic competition provides. Hence, prices under monopolistic competition are not strictly comparable with prices under perfect competition. It is possible that consumer surplus is greater under monopolistic competition, implying that monopolistic competition may not be inefficient.

Multiple-Choice Questions

1. a

2. d

3. c

4. b

5. d

6. c (The incentive to cheat on a cartel arrangement would not be completely eliminated by the policy of meeting the competition.)

7. b

8. a (Firm 1's payoff is higher with strategy A, regardless of whether firm 2 adopts strategy A or strategy B.)

9. a

10. d

Chapter 11
MANAGING THE CORPORATION: CORPORATE GOVERNANCE

• LEARNING OBJECTIVES

After completing this chapter, you should be able to

1. Distinguish between internal and external monitors.

2. Understand how external monitors constrain the behavior of managers to maximize profits, and discuss what factors determine the effectiveness of external monitors.

3. Understand how internal monitors constrain the behavior of managers to act in the interest of owners, and discuss what factors determine the effectiveness of internal monitors.

4. Define tender offers, and explain the role of free riders in limiting the effectiveness of tender offers.

5. Explain how different treatments of nontendered shares or having minority ownership in a company increase the payoffs to tender offers.

6. Define expense preference, and contrast the incentives for expense preference behavior with and without a profit constraint.

7. Explain why express preference behavior is more likely when ownership is separated from management.

8. Define *ex post settling up* and explain how its use by a board of directors can force management to pay for expense preference behavior.

9. Discuss principal agent problems as they relate to corporate governance.

10. Evaluate the relation between corporate performance and executive compensation.

11. Evaluate the consequences of recent takeover activity.

• CHAPTER OVERVIEW

Profit Maximization: Assumption vs. Practice

Up to this point, the text has assumed that business firms attempt to maximize profit. This chapter scrutinizes that assumption, investigating the effects of separating ownership and control on the profit-maximization incentive.

Figure 11-1 presents the relation between company profit (π) and managerial compensation (E). The curve TT' illustrates the relation between profit and managerial compensation. If compensation were zero, profit would be negative, since the firm could attract only poor quality managers, and those managers would embezzle from the firm. As compensation increases, profit increases until, at E^*, the firm achieves maximum profit of π^*. If the owner pays more than E^*, profit declines due to **expense preference** behavior.

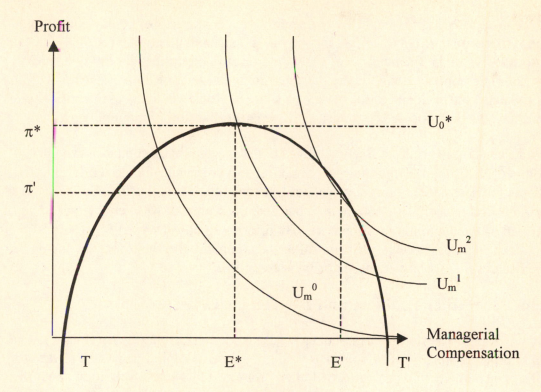

Figure 11-1

If we assume the firm has a single owner, it is clear that the owner would want to pay E^*. That is, the single owner's indifference map would be parallel to the horizontal axis; the owner is indifferent to the level of managerial compensation as long as profit is maximized. If there is **separation of ownership and control**, however, a different story develops. If managers determine their own compensation, then their indifference map will reflect a trade-off between profits (that go to shareholders) and their own compensation. The way Figure 11-1 is drawn, managers do not maximize utility by maximizing either managerial compensation or company profits. Instead, managers select a combination of profit and their own compensation that satisfies them. If the owner(s) of the company wish to obtain profit π^*, instead of merely profit π', they should find a way of tying managerial compensation to company performance. This can be accomplished with either external monitors or internal monitors.

External Monitors: Product and Capital Markets

The **product market** monitors managerial performance with economic profit and loss. We learned in Chapter 8 that a competitive market generates zero economic profit in the long run if managerial talent is in perfectly elastic supply. If some managers are indeed more talented, they will receive payments, perhaps in the form of economic rent, from the owners of their companies. **Capital markets** guarantee that the value of ownership shares (common stock) reflect the long-run profit potential of the companies. Therefore, investors in companies selling in competitive product markets will receive a normal return on their ownership shares.

If the product market is imperfectly competitive, economic profits may persist in the long run if there are barriers to entry. If companies distribute monopoly (or oligopoly) profits through dividends, financial investors would offer higher prices for the shares of monopoly companies than for the shares of competitive companies. Eventually, the ratio of the expected dividend to the price of a share of stock would equal the normal rate of return. This is a process economists call the **capitalization** of monopoly profits.

If a large enough group of financial investors suspected that a company—whether competitive or monopolistic—was not maximizing profit, they could **tender** an offer for shares in excess of the current price, but less than the potential price. Suppose the shares in XYZ corporation were selling at S' because the company was generating profits of π' instead of the maximum profits of π^*. By offering to buy shares at S'', where $S^* > S'' > S'$, the speculators hope to gain control of the company, fire the managers paying themselves E', and hire a new set of managers for E^*.

The Free Rider Problem and the Tender Offer

By purchasing the shares in a company that is underperforming (generating less than the maximum possible profits), speculators hope to receive capital gains as a reward for their efforts. There are two problems with their strategy: (1) Their information about the company's profit potential may be erroneous, in which case the speculators will lose the difference between S'' and S'. (2) The speculators' information may be correct, but current shareholders may interpret the tender as evidence that the company is indeed undervalued. By not accepting the tender offer, alert shareholders expect to reap not $S''-S'$, but S^*-S'. If they succeed, they receive the entire gain without risking their money or expending their effort; they are **free riders**. So, if free riding is prevalent enough, tender offers may fail.

There are two potential solutions to the free-rider problem. First, corporate charters may allow the new owners to discriminate against the shareholders who held onto their stock. By tying higher dividends (and hence, capital gains) to the tendered shares, the incentive for free-riding is reduced. Second, speculators may quietly accumulate sufficient shares in a company before tendering a takeover offer that the capital gain on the shares owned before the tender offer is sufficient to compensate them for the risk and cost of the takeover.

Internal Monitors of Management

We have already seen in Figure 11-1 that one of the impediments to the excessive compensation of managers is a single owner of a company. If there is one residual claimant, that person has the incentive to closely monitor managerial behavior and assure that both the optimal level of compensation and the maximum level of profit are realized. Indeed, it is typical that the single stockholders of privately held corporations both chair the board of directors and act as chief executive officer.

The second internal monitor of managerial behavior is the **board of directors.** The legal duty of the board of directors is to look after the financial interest of the owners of the corporation. Typically, however, the board is composed of part-time workers who receive information from managers themselves. This creates a conflict of interest for board members: Their duty is to serve stockholders, but their rewards come from management. The name for this conflict of interest is the **agency problem.**

Agency Problems

A principal-agent relationship exists whenever an agent makes decisions that affect the well-being of the principal. In a corporation, the agents are managers and the principals are owner-stockholders. Agency problems reflect the fact that the interests of the agents–their own income and wealth–often conflict with maximizing the income and wealth of the stockholders. With a proprietorship or single-owner corporation, there is no conflict. The owner would pay management just enough, E^*, to maximize profit at π^*. If the owner wishes to trade profits against other goals, that is her right. **Expense preference** is the excess of expenses over the level that maximizes the firm's profits. In **Figure 11-2,** profits are π^* when expense preference is zero. At point **A** the owner-manager values a dollar of expense preference more than a dollar of profits, so profits decline to π' and expense preference increases to E' at point **B.**

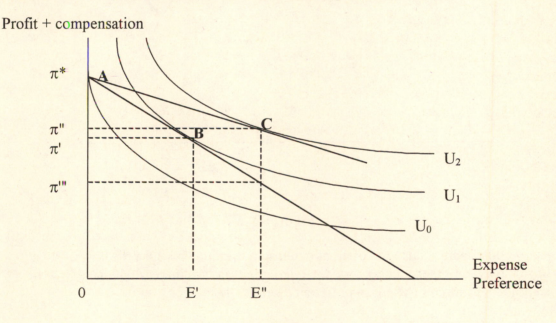

Figure 11-2

If the owner sold some of her shares to a passive investor, she could invest the proceeds and continue to receive π^* from her total investments, including her remaining shares of her business. However, the effect of expense preference behavior is now borne by the original owner and the new owner; the former proprietor now sacrifices less than $1 in profit for another dollar's worth of expense preference. Predictably, the manager will operate at point **C,** increasing expense preference to E'' and still enjoy π'' in profit plus compensation, even though the total company profit declines to π'''. The agency problem occurs because corporate managers typically own a very small percentage of corporate stock, so the costs to them of expense preference behavior are very low.

When the corporation is operating under a profit constraint, economists predict that expense preference behavior becomes more pronounced. In **Figure 11-3,** the profit-possibility frontier is flattened because the firm is constrained to make no more than $\pi_r <$ π^*. If executives were paid E^*, the firm would be required to reduce price to generate a profit of π'. This outcome would benefit the firm's customers at the expense of stock-holders. Because stockholders can receive no more than π' anyway, management could reduce profit to π' by increasing their own compensation to E'.

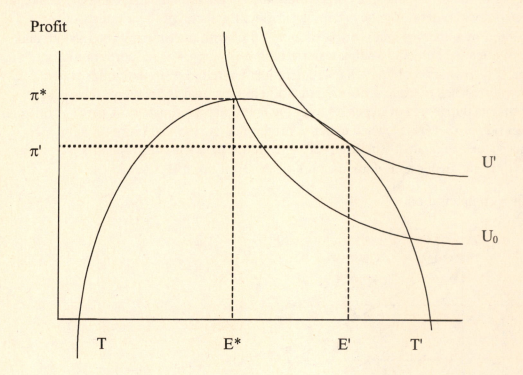

Figure 11-3

If profit constraints reduce the price of expense preference because the cost of such behavior is zero to the stockholders, then deregulation will increase the incentive for stockholders to monitor expense preference behavior.

• KEY TERMS

External monitors The product market assures that any time costs are not minimized, profit declines. The capital market allows companies that are under-performing to be taken over by speculators who can change management as a way of reaping capital gains.

Internal monitors The greater the concentration of ownership, the greater the incentive of owners to police the behavior of managers. In the absence of concentrated ownership, the board of directors serves as an internal monitor. The problem with the board of directors is that they may depend on management for information and remuneration.

Product market The market for the final good or service a firm produces. The product market generates economic profit or loss based on the efficiency of the operation.

Capital market The market for ownership shares of corporations. If a company is not run efficiently, financial investors can use the capital market to gain control of the firm, subsequently firing management and running the company more efficiently.

Tender offer An offer, made by an individual or group to pay a higher price than the market value of each share of stock, provided shareholders tender a specified number of shares.

Free rider problem and the tender offer The process whereby some stockholders, who perceive that a tender offer will lead to still higher stock prices in the future, hold their stock rather than selling, making it difficult for investors to acquire a sufficient number of shares to control the company and displace management.

Expense preference The tendency of managers to increase expenditures on support staff and other office perks as a way of padding their own compensation.

Profit constraint and expense preference When profits are restricted by regulatory bodies, the ability of managers engage in expense preference behavior with little or no direct cost to owners, thus reducing the incentive of owners to police managerial behavior.

Ex post settling up. The process whereby the board of directors may force managers to bear the cost of expense preference behavior by reducing salary or bonus by all or part of expenses that cannot justified on efficiency grounds.

Separation of ownership from management A principal-agent problem encountered in corporations. When owners (shareholders) are distinct from managers (who own but a small share of the company), the desires of managers to maximize their own utility will clash with the desires of owners to maximize their wealth.

Regulated firm operating under profit constraint When the profit a firm may earn is limited by regulation, managers will find it easier to achieve goals that would otherwise be at odds with the desires of owners. Once the allowable rate of profit is achieved, all executive perquisites are free.

Deregulation and import competition When profit constraints are removed incumbent managers are often unable to cope with a more competitive market. This is especially the case with the removal of trade barriers which previously protected industries from foreign competition. This inability of management to cope makes such firms ripe for takeover bids.

Targets and acquirers Evidence indicates that after the announcement of a takeover bid, the market price of shares in the target company increases dramatically, while increases in the price of the acquiring company are subject to a more modest increase. The combined value of targets and acquirers consistently increase 7 to 8 percent.

• **Problems**

1. **Chart 11-1** depicts the indifference map for the manager of a firm. The manager gets utility from both management compensation and expense preference. Suppose that this manager's maximum compensation per year (including bonuses) is $100,000. The board of directors carefully monitors the manager and, through ex post settling up, ensures that expenditure on expense preference results in a dollar-for-dollar reduction in manager compensation.

   a. Draw the manager's budget constraint between manager compensation and expense preference in Chart 11-1.

Chart 11-1

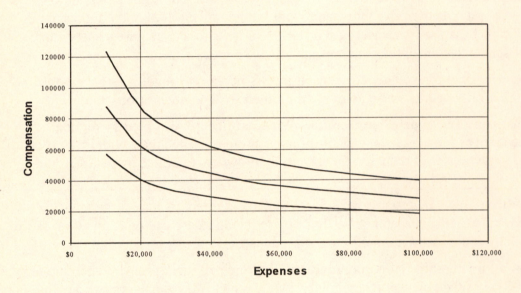

   b. What is the slope of the budget constraint?

   _____

   c. What does this slope imply about the cost of expense preference behavior to the manager?

   _____

   d. What combination of manager compensation and expense preference will the manager select?

   _____

   e. Does this combination of expense preference and manager compensation maximize profit? Explain your answer.

   _____

   _____

   _____

f. Why doesn't the manager pick the point of maximum managerial compensation?

_____

_____

2. Suppose the manager in **Chart 11-2** is the sole owner of a firm so that any expense preference reduces her profits dollar per dollar. She pays herself a salary of $25,000 in addition to profits. Maximum profits for this firm would be $50,000 per year.

Chart 11-2

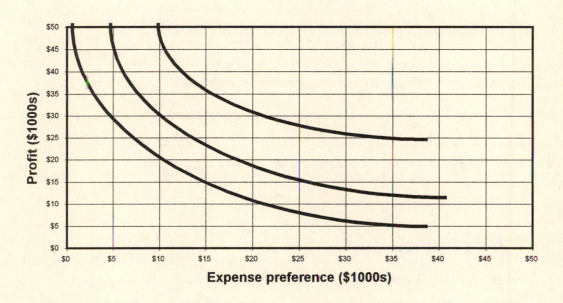

a. Draw the manager's budget constraint between profits and expense preference on Chart 11-2.

b. What is the slope of the budget constraint?

_____

c. What does this slope imply about the cost of expense preference behavior to the manager?

_____

d. What combination of manager compensation and expense preference will the manager select?

_____

e. Does this combination of expense preference and manager compensation maximize profit? Explain your answer.

_____

_____

_____

f. Why doesn't the manager pick the point of maximum profit?

_____

_____

3. Suppose that the manager in problem 2 sells the firm to her brother, who is now the sole shareholder. He retains his sister as manager at a salary of $25,000 per year. He retires to the coast secure in the belief that his firm is in good hands.

a. How much does $1 in expense preference cost the manager?

_____

b. How much does $1 worth of expense preference cost the brother?

_____

c. If the manager chooses to maximize expense preference, what can we infer?

_____

_____

d. If the manager chooses to maximize profit, what can we infer?

_____

_____

• TRUE-FALSE QUESTIONS

For each of the following statements, indicate whether the statement is true (agrees with economic theory), false (is contradicted by economic theory), or uncertain (could be true or false; not enough information is given), and briefly explain your answer.

1. The assumption that the manager(s) of a firm maximize profit is just as likely to be true for corporations run by non-owner managers as for single-owner proprietorships.

_____

_____

_____

_____

2. Students at a university want easy courses and high grades. Alumni want challenging courses with low grades. This is an example of a principal-agent problem.

_____

_____

_____

_____

3. Firms in industries that have recently been deregulated are more likely to be taken over by corporate raiders than are firms in industries that have never been regulated.

    _____

    _____

    _____

    _____

4. Evidence indicates that the stock prices of companies that are the targets of acquisitions appreciate more than do the stock prices of acquiring firms.

    _____

    _____

    _____

    _____

5. When managers are forced to bear $1 in lost salary for each $1 of expense preference behavior, profits will be higher than when the behavior of managers is not so monitored.

    _____

    _____

    _____

• MULTIPLE CHOICE QUESTIONS

1. Which of the following is an example of a free-rider problem?

    a. not contributing to National Public Radio

    b. buying most items on discount

    c. hitch hiking

    d. buying an airline ticket and giving it to a friend

2. When a tender offer is made, it is likely that the share price of the acquisition target will subsequently

    a. fall.

    b. rise.

    c. remain unchanged.

    d. move in some direction, but we cannot tell without knowing which company is involved.

3. Which of the following is *not* an external monitor of management?

   a. board of directors.

   b. threat of takeover.

   c. loss of market share.

   d, competition from other firms.

4. If Fred owns 50 percent of the company that he manages and he spends $10,000 on expense preference, he will experience a reduction in his own profits of

   a. $500.

   b. $1,000.

   c. $5,000.

   d. $10,000.

5. Which of the following constitutes a principal-agent problem?

   a. The pitcher wants the umpire to call strikes. The umpire calls 'em as he sees 'em.

   b. The linesman wants to score a goal. The goalie tries to prevent the score.

   c. The author wants the publisher to maximize revenue. The publisher wishes to maximize profit.

   d. None of the above.

6. If a firm is regulated by a government agency, the level of expense preference in comparison to an unregulated firm will

   a. be lower.

   b. be similar.

   c. be higher.

   d. depend on the proportion of shares owned by managers.

7. When one company acquires another company

   a. the share prices of both companies will increase by the same percentage.

   b. the share prices of the acquiring company will increase by a greater percentage than will the share price of the acquired company.

   c. the share prices of the acquired company will rise by a greater percentage than the share price of the acquiring company.

   d. the share price of one company will increase while the share price of the other company will decrease.

8. The fact that there has been a decline in performance-based compensation of managers over the last few years indicates that

    a. internal monitoring of firms is effective.

    b. external monitoring of firms is effective.

    c. internal monitoring of firms is ineffective.

    d. external monitoring of firms is ineffective.

9. Which of the following types of firms appear most likely to be the target of a takeover bid?

    a. A family-owned business

    b. An unregulated firm

    c. A regulated firm

    d. A recently deregulated firm

10. Takeovers of firms appear to

    a. increase wealth.

    b. decrease wealth.

    c. leave wealth unchanged.

    d. increase expense preference.

• ANSWERS TO PROBLEMS, TRUE-FALSE, AND MULTIPLE CHOICE QUESTIONS

Answers to Problems

1. a.

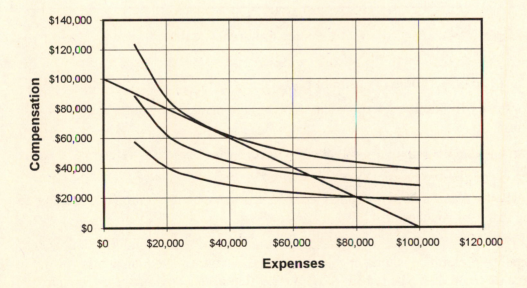

Chart 11-1a

b. The slope of the budget line is -1.

c. Each extra dollar of expense preference implies $1 less in manager compensation. The manager bears the full cost of expense preference.

d. In this example, expense preference = $30,000, and manager compensation = $70,000.

e. This combination does maximize profit because the firm saves $30,000 in manager compensation, which exactly offsets the $30,000 cost of expense preference.

f. When managerial compensation = $100,000 the manager is willing to sacrifice more than $1 in compensation for $1 in expense preference. The reason might be that expense preference is not subject to income taxation.

2. a.

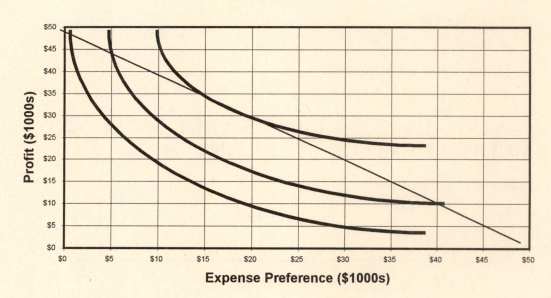

Graph 11-2a

b. The slope of the budget constraint is -1.

c. For each extra dollar of expense preference, the manager must give up $1 in profit.

d. In this example, maximum satisfaction occurs when expense preference = $20,000 and profit = $30,000.

e. This combination does *not* maximize profit, since expense preference is a cost to the firm that reduces profit.

f. At the point of maximum profit, the marginal rate of substitution of profit for expense preference is greater than 1 in absolute value. The manager is willing to give up more than $1 in profit to obtain another dollar of expense preference.

This could be explained by the double taxation of profit, whereas expense preference is tax exempt.

3. a. As long as the owner does not monitor his sister's behavior, each $1 of expense preference costs the manager $0.

   b. Each $1 of expense preference costs the brother $1 in lost profit.

   c. That the manager is maximizing her own satisfaction, without regard to the satisfaction of her brother, and that the brother is unwilling or unable to monitor his sister's behavior.

   d. That the sister cares more for her brother than for herself. Perhaps she expects to inherit.

True-False Questions

1. *False*. The separation of ownership from control in the corporation implies that managers are less likely to maximize profits than would be the case if the firm were managed by a single proprietor.

2. *False*. Neither students nor alumni set grading policies, and neither acts as the other's agent. This is simply a conflict of goals between different groups.

3. *True*. Managers of newly deregulated firms may be slow to adapt to the reduced constraints and profit opportunities of the deregulated environment. Consequently, there are more likely to be unexploited profits for newly regulated firms, which invites takeover bids.

4. *True*. Target firms typically are not realizing their profit potential, whereas the acquirers are realizing theirs. This implies that the value of the former will appreciate relative to the latter, although the latter will also appreciate.

5. *True*. Managers will select that combination of compensation and expense preference that maximizes utility. An increase in the relative price of expense preference behavior will reduce the quantity selected, *ceteris paribus*.

Answers to Multiple-Choice Questions

1. a
2. a
3. a
4. c
5. d
6. c
7. c
8. c
9. d
10. a

Chapter 12

PRICE DISCRIMINATION

• LEARNING OBJECTIVES

After completing this chapter, you should be able to

1. Distinguish between first-, second-, and third-degree price discrimination, and explain how price discrimination increases profits.

2. Explain why first-degree price discrimination causes the same rate of output that would prevail if a monopoly market were perfectly competitive.

3. Understand how price discrimination transfers consumer surplus--in part or in total--to the producer.

4. Describe the conditions necessary for a firm to practice price discrimination.

5. Comprehend how a firm practicing third-degree price discrimination maximizes total revenue by allocating a fixed number of units so that marginal revenues in the two markets are equal.

6. Explain why a price discriminating monopolist absorbs the freight costs of transporting a good to a distant location.

7. Determine the two-part tariff that maximizes profits in the case of a single user or similar consumers.

8. Understand why, if the demand functions of consumers differ, the uniform price that maximizes profits will not equal marginal cost.

9. Elucidate why leasing is preferred to selling if arbitrage is possible or if a firm does not know which of its consumers are intensive users of its product.

• CHAPTER OVERVIEW

Price Discrimination

A monopolist can increase revenue by practicing **price discrimination,** which is the practice of charging different prices for different units of a commodity. A price maker uses price discrimination in an attempt to transform **consumer surplus** into revenue. This practice is known as **revenue enhancement.** In order to accomplish price discrimination, a seller must have some degree of monopoly power, some knowledge of the *price elasticity of demand* for different groups of customers, and an ability to prevent **arbitrage**. Arbitrage is the practice of buying at a lower price and reselling at a higher price. For obvious reasons, it is easier to prevent arbitrage with services than with the sale of goods.

First-Degree Price Discrimination

Perfect or first-degree price discrimination maximizes revenue enhancement by allowing the seller to charge the highest price for each subsequent unit sold. **Figure 12-1** shows the inverse demand curve, D^{-1} confronting a first-degree discriminating monopolist. Another name for the inverse demand curve is the **marginal value function**, because it indicates the maximum price that consumers will pay for each unit offered. The intercept of the marginal value function is P_{max}, which is the price at which quantity demanded falls to zero. The slope of the inverse demand curve is $-b$; the seller must reduce the price by \$b to sell one more unit. For simplicity, we assume that the seller faces a constant marginal cost of MC. A first-degree discriminating monopolist would set price of the first unit at $P_{max} - b$, the second unit would be sold at $P_{max} - 2b$, the third unit at $P_{max} - 3b$, and so forth, until the last (n^{th}) unit is sold for $P_{max} - nb = MC$.

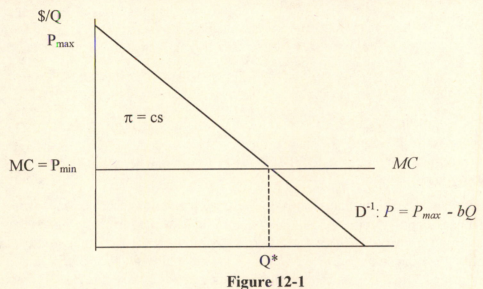

Figure 12-1

Under first-degree price discrimination, prices charged range along the demand curve from a high of P_{max} (the vertical intercept of the inverse demand curve) to a minimum of $P_{min} = MC$. This is marginal cost pricing only in the marginal sense: Output expands and the price declines until *marginal price* equals marginal cost. Under perfect competition, the area of triangle $P_{max}AP_{min}$ is consumer surplus. Under first-degree price discrimination, all potential consumer surplus is transferred to the seller, so area $P_{max}AP_{min}$ represents the maximum profit from price discrimination.

Second-Degree Price Discrimination

Second-degree price discrimination is also called **block pricing**, since this form of price discrimination entails offering a limited number of prices, with lower prices being associated with larger purchases. As such, second-degree price discrimination allows consumers to enjoy some surplus, unlike first-degree price discrimination. **Table 12-1** illustrates the difference.

Table 12-1 presents six different groups of consumers. For group 1, P(1) starts at \$15 for the first unit and falls by \$1 for each subsequent unit. A first-degree price-discriminating monopolist would charge members of this group \$120 to consume 15 units, leaving this group with a consumer surplus of zero. Members of group 2 would pay \$22 for the first unit, and their marginal value on the commodity declines by \$2 per unit. A perfect price discriminator could extract \$132 for 11 units or more. A first degree price discriminator could extract \$90 from group 3 for 10 units; \$108 from group 4 for 8 units, \$75 from group 5 (5 units), and \$100 from group 6 (4 units).

Table 12-1

Unit	P(1)	P(2)	P(3)	P(4)	P(5)	P(6)
1	$15	$22	$18	$24	$18	$20
2	$14	$20	$16	$21	$15	$16
3	$13	$18	$14	$18	$12	$12
4	$12	$16	$12	$15	$9	$8
5	$11	$14	$10	$12	$6	$4
6	$10	$12	$8	$9	$3	
7	$9	$10	$6	$6		
8	$8	$8	$4	$3		
9	$7	$6	$2	$0		
10	$6	$4	$0			
11	$5	$2				
12	$4	$0				
13	$3					
14	$2					
15	$1					
Total Value	$120	$132	$90	$108	$63	$60

A second-degree price discriminator does not have such detailed information. However, if he offers a package of 15 units of $120, groups 1 and 2 would purchase that package. This implies a unit price of $120/15 = $8. Group 1 would get no consumer surplus, but group 2 would get a consumer surplus of $12. A package of 9 units for $90 would entice members of groups 3 and 4, even though the per unit price is $9. In this case, members of group 4 would obtain a consumer surplus of $18. Finally a package with 5 units could be sold to members of groups 3 and 4 for $60 each, for a unit price of $12. In this case, members of group 3 would obtain a surplus of $3. If the seller offered the 5-unit package for $50 ($10 unit price), members of both groups 5 and 6 would realize a surplus.

Third-Degree Price Discrimination

Third-degree price discrimination is the most prevalent form of price discrimination because it requires the least amount of information. Third-degree price discrimination entails recognizing different groups of customers, estimating the elasticity of demand for these groups, and charging prices consistent with those elasticities. One obvious form of price discrimination is the practice of charging lower movie-ticket prices for children. Because adults have high opportunity costs of time, their demand for movie tickets is relatively price inelastic. An economist who consults for $50 per hour must incur an opportunity cost of $100 to see a 2-hour movie. For that economist, doubling of ticket prices from $5 to $10 would represent only a 4.76 percent increase in the full price of seeing a movie.[1] If the economist can hire a sitter for $5 per hour, she may leave the kids at home if the theater also charges $10 for children's tickets.

Table 12-2 presents the demand conditions for adults' and children's tickets at the Picture-Picture Show. Because the marginal cost of one more patron is zero, the theater

---

[1] See Chapter 4.

operator will maximize profit by maximizing revenue. The proprietor confronts two inverse demand equations. The demand equation for adults' tickets is $P_a = \$15 - .1Q_a$. Adult tickets are priced out of the market at \$15. At each quantity, the price of *all* adults' tickets must be reduced by 10 cents in order to sell one more ticket. Since each adult patron will buy only one ticket, different patrons have different marginal values. But all adult patrons must be charged the same price.

Merely by hiring an usher with minimal depth perception, the theater owner can discriminate between adults' and children's ticket prices. As indicated above, the demand for adults' tickets is likely to be much less price-elastic than the demand for children's tickets. We assume that the inverse demand (marginal value) function for children's tickets is given by $P_c = \$7.50 - .05Q_c$. The most that would be paid for a child's ticket is \$7.50, and the children's ticket price must be cut by 5 cents to sell an additional one.

Table 12.2

Ticket Price	Adult tickets Demanded	Adults' Ticket Revenue	Adults' Price Elasticity	Children's Tickets Demanded	Children's Ticket Revenue	Children's Price Elasticity	Total Tickets Demanded	Total Revenue	Total Price Elasticity
$15.00	0	$0.00		0	$0.00		0	$0.00	
$14.00	10	$140.00	-14.00	0	$0.00		10	$140.00	-14.00
$13.00	20	$260.00	-6.50	0	$0.00		20	$260.00	-6.50
$12.00	30	$360.00	-4.00	0	$0.00		30	$360.00	-4.00
$11.00	40	$440.00	-2.75	0	$0.00		40	$440.00	-2.75
$10.00	50	$500.00	-2.00	0	$0.00		50	$500.00	-2.00
$9.00	60	$540.00	-1.50	0	$0.00		60	$540.00	-1.50
$8.00	70	$560.00	-1.14	0	$0.00		70	$560.00	-1.14
$7.50	75	$562.50	-1.00	0	$0.00		75	$562.50	-1.00
$7.00	80	$560.00	-0.88	10	$70.00	-14.00	90	$630.00	-2.33
$6.50	85	$552.50	-0.76	20	$130.00	-6.50	105	$682.50	-1.86
$6.00	90	$540.00	-0.67	30	$180.00	-4.00	120	$720.00	-1.50
$5.50	95	$522.50	-0.58	40	$220.00	-2.75	135	$742.50	-1.22
$5.00	100	$500.00	-0.50	50	$250.00	-2.00	150	$750.00	-1.00
$4.50	105	$472.50	-0.43	60	$270.00	-1.50	165	$742.50	-0.82
$4.00	110	$440.00	-0.36	70	$280.00	-1.14	180	$720.00	-0.67
$3.75	113	$421.88	-0.33	75	$281.25	-1.00	188	$703.13	-0.60
$3.50	115	$402.50	-0.30	80	$280.00	-0.88	195	$682.50	-0.54
$3.00	120	$360.00	-0.25	90	$270.00	-0.67	210	$630.00	-0.43
$2.50	125	$312.50	-0.20	100	$250.00	-0.50	225	$562.50	-0.33
$2.00	130	$260.00	-0.15	110	$220.00	-0.36	240	$480.00	-0.25
$1.50	135	$202.50	-0.11	120	$180.00	-0.25	255	$382.50	-0.18
$1.00	140	$140.00	-0.07	130	$130.00	-0.15	270	$270.00	-0.11
$0.50	145	$72.50	-0.03	140	$70.00	-0.07	285	$142.50	-0.05

If price discrimination were not feasible, the theater operator would charge the uniform ticket price that maximizes total revenue. This would require a uniform price of \$5.00, because at that price the elasticity of demand is -1. At that price the theater would sell 150 tickets and realize revenue of \$750 per showing. But such a price would leave the operator with a dilemma. The price elasticity of demand for adults' tickets when $P_a = \$5$ is -0.5; adults' ticket revenue could be increased by increasing the adults' ticket price. When $P_c = \$5$, the price elasticity of demand for children's tickets is -2. Children's ticket revenue could be increased if children's ticket prices were reduced. Splitting the market solves the dilemma. Children under 12 pay $3.75, and everyone over 12 pays $7.50. Total revenue with price discrimination equals $562.50 from adults and $281.25 from children, for a total of $843.75. The theater increases revenue by $93.75 by splitting the market on the basis of price elasticity of demand.

If a firm experiences a positive marginal cost, maximizing profit implies equating the marginal revenue in each submarket to the marginal cost for the total rate of output. Note that the movie theater example is actually a special case of this rule. When the marginal cost equals zero, the marginal revenue in each sub-market (e.g., for adults' and children's tickets) will each be set equal to zero.

Figure 12-2 shows a market with two groups of consumers. Group 1 has a fairly inelastic demand, while group 2 has a fairly elastic demand. For each inverse demand function, the seller estimates the marginal revenue function. By equating the marginal revenue in each market, the composite marginal revenue function, ΣMR, is generated. The rate of output is determined in the third panel, where $\Sigma MR = MC$. Once the common marginal revenue is determined, the output is distributed between the two groups so that $MR_1 = MR_2 = MC$. Note that group 1, with the less elastic demand, pays the higher price, while group 2, with the more elastic demand, pays the lower price.

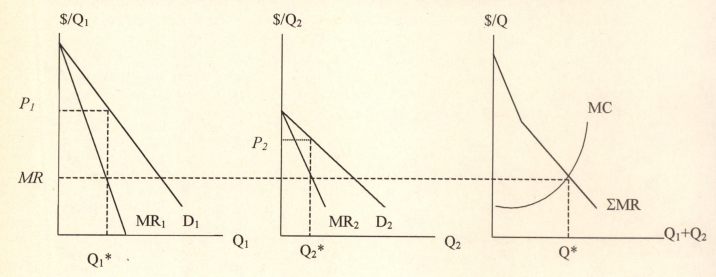

Figure 12-2

Price Discrimination and Arbitrage

When arbitrage can be practiced at little or no cost, price discrimination is difficult. For instance, campus bookstores typically give discounts on textbooks to faculty. The price elasticity of demand for textbooks by faculty is greater than the demand by students, since faculty are more knowledgeable about alternative prices, can order texts directly from publishers, and do not have to worry about exams. If faculty members regularly purchased books on behalf of students, this form of price discrimination would soon come to an end.

Another form of price discrimination that is vulnerable to arbitrage is the practice of selling prescription drugs under an expensive brand name as well as under an equivalent, but cheaper, generic name. Many health insurance plans routinely require substituting the cheaper generic drug for the more expensive brand named drug, much to the chagrin of the drug companies.

Spatial Price Discrimination

One way that sellers can deter arbitrage is by absorbing freight costs. It is not unusual for companies to export a good at a price lower than the domestic price. This is an example of **spatial price discrimination.** Those companies correctly reason that since overhead costs are covered in the domestic market, the commodity can be shipped to other countries at a price only slightly greater than variable cost. The limit to the domestic-foreign price differential, however, is the cost of shipping the product back from the low price foreign market to the high priced domestic market. This often leads companies to lobby governments for import restrictions on their own products. Actually, international trade is just another form of arbitrage.

Two-Part Tariffs

Two-part tariffs entail the payment of a fixed fee that gives the consumer the right to purchase units of a good at a specified price. The seller's revenue equals the fee plus the product of price times quantity. When there is a single customer, or many customers with the same demand equation, using a two-part tariff is equivalent to first-degree price discrimination. The seller sets the unit price equal to marginal cost and sets the periodic fee equal to consumer surplus. When customers differ in their marginal value functions, and when the seller either cannot estimate their consumer surpluses, or the seller cannot prevent arbitrage, the periodic fee will not capture all of consumer surplus. In this case, the two-part tariff will function as second-degree price discrimination.

• KEY TERMS

Revenue enhancement The practice of transforming the consumer surplus that would occur under competitive market conditions into monopoly profits through the use of price discrimination.

First-degree price discrimination   The practice of charging the highest price the market will bear for each unit produced, thereby completely transforming all consumer surplus into monopoly revenue.

Second-degree price discrimination The practice of charging different uniform prices to each customer. Typically, second-degree price discrimination takes the form of block pricing.

Third-degree price discrimination The most common form of price discrimination, whereby consumers are separated into identifiable groups with different price elasticities of demand. The group(s) whose demand is the most price-elastic pay the lowest price(s) and the group(s) with the least elastic demand pay the highest price(s).

Grouping consumers Segmenting markets so that all consumers with the same price elasticity of demand pay the same price.

Equating marginal revenue across markets In order to maximize profit with price discrimination, the seller sells each unit for the highest marginal revenue it will bring.

This implies that prices will be set so that the marginal revenue is the same in all markets. Profit is thereby maximized when the common marginal revenue in each market equals the marginal cost for all the markets.

Setting prices based on elasticity of demand Since $MR = P(1 + 1/E)$, equating marginal revenue in all markets implies that markets with more elastic demand will experience lower prices than will markets with less elastic demand. Of course, for marginal revenue to be nonnegative in all markets, demand must not be price-inelastic in any market.

Preventing arbitrage Price discrimination will not enhance revenues if customers paying lower prices can easily resell to customers who would otherwise be charged higher prices.

Bundling reduces consumer surplus When customers have differing, but unknown willingness to pay for close substitutes--like different professional team logos or different makes of model cars--the seller can capture some consumer surplus by bundling products together, so that the average price for bundled products is greater than the uniform price if products were not bundled.

Two-part tariff Charging a fee for the right to purchase a product at a uniform price. If all customers have uniform tastes, the optimal two-part tariff sets the uniform price equal to marginal cost and the periodic fee equal to (what would be) consumer surplus.

Leasing vs. selling Leasing a product may make it easier to practice price discrimination by preventing arbitrage and by facilitating the monitoring of product use.

• PROBLEMS

1. **Chart 12-1** shows the market demand curve, marginal revenue curve and marginal cost curve facing a monopolist.

   a. Fill in the information below, assuming that the monopoly charges all customers a uniform monopoly price.

   i)   Monopoly price: _____

   ii) Output: _____

   iii) Total revenue: _____

   iv) Monopoly profit: _____

   v)   Consumer surplus: _____

Graph 12-1

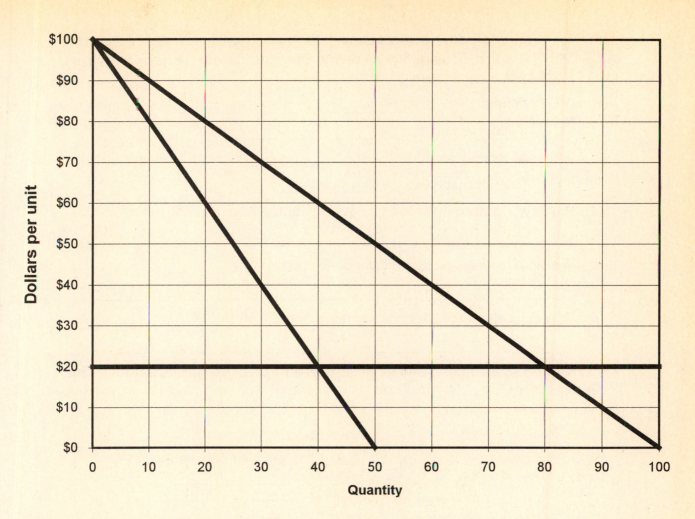

Dollars per unit (y-axis): $100, $90, $80, $70, $60, $50, $40, $30, $20, $10, $0

Quantity (x-axis): 0, 10, 20, 30, 40, 50, 60, 70, 80, 90, 100

b. Fill in the information below assuming that the monopoly in Chart 12-1 practices first-degree prices discrimination.

i)   Maximum price: _____

ii) Minimum price: _____

iii) Output: _____

iv) Total revenue: _____

v)   Monopoly profit: _____

vi) Consumer surplus: _____

c. Fill in the information below assuming that the monopoly in Chart 12-1 charges $80 for the first 20 units, $60 for the next 20 units, $40 for the next 20 units, and $20 for any additional units.

   i)   Output: _____

   ii)   Total revenue: _____

   iii)   Monopoly profit: _____

   iv)   Consumer surplus: _____

d. What type of price discrimination is being practiced in part c?

_____

e. Which of the three pricing schemes maximizes profit?

_____

f. Why don't all monopolies practice this scheme at all times?

_____

2. **Table 12-3** shows the demand for plane trips for tourists and the market for business travelers for Fly by Night Airlines. For simplicity, we assume that the marginal cost of providing plane trips is zero for both tourists and business travelers.

Table 12-3

Fare	Q(tourist)	TR(tourist)	Q(business)	TR(business)	Total Revenue
$1,000	0	_____	0	_____	_____
$900	0	_____	100	_____	_____
$800	0	_____	200	_____	_____
$700	0	_____	300	_____	_____
$600	200	_____	400	_____	_____
$500	400	_____	500	_____	_____
$400	600	_____	600	_____	_____
$300	800	_____	700	_____	_____
$200	1000	_____	800	_____	_____
$100	1200	_____	900	_____	_____

a. Fill in the total revenue columns for tourists and business travelers as well as for overall total revenue.

b. If the airline must charge all passengers the same fare, what fare will maximize total revenue?

_____

c. What is the price elasticity of demand for each group at the price in part b?

   Tourists _____

   Business travelers _____

d. If the airline practices third-degree price discrimination, what fare will it charge each group?

Tourists _____

Business travelers _____

e. What is the effect of price discrimination on the airline's profits?

_____

_____

3. The following problem concerns two geographically isolated sets of consumers served by a monopolist. The inverse demand equations are as follows for market 1 and market 2: $P_1 = 8 - 0.5Q_1$; $P_2 = 10 - Q_2$. The plant that produces the good is located in town 1, and the transportation cost is zero to customers in that town. The cost of shipping to town 2 is \$1 per unit. Marginal cost is constant at \$2.

a. Write the expression for total revenue in each market

Market 1: _____

Market 2: _____

b. What is the expression for marginal revenue in each market?

Market 1: _____

Market 2: _____

c. What is the profit-maximizing price _____ and quantity _____ in market 1? (Hint: Set MC = MR$_1$ and solve for Q$_1$; then find P$_1$.)

d. What is the profit-maximizing price _____ and quantity _____ in market 2? (Hint: Set MC = NMR$_2$ and solve for Q$_2$; then find P$_2$.)

e. If the two towns were not isolated, would there be any arbitrage possibilities? _____ Briefly explain your answer. _____

_____

4. **Chart 12-2** shows market demand for a monopolist who seeks to maximize profit using a two-part tariff structure.

a. What is the per unit charge by the monopolist in Chart 12-2?

_____

b. What is the fixed fee charged by the monopolist?

_____

c. What is monopoly profit under the two-part tariff structure?

_____

d. What is consumer surplus under the two-part tariff structure?

_____

e. What type of discrimination does this resemble?

_____

Chart 12-2

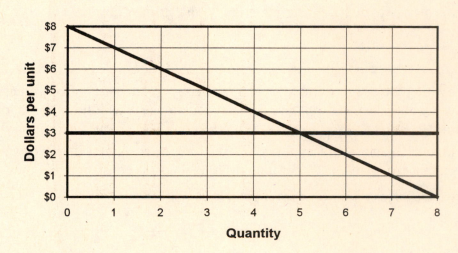

• TRUE-FALSE QUESTIONS

For each of the following statements, indicate whether the statement is true (agrees with economic theory), false (is contradicted by economic theory), or uncertain (could be true or false; not enough information is given), and briefly explain your answer.

1. Because perfect competition and first-degree price discrimination both result in the rate of output where marginal cost equals (marginal) price, both types of economic organization yield equivalent consumer surplus.

_____

_____

_____

_____

2. Bundling always constitutes second-degree price discrimination.

_____

_____

_____

_____

3. Third-degree price discrimination will not pay if different groups of consumers have the same price elasticity of demand.

_____

_____

_____

_____

4. Arbitrage is an impediment to price discrimination.

_____

_____

_____

_____

5. Price discrimination reduces economic welfare.

_____

_____

_____

_____

• MULTIPLE-CHOICE QUESTIONS

1. If soap is sold at a lower price per bar when two bars are packaged together than when one bar is packaged alone, this is an example of

   a. competitive market pricing.

   b. first-degree price discrimination.

   c. second-degree price discrimination.

   d. third-degree price discrimination.

2. If senior citizens travel for reduced fares on buses, this is an example of

   a. competitive market pricing.

   b. first-degree price discrimination.

   c. second-degree price discrimination.

   d. third-degree price discrimination.

3. Which of the following limits the ability of a firm to engage in price discrimination?

    a. identical price elasticity of demand for different groups of customers

    b. competitive market conditions

    c. costless arbitrage between groups paying different prices

    d. all of the above

4. It costs $3.75 to have a woman's shirt laundered at the local cleaner and $1.25 to have a man's shirt laundered -- a cost difference the cleaner attributes to the higher cost of pressing women's shirts. A possible alternative explanation might be

    a. third-degree price discrimination because women's elasticity of demand is less than men's elasticity of demand.

    b. third-degree price discrimination because women's elasticity of demand is greater than men's elasticity of demand.

    c. second-degree price discrimination.

    d. first-degree price discrimination.

5. For two geographically separated markets served by a monopolist, where the plant is located in town 1 and town 2 is a distant, identical market and for which arbitrage is not possible, market equilibrium implies

    a. price in town 1 > price in town 2.

    b. price in town 2 > price in town 1.

    c. price in town 2 = price in town 1 plus per unit transportation cost.

    d. b and c are both correct.

6. For two geographically separated markets served by a monopolist, where the plant is located in town 1 and town 2 is a distant, identical market and for which arbitrage is costless, market equilibrium requires

    a. price in town 1 > price in town 2.

    b. price in town 2 > price in town 1.

    c. price in town 2 = price in town 1 plus per unit transportation cost.

    d. b and c are both correct.

7. A firm should seek to expand into a new market so long as

    a. marginal revenue$_{new}$ is less than marginal revenue$_{old}$.

    b. marginal revenue$_{new}$ is more than marginal revenue$_{old}$.

    c. marginal cost$_{new}$ is less than marginal cost$_{old}$.

    d. marginal cost$_{new}$ is more than marginal cost$_{old}$.

8. Under a two-part tariff structure with identical consumers,

    a. consumer surplus equals zero.

    b. consumer surplus equals competitive industry surplus.

    c. consumer surplus is positive.

    d. consumer surplus is negative.

9. Under a two-part tariff structure with nonidentical consumers

    a. consumer surplus equals zero.

    b. consumer surplus equals competitive industry surplus.

    c. consumer surplus is positive.

    d. consumer surplus is negative.

10. Compared to other monopolists, price discriminators produce _____ output.

    a. more

    b. quite a bit less

    c. the same

    d. a little less

• ANSWERS TO PROBLEMS, TRUE-FALSE AND MULTIPLE-CHOICE QUESTIONS

Answers to Problems

1. a. For the non-discriminating monopolist

    i)   Monopoly price = $60

    ii)   Output = 40 units

    iii)   Total revenue = ($60)(40) = $2,400

    iv)   Monopoly profit = TR - TC = $2400 - ($20)(40) = $1,600

    v)   Consumer surplus = 1/2(100-60)(40) = $800

    b. For the first-degree discriminating monopolist

    i)   Maximum price = $100 (vertical intercept of demand curve)

    ii)   Minimum price = marginal cost = $20

    iii)   Output = 80 units

    iv)   Total revenue = 1/2(100-80)80+20*80 = $4,800

    v)   Monopoly profit = $4,800 - 20(80) = $3,200

    vi)   Consumer surplus = 0.

c. If the monopoly practices block pricing

    i)   Output = 80 units.

    ii)   Total revenue = $80(20) + $60(20) + $40(20) + $20(20) = $4,000

    iii)   Monopoly profit = $4,000 - $20(80) = $2,400.

    iv)   Consumer surplus = $3,200 - $2,400 = $800

d. In part c, the firm is practicing second-degree price discrimination.

e. First-degree price discrimination returns the largest profit.

f. Monopoly sellers do not always practice first degree price discrimination because they do not always know the maximum price offered for each unit, or they cannot sort consumers strictly by their highest ability to pay.

2. a.
Table 12-3a

Fare	Q(tourist)	TR(Tourist)	Q(Business)	TR(Business)	Total Revenue
$1,000	0	$0	0	$0	$0
$900	0	$0	100	$90,000	$90,000
$800	0	$0	200	$160,000	$160,000
$700	0	$0	300	$210,000	$210,000
$600	200	$120,000	400	$240,000	$360,000
$500	400	$200,000	500	$250,000	$450,000
$400	600	$240,000	600	$240,000	$480,000
$300	800	$240,000	700	$210,000	$450,000
$200	1000	$200,000	800	$160,000	$360,000
$100	1200	$120,000	900	$90,000	$210,000

3.

b. If the airline must charge all passengers the same fare, a fare of $400 will maximize total revenue at $480,000.

c. At the $400 fare, the price elasticity for each group is

$$\text{Tourists: } E_T = -2\left(\frac{400}{600}\right) = -1.33$$

$$\text{Business travelers: } E_B = -1\left(\frac{400}{600}\right) = -0.67$$

d. If the airline practices third-degree price discrimination, the fares will be

Tourists: $P_T = \$350$, $Q_T = 750$, $Revenue = \$245,000$

Business travelers: $P_B = \$500$, $Q_B = 500$, $\$250,000$

e. Price discrimination increases revenue by $15,000. Since costs remain constant, profit also increases by $15,000.

3. a. Total revenue in market 1: $R_1 = (8 - 0.5Q_1)Q_1 = 8Q_1 - 0.5Q_1^2$

Total revenue in market 2: $R_2 = (10 - Q_2)Q_2 = 10Q_2 - Q_2^2$

b. $MR_1 = 8 - Q_1$

$$MR_2 = 10 - 2Q_2$$

   c. $MC = MR_1 \rightarrow 2 = 8 - Q_1 \rightarrow Q_1^* = 6; \; P_1 = 8 - 0.5(6) = \$5$

   d. $MC = NMR_1 \rightarrow 2 = 10 - 2Q_2 - 1 \rightarrow Q_2^* = 3.5; \; P_1 = 10 - (3.5) = \$6.5$

   e. If the two towns were not isolated, there *would* be arbitrage possibilities. The product could be bought in market 1, shipped to market 2, and sold for $6, cutting the seller's profit margin.

4. a. The seller would charge a unit price equal to marginal cost = $3.

   b. The fixed fee charged by the monopolist would equal consumer surplus = $\frac{1}{2}(8-3)(5) = 12.5$.

   c. Monopoly profit = confiscated consumer surplus = $12.50.

   d. The consumer surplus is zero.

   e. This two-part tariff scheme resembles first-degree price discrimination.

Answers to True-False Questions

1. *False*. The price output combination under perfect competition *maximizes* consumer surplus. A first-degree price discriminating monopoly *minimizes* consumer surplus. Therefore, consumer surplus is not equivalent under the two pricing schemes.

2. *False*. Bundling may reflect economies of packaging or marketing, which, under competitive market conditions, would reduce the unit prices paid by consumers. Hence, although second-degree price discrimination typically involves bundling, not all bundling is second-degree price discrimination.

3. *True*. Price discrimination involves charging different prices to different consumers. For price makers, $P_i = MC(1 + \frac{1}{E_i})$. Since marginal costs will be the same, prices will also be the same if the elasticities of demand are identical for different consumers.

4. *True*. With arbitrage, the group paying the lower price will resell the product to the group being charged the higher price. Hence, only trades at the lower price will occur, and price discrimination will fail.

5. *Uncertain*. Price discrimination reduces consumer surplus, making buyers, as a group, worse off. However, some buyers paying lower prices than would prevail under single-price monopoly gain with second- or third-degree price discrimination. Furthermore, sellers are better off. With some economic agents being better off and others being worse off, we do not have sufficient information to make a judgement about economic welfare.

Answers to Multiple-Choice Questions

1. c (the answer could also be a--see true-false question 2).

2. d   3. d   4. a   5. b   6. d   7. b

8. a (the answer could be c if information about consumer demand is imperfect.)

9. c   10. a

Chapter 13

THE FREE RIDER PROBLEM AND PRICES

• LEARNING OBJECTIVES

After completing this chapter, you should be able to

1. Recognize and evaluate the free rider problem in a variety of market situations.

2. Explain why a manufacturer will maximize profit by allowing free entry of bona fide retailers to sell a product whose features are familiar to customers.

3. Evaluate how consumer ignorance of product characteristics changes the incentive of the manufacturer to control who and how many retail firms sell its product.

4. Define a special service and explain how it shifts the wholesale and retail demand functions to the right.

5. Explain how resale price maintenance provides a greater incentive for retailers to provide special services.

6. Understand how resale price maintenance can facilitate a cartel.

7. Relate quality certification to the problem of free-riding in pricing.

• CHAPTER OVERVIEW

Free rider problems

The term **free rider** was born in the Depression-era practice of hobos riding in railroad boxcars, evading the ticket price, and "riding free." The railroads were understandably upset by the practice and hired guards armed with billy clubs to discourage it. Many a vagrant would complain of the unfairness of being tossed off a train, since the boxcars were already moving, and it cost virtually no fuel for the railroads to tolerate a few free riders. "What if everyone thought as you do?" a more erudite guard would often inquire. "Then I'd be pretty foolish if I didn't take advantage of free rides myself," was often the reply.

Free-riding is a problem precisely because everybody does it. In this chapter Professor Pashigian illustrates free-riding in labor markets (where key employees walk off with company secrets), and in retailing. To really appreciate the richness of this chapter, keep in mind that market entry is itself a type of free riding. Some pioneering firm takes the risk of introducing a new product or opening a new location. When the firm succeeds and earns economic profit, the market is flooded with imitators.

Manufacturers and retailers

When selling a familiar product, a manufacturer maximizes profit by allowing free entry of bone fide retailers into the industry. Free entry guarantees that retailers operate at the minimum point on their long-run average cost curves. This efficiency of retailing minimizes the retail markup. Since the wholesale demand curve is obtained by subtracting the retail markup from the market (retail) demand curve, the lower the markup, the higher the price the manufacturer receives. It is perplexing why manufacturers would object to cut-rate retailers entering the market.

One answer to this puzzle lies in **special services.** A special service typically involves educational activities like displays, demonstrations of product operation, and knowledgeable sales personnel who can answer customer questions. Because special services are part of the marketing effort, they are provided free of charge to potential customers. The free rider problem arises because customers shop around. Once they are informed about a product's characteristics and are convinced to buy, they may purchase the item at a discount store (or via the Internet or mail order) that does not provide special services. When discount sellers ride free, full service retailers will ultimately be driven out of business as more and more buyers learn that they don't have to pay for special services through a higher price. And when the manufacturer cannot rely on retailers to provide special services, the demand for the manufacturer's product will decline.

Resale Price Maintenance

Under **resale price maintenance (RPM)**, the manufacturer prohibits retailers from selling below a minimum suggested price. A floor on prices encourages the provision of special services, since retailers are precluded from price competition below the floor. The special services shift the manufacturer's demand function rightward and lead to more sales and higher profits for the manufacturer. A select group of retailers make profits under RPM.

Free rider problems are more common with new rather than established products, so a manufacturer is more likely to use RPM early in the product life cycle. RPM is more common with complex durable or technical goods and when the cost of the consumer's time is low relative to the cost of the product.

The law is ambiguous as to whether RPMs violate **antitrust regulations**. The free rider problem can be addressed in other ways. Firms may operate demonstration stores that provide information but do not sell products. Alternatively, firms may subsidize stores that offer special services. However, if manufacturers lower the wholesale price to stores providing special services, they may be violating the **Robinson-Packman Act,** which prohibits firms from charging retailers different prices unless the differences are cost-justified.

A manufacturer who voluntarily eliminates an existing RPM agreement is signaling that the provision of special services is no longer necessary because the product is now familiar. The elimination of special services reduces minimum long-run average operating costs in the retail industry while leaving the retail demand function unchanged. Equilibrium retail margins decline as new retailers enter the industry, output increases, and manufacturer's profits increase.

RPM may facilitate the development and maintenance of a cartel by reducing the possibility of price competition among cartel members. Retail price maintenance agreements in the absence of a need for special services would constitute at least circumstantial evidence of collusive pricing.

The Certification Function

Retail price maintenance may eliminate another form of free riding. A quality retailer often performs a **certification function** through its decision to stock certain brands. Certification of a new brand typically requires considerable testing and other costly activities. The retailer would expect to recoup these expenses through a higher markup. If the same product is available from a discount retailer, customers can free-ride on the quality assurance provided by the quality retailer. Eventually, the certification function may prove unprofitable. If it is discontinued, demand for the manufacturer's product will be reduced. The manufacturer can refuse to supply to low-price retailers or can enact retail price maintenance agreements with retailers to remove the option of free-riding by consumers.

• KEY TERMS

Free rider problem The problem that occurs when valuable general information or goods can be appropriated by other agents without compensating the owner of the information or goods.

Free entry of retailers The optimal policy for a manufacturer of a well-known product. Free entry guarantees that retailers operate at minimum long-run average cost, which reduces the margin between the retail and wholesale prices. This assures the retailer of receiving the maximum profit for its product.

Educational information Information about the quality or characteristics of a good or service provided free to potential customers prior to sale. Because retailers cannot easily charge for educational information, its provision is particularly susceptible to free-riding. Typically, a customer will learn of a product's characteristics at a full-service store, and then buy the product at a lower price at a discount store, on the Internet, or through mail order, thus avoiding paying the cost of providing educational information.

Special services A number of different services, provided before or after sale, that enhance the demand for a manufacturer's product. Providing educational information is one type of special service. Others include *quality certification*, providing after-sale repair and warranty work, and monitoring consumer satisfaction. Like educational information, special services are subject to a free rider problem because buyers may purchase the product at a lower price after they have used special services to inform their buying decision.

Resale price maintenance (RPM) A contractual agreement whereby a retailer agrees not to sell an item below a minimum suggested price (or range of prices) in exchange for the right to sell merchandise. Once considered a simple provision of contract law, resale price maintenance agreements fell into disfavor because they could serve to stabilize a cartel pricing conspiracy. Recently courts have entertained arguments that there may be legitimate reasons for using RPMs that do not involve restraint of trade.

Nonprice competition The use of tactics other than price cuts to attract customers, including advertising, special services, and providing educational information.

Quality certification A service of quality retailers whereby carrying a manufacturer's product extends quality assurance to potential customers. There is a free rider problem here, because once the product is subject to the halo effect, other retailers will also enjoy the increased demand for the product without incurring the costs of quality assurance.

• PROBLEMS

1. Suppose that a manufacturer wishes to sell 2 million units of a familiar product and knows that consumers will purchase this amount with a retail price of $12. Minimum long-run average operating cost for retailers in this industry occurs at an output of 1,000 units. At output = 1,000, AOC_L = $2.

   a. What wholesale price should the manufacturer charge to achieve the goal of 2 million sales?

   _____

   b. How many retailers will agree to carry the manufacturer's product?

   _____

   c. What is the manufacturer's revenue?

   _____

   d. What profits do retailers earn on this product?

   _____

2. Suppose that the manufacturer in problem 1 introduces a new product whose quality and characteristics are unknown to the public. The manufacturer has estimated that 2 million units can be sold at $10 each if the public remains ignorant of the quality before buying (eventually word of mouth will generate some sales), but that with special services, 2 million units can be sold for $15 each. Special services would average $2 per unit for each store that sold 1,000 units. Assume that retailers experience minimum AOC_L of $2 at q = 1000 without special services or AOC_L of $4 with special services, also selling 1,000 units.

   a. Fill in the information below, assuming that all stores provide special services.

   i)   Retail price of 2 million units: _____

   ii)   Wholesale price of 2 million units: _____

   iii)   Total revenue for the manufacturer: _____

   iv)   Profits for the retailers: _____

   b. Suppose that 25 percent of the retailers decide to reduce their price by $1 and discontinue the special services.

   i)   What happens to the profit of the discount retailers? _____

   _____

ii)   Will the 75 percent of retailers still offering special services continue to offer those services?

_____

_____

iii)   What happens to the inverse demand for the manufacturer's product?

_____

_____

iv)   What ultimately happens to the manufacturer's wholesale price?

_____

_____

v)   What ultimately happens to the manufacturer's revenue?

_____

_____

3. What advise, if any, could you offer to the manufacturer?

_____

_____

_____

• TRUE-FALSE QUESTIONS

For each of the following statements, indicate whether the statement is true (agrees with economic theory), false (is contradicted by economic theory), or uncertain (could be true or false; not enough information is given), and briefly explain your answer.

1. It is generally in the interests of a manufacturer to restrict the number of retailers that sell its product.

_____

_____

_____

_____

2. Typically, special services are jointly produced with a commodity and cannot be stripped from the commodity and sold separately.

_____

_____

_____

_____

3. Resale price maintenance eliminates free-riding by consumers, who can purchase the product without paying for special services.

_____

_____

_____

_____

4. Resale price maintenance may induce other forms of nonprice competition besides the provision of special services.

_____

_____

_____

_____

5. A quality retailer has a reputation picking quality products. A manufacturer is better off signing an exclusive dealership arrangement with the quality retailer than employing resale price maintenance agreements with a number of competitive retailers.

_____

_____

_____

_____

• MULTIPLE CHOICE QUESTIONS

1. Which of the following is an example of free-riding in the retail industry?

   a. buying stock only from a discount manufacturer

   b. stocking only name-brand clothing

   c. buying the same stock as a prestigious retailer

   d. buying early for each season

2. When a product's features are familiar to consumers, the manufacturer of that product can maximize profits by

   a. not seeking to influence the number of retailers.

   b. restricting the number of retailers.

   c. subsidizing retailers.

   d. screening retailers for the quality of their special services.

3. When products are familiar to consumers, retailers make

   a. zero profits in the long run.

   b. positive profits in the long run.

   c. profits equal to AOC_L minus R^*.

   d. profits sufficient to cover the cost of special services.

4. Resale price maintenance is most likely to be found in which of the following industries?

   a. knives and forks

   b. garden rakes

   c. medical equipment

   d. cigarettes

5. A retailer supplying special services

   a. has higher AOC_L than a discount store.

   b. will make a profit as long as all of its competitors also provide special services.

   c. will make a profit as long as only some of its competitors offer special services.

   d. reduces the profits of a manufacturer of an unfamiliar product.

6. One problem with RPM for the manufacturer is that

   a. it can lead to the breakup of profitable cartels.

   b. it will reduce the profits of the manufacturer.

   c. it discourages the production of special services.

   d. it may be illegal.

7. With resale price maintenance, as compared to free entry of retailers, retail margins on unfamiliar products will be

   a. the same.

   b. higher.

   c. lower.

   d. impossible to determine without additional information.

8. Quantity of output of an unfamiliar product under RPM will be:

   a. the same.

   b. higher.

   c. lower.

   d. impossible to determine without additional information.

9. If a manufacturer stops an existing RPM program, it is *probably* because

    a. firms are cheating by not offering special services.

    b. advertising is a better way of educating consumers about complicated products.

    c. demonstration stores are a better way of educating consumers about complicated products.

    d. the product has become familiar.

10. If a designer refuses to sell to a discounter, it is probably because

    a. the cost of selling to discounters is higher.

    b. the designer wants to reward stores that perform a certification function.

    c. the designer seeks monopoly profits.

    d. of none of the above reasons.

• ANSWERS TO PROBLEMS, TRUE-FALSE, AND MULTIPLE-CHOICE QUESTIONS

Answers to Problems

1. a. $10

    b. 2,000 stores will carry the merchandise.

    e. Revenue = $10(2 million) = $20 million

    f. Retailers earn $0 economic profit, due to free entry.

2. a. i) $15

       ii) $11

       iii) $22 million

       iv) $0, again, due to free entry

    b. i) The discount retailers will *temporarily* experience positive economic profits. These profits will decline after other retailers drop their special services.

       ii) The retailers still offering special services will experience economic losses (they will have many shoppers receiving costly services, but will have fewer sales than the discount sellers). Eventually, they will stop offering special services and their profits will return to normal.

       iii) As retailers discontinue special services, the demand curve shifts down so that $12 is the market clearing price for 2 million units.

       iv) The manufacturer's wholesale price will decline to $10.

       v) The manufacturer's revenue will decline to $20 million.

3. This manufacturer should consider resale price maintenance agreements with its retailers. Without the ability to cut the price, the discount sellers will lose their competitive advantage. Retailers will be forced to offer special services through nonprice competition.

Answers to True-False Questions

1. *False*. When there is free entry of retailers selling a familiar product, competition drives the retail margin to its lowest sustainable level. This, in turn, maximizes the wholesale price. It may be in the interest of a retailer to screen retailers to police special services and to encourage quality retailers to grant quality assurance.

2. *Uncertain*. Special services are jointly produced with the *sale* of a commodity (typically, special services are produced at the retail, not the wholesale, level). Special services usually cannot be sold separately, since consumers do not demand information about a commodity if they haven't yet decided to purchase it. However, free-riding discount retailers strip the special services from the commodity.

3. *True*. By discouraging deep discounts, RPM agreements force sellers to engage in nonprice competition, which typically involves providing special services.

4. *True*. Other forms of nonprice competition besides the provision of special services that RPM may cause are location closer to consumers, high-pressure selling, and persuasive (as opposed to informative) advertising.

5. *Uncertain*. Signing an exclusive dealership relation with the quality retailer gives the retailer monopoly control over the price, which could reduce the price received by the manufacturer. However, RPMs are not a perfect substitute for quality assurance, since special services are not equivalent to quality assurance.

Multiple Choice

1. c   (The store is free-riding on the research the prestigious retailer).

2. a

3. a   (Competition eliminates profit, as long as retailers are not price makers.)

4. c (The seller will have more information than the buyer.)

5. a   (RPMs, by themselves, are not barriers to entry, so do not cause profits.)

6. d

7. b   (The margin must be high enough to cover the cost of special services.)

8. d   (Providing special services will increase the demand, but the higher price will reduce the quantity demanded, so we cannot say, *a priori*.)

9. d   (While a, b, or c might happen, d is usually bound to happen.)

10. b

Chapter 14

MARKET BEHAVIOR WITH ASYMMETRIC INFORMATION

• LEARNING OBJECTIVES

After completing this chapter, you should be able to

1. Explain how problems of asymmetric information arise.

2. Find equilibrium price and quantity in a market with complete information.

3. Construct a hybrid supply function for a good supplied as either a gem or a lemon, with product quality indistinguishable to buyers.

4. Spell out the characteristics of equilibrium in which only lemons trade.

5. Explain the conditions necessary for a pooling equilibrium to be established.

6. Calculate the loss to a seller from selling a gem in a pooled market.

7. Describe the institutions that have developed to overcome the problem of adverse selection.

8. Identify the circumstances in which a firm will promise a high-quality product but deliver a low-quality product.

9. Explain how charging a price premium and making nonsalvageable investments give firms a greater incentive to forego short-term profits in favor of winning repeat business.

10. Understand present value and use this concept to compare the present and future profit from delivering inferior and quality merchandise.

11. Explain the different incentives of competitive and monopoly firms to promise high quality and deliver low-quality merchandise.

• CHAPTER OVERVIEW

Asymmetric Information

Asymmetric information exists when one side of a potential transaction has more information than the other side. When asymmetric information exists, buyers become wary of the quality of the goods they are purchasing. A market with high-quality **gems** and low-quality **lemons** will have two different prices only if buyers can determine a good's quality *before* making their purchases. **Figure 14-1** shows the separate markets for gems and lemons when there is **complete information.** We assume that the market for used cars contains N items, with fraction f being gems and $(1-f)$ being lemons. In the lemon market, S_l is the price sellers demand for lemons and B_l is the offer price from buyers. As long as $B_l > S_l$, all the lemons will be sold at a price of B_l. In the gem market, S_g is the price offered by sellers and B_g is the price offered by buyers of gems. As long as $B_g > S_g$, all fN gems are sold at a price of B_g.

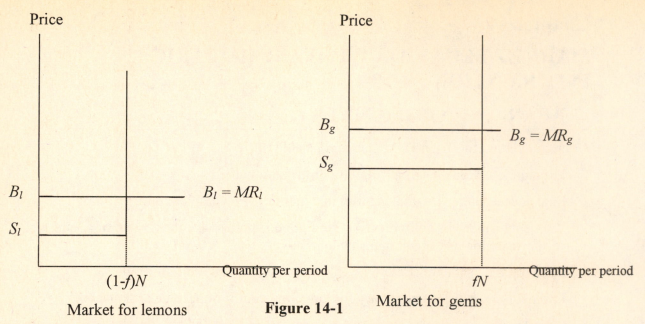

Market for lemons   **Figure 14-1**   Market for gems

When sellers know the quality of used cars, but buyers cannot determine that quality until after they have made purchases, we have a market with asymmetric information. The prudent buyer would base his/her bid price on the average of the value of a lemon (B_l) and the value of a gem, (B_g): $P_b = fB_g + (1-f)B_l$. The **hybrid supply function** shows the behavior of sellers who know the quality of the cars they sell. At the offer price for lemons, S_l, only lemons are sold. When the quantity of lemons is exhausted, the supply curve rises vertically to price S_g, and the supply curve is again horizontal until all gems are exhausted, and the supply curve becomes vertical again. **Figure 14-2** shows two different equilibrium solutions. In the left panel, the bid price, P_b, exceeds the offer price for lemons but is less than the offer price for gems. In this case, only lemons are sold, and once buyers realize this, the bid price will drop to S_l. In the right panel, the proportion of gems is high enough so that $P_b = fB_g + (1-f)B_l > S_g$. In this case, both gems and lemons are traded. Those buyers lucky enough to pick gems are happy, because the price they paid is less than the value of a gem to them ($P_b < B_g$). The unlucky buyers who end up with lemons are likely to regret their purchases since the price they paid is greater than the value of a lemon to them ($P_b > B_l$).

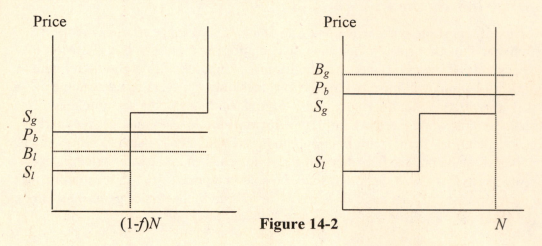

Figure 14-2

If we relax the simplifying assumption that there are only two types of homogenous goods, lemons and gems, and look instead at a more realistic assumption of continuous quality variation between those two extremes, we see that asymmetric information can lead to a market-destroying **adverse selection** problem. Unable to determine the quality of a used car before they buy it, potential buyers offer the price for a car of average quality. However, only owners of cars of below-average quality will offer to sell at that price. Virtually all buyers will be disappointed, and as word is passed, the bid price will fall, further reducing the quality of cars offered for sale. Ultimately, buyers may be unwilling to purchase any cars because they know only the lowest quality cars will be offered.

As Professor Pashigian explains, adverse selection due to asymmetric information can create demand curves that are positively sloped over the lower price ranges. Buyers learn that the market price sets the upper limit for the quality of a car. So as price falls, there are two counteracting effects. The usual negative substitution effect occurs, where quantity demanded decreases as price increases, *assuming that quality is held constant.* The quality effect implies that as price decreases, quantity demanded also decreases. At very low prices, the quality effect becomes stronger than the substitution effect, and the demand curve takes on a positive slope.

In **Figure 14-3**, if the supply curve is S_0, a typical equilibrium is achieved, at P_0, in the negatively sloped portion of the demand curve. This equilibrium could occur when used cars are in relatively short supply, so buyers in need of transportation would be willing to buy and fix up a lemon. If the supply curve shifts to $S_1 S_1$, the demand curve lies everywhere above the supply curve, so at any price a surplus exists, and price and quantity fall to zero.

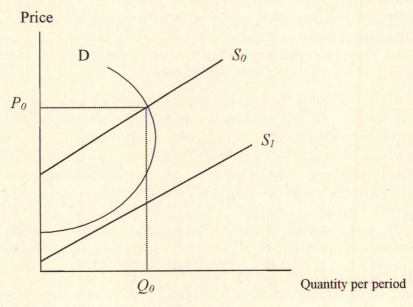

Figure 14-3

Owners of gems have an incentive to differentiate their cars from lemons. Three methods they use are **warranties**, **testing**, and **reputation.** Warranties can be costly to enforce and may lead to problems of **moral hazard**—the behavioral change induced by the reduction in the cost of reckless behavior. People who have insurance may take less care to avoid accidents if the harm they suffer for accidents is diminished by insurance. People who have warranties may take less care in their buying decisions, believing any that mistakes they make can be corrected costlessly. Testing of a product can eliminate some uncertainty for buyers, but testing also involves costs. There is the obvious risk of quality certification offered by a seller who has an incentive to cheat. When a seller has a reputation for honesty to protect, the incentive to misrepresent a product is reduced.

Asymmetric Information and Potential Cheating

When the seller knows more about product quality than the buyer, the seller has an incentive to misrepresent the quality of a product. Ironically, a perfectly competitive seller has a stronger incentive to cheat on product quality than does a monopoly seller. The monopoly seller has positive economic profits and a concern for repeat customers that a competitive firm does not have. By cheating, that monopolist can obtain higher profits in the present but will lose profits in the future because customers will not return and may pass the word to friends. Indeed, the monopolist could lose its franchise if enough customers complain. As Professor Pashigian shows, the monopolist will cheat only if the profits from cheating exceed the **present value of** the future profits from not cheating. Suppose profits without cheating are $500 per year. If the market rate of interest is 10 percent, the present value of the profit stream into the indefinite future approaches $5,000, since an $500 is a 10 percent return on an investment of $5,000. Only if cheating would generate one-time profits of $5,000 or more would it make economic sense for the monopolist to cheat.

A competitive firm will have less to lose by cheating. The competitive firm can expect zero profit in the long run. Competitive sellers who cheat receive positive profits now because their revenue is based on the promise of a high-quality product while the cost is that of a low-quality product. When they lose repeat business, they simply exit the industry and receive zero profits somewhere else.

Although government regulation—detecting and punishing fraudulent firms—is an obvious option, competitive sellers can and do signal their honesty to would-be customers. If competitive sellers face the prospect of positive economic profit, they will have a weaker incentive to cheat, just as a monopoly firm would. By charging a **price premium**, honest firms signal that they have too much to lose by fraudulent promises. This promise must be ratified by the actual experience of customers who pass the word that the higher priced sellers to offer a superior product. Once the honest sellers' reputations are established, new entrants cannot attract customers by offering a price below this premium. Consumers will infer that this lower price means a product of inferior quality.

Firms cannot enter this industry by offering lower prices so they use **nonprice competition. Nonsalvageable**, firm specific investments send customers the signal that the firm will suffer large capital losses if it cheats on quality and must exit the industry. If possible, these capital improvements will provide services that customers value and, therefore, all firms must offer them to be competitive. This strategy raises costs, eliminates profits, and discourages cheating on quality.

When the required price premium is unknown, consumers must infer from observing the capital investments of a firm whether or not this firm has made a sufficiently large nonsalvageable investment to deter it from cheating. Such an assessment of nonsalvageable capital investment is difficult to make, so the possibility of cheating by a firm is greater when the price premium is unknown.

• KEY TERMS

Asymmetric information A situation in which one party to a trade has more information than the other, leading the uninformed party to be wary of being cheated, reducing the bid or offer price, and, in extreme situations, precluding trade entirely.

Adverse selection A consequence of asymmetric information whereby superior products are driven from the market because buyers are not capable of judging product quality prior to the trade and therefore offer prices only for products of average quality. The insurance market is one market in which buyers have more information about their health or driving habits than does the insurance company, so that only high-risk customers may buy auto insurance and only people in poor health buy health insurance.

Bid price The price proposed by a buyer.

Offer price The price tendered by the seller.

Hybrid supply function A supply function containing a mix of high- and low-quality products, such as the market for used cars. The price that elicits high quality products is greater than the price resulting in the offer of low-quality products.

Pooling equilibrium An equilibrium price sufficiently high for both good and poor quality products to be purchased. At this price, customers receiving lemons are disappointed, but customers receiving gems are delighted.

Warranties Contracts offered by the seller promising to make good the difference between the price paid and the actual quality of a good. Warranties can be costly to enforce and cause moral hazard problems for the buyer.

Testing The use of objective analysis to verify the quality of a product prior to purchase. The danger here is that the testing may be expensive or biased. High-priced goods are more likely than low priced goods to be tested.

Reputation A long-term relationship between buyer and seller that can deter fraud, particularly if the buyer is willing to pay a price premium that would be lost if the reputation of the seller is damaged.

Moral hazard problem The condition encountered when economic agents are insured they reduce their diligence in taking precautionary measures.

Incentive to cheat A condition encountered in a market with asymmetric information when a seller achieves economic profit in the short run by delivering a product of lower quality than promised. An amoral seller will weigh the present value of future profits (without cheating) against the value of profits from cheating.

Present value The amount of money that must be invested today to obtain a specified amount of money in the future. The present value of F dollars in the future, at an interest rate of i, t periods in the future is $PV = \dfrac{F}{(1+i)^t}$. If the payment is made annually into the indefinite future, the present value approaches F/i.

Price premium A payment above the competitive price that generates economic profit and thus deters a seller in a market with asymmetric information from cheating.

Nonsalvageable investments Capital expenditures sufficient to signal to customers that a firm has too much to lose by cheating, since such investments are useless in any other industry.

• PROBLEMS

1. Suppose that there are 5,000 1988 Excaliburs in existence and 40 percent would be considered gems, but the rest are lemons. A consumer would bid $5,000 for a gem but would pay only $3,500 for a lemon. Sellers would accept $4,500 for a gem and $3,000 for a lemon. Assume that demand is perfectly elastic.

   a. What are the equilibrium price _____ and quantity _____ of gems?

   b. What are the equilibrium price _____ and quantity _____ of lemons?

   c. Now, suppose that consumers are unable to tell whether a *particular* car is a gem or a lemon before they purchase it. What is the maximum price that a customer is willing to pay for a car chosen at random? _____.

   d. What is the equilibrium price _____ and quantity _____ in the pooled equilibrium?

   e. How many gems are sold? _____

   f. How many lemons are sold? _____

   g. What name do economists give to this market outcome?

   _____

   h. Suppose that new information is presented on "Car Talk," and consumers realize that the fraction of gems is really 80 percent. However, they still have no way of telling whether a *particular* car is a lemon or a gem. What is the maximum price a consumer would offer for a randomly selected car?

   _____

   i. What are the pooled equilibrium price and quantity?

      Price: _____ Quantity of gems: _____ Quantity of lemons: _____

2. Suppose that a monopoly firm can earn profits of $100,000 per year forever if it delivers a promised high-quality product, or earn $1,000,000 in one year if it cheats and delivers a low-quality product. If the latter occurs, consumers would refuse to buy any more of the good and the firm would shut down. The interest rate is 8 percent.

   a. What is the present value of the $1,000,000 profit for cheating?

   _____

b. What is the present value of the $100,000 a year from not cheating?

_____

c. If the owner of the monopoly is amoral, will the monopoly cheat or not? Explain your answer.

_____

_____

_____

d. Suppose the interest rate increased to 12 percent. How would this affect the monopolist's decision?

_____

_____

_____

e. Suppose that regulation imposes a $50,000 cap on monopoly profit if the firm does not cheat, but the firm can still receive profits of $1,000,000 by cheating. Would the firm cheat at a market rate of interest of 8 percent? Explain.

_____

_____

_____

3. Suppose that a competitive firm is contemplating cheating in a market with asymmetric information. The firm can receive a one-time $100,000 economic profit in one year by cheating and exit the industry, or it can receive $0 economic profit forever by not cheating. The interest rate = 8 percent.

a. What is the present value of the economic profit from not cheating?

_____

b. What is the present value of the economic profit from cheating?

_____

c. What is an amoral owner of such a firm likely to do?

_____

d. Is the decision sensitive to changes in the interest rate? Explain.

_____

_____

_____

e. Suppose that consumers signal a willingness to pay a price premium to honest sellers that would result in profits of $10,000 per year. The interest rate = 8 percent.

   i) What is the present value of profits from not cheating?

   _____

   ii) What is the present value of the profit from cheating?

   _____

   iii) What decision would an amoral producer make?

   _____

   _____

f. Finally, suppose that new firms want to enter this industry. Approximately what size nonsalvageable investments would they have to make to entice consumers to buy from them, assuming consumers are well informed about the price premium?

   _____

   _____

   _____

• TRUE-FALSE QUESTIONS

For each of the following statements, indicate whether the statement is true (agrees with economic theory), false (is contradicted by economic theory), or uncertain (could be true or false; not enough information is given), and briefly explain your answer.

1. When sellers have more information than buyers do about the quality of their wares, and when buyers cannot discern quality prior to purchase, all sellers will receive higher prices than they will when buyers can discern product quality prior to sale.

   _____

   _____

   _____

2. The best way to get rid of a pesky insurance salesperson is to become very enthusiastic about buying insurance.

   _____

   _____

   _____

3. Gresham's law, that "bad money drives out good," is an example of adverse selection.

   _____

   _____

   _____

4. According to the problem of moral hazard, driver's-side air bags on cars may actually contribute to automobile accidents.

_____

_____

_____

5. Banks that invest in huge expensive vaults, which could never be moved if the bank went out of business, are signaling their honesty to customers.

_____

_____

_____

• MULTIPLE-CHOICE QUESTIONS

1. Which of the following is an example of adverse selection?

   a. quality of used cars

   b. membership in AAA

   c. walk-in to purchase auto insurance

   d. all the above

2. Having purchased ski-vacation insurance, I don't look where I'm going and run into a tree on the ski slopes. This is an example of

   a. adverse selection.

   b. moral hazard.

   c. asymmetric information.

   d. nonsalvageable investment.

3. Gems make up 50 percent of all used cars. Consumers would pay $10,000 for a gem or $7,000 for a lemon. How much would a buyer be willing to pay for a car picked at random?

   a. $7,000

   b. $8,000

   c. $8,500

   d. $10,000

4. A lemon owner will supply a particular used car for $5,000, but a gem owner requires $7,000. Twenty percent of cars are gems. If consumers would pay $8,000 for a gem or $6,000 for a lemon, then

    a. no cars are supplied.

    b. only lemons are supplied.

    c. only gems are supplied.

    d. both lemons and gems are supplied.

5. Good pizza costs $1.75 per slice to make and sells for $2.50 while poor pizza costs $1.00 per slice to make and sells for $1.25. If Joe's pizza enters the market and charges a price of $1.75, consumers are likely to infer

    a. Joe has found a way of producing premium pizza at lower cost.

    b. Joe is offering a low-quality pizza.

    c. Joe has a greater volume of sales.

    d. Joe is offering special services.

6. Competitive firms, in long-run equilibrium, with asymmetric information make

    a. positive profits.

    b. zero profits.

    c. negative profits.

    d. salvageable investments.

7. Which of the following is a nonsalvageable investment made by Joe's Pizza Parlor?

    a. redecorating the restaurant in rustic Italian style.

    b. hiring attractive staff.

    c. purchase of expensive cheese to put on the pizza.

    d. purchase of a desktop pc to keep books.

8. If the discount rate is 5 percent, the present value of $100 received at the end of this year is

    a. $105.00.

    b. $100.00.

    c. $99.95.

    d. $95.24.

9. If the discount rate is 5 percent, the present value of a $100 indefinite income stream is

   a. $500.

   b. $1,000.

   c. $1,500.

   d. $2,000.

10. Which of the following happens in an industry with asymmetric information in long-run equilibrium?

   a. Consumers will purchase from new entrants offering lower prices.

   b. Firms will misrepresent product quality.

   c. Firms will make long-run profits.

   d. None of the above.

• ANSWERS TO PROBLEMS, TRUE-FALSE AND MULTIPLE-CHOICE QUESTIONS

Answers to Problems

1. a. Equilibrium price of gems = $5,000 and quantity = 2,000.

   b. Equilibrium price of lemons = $3,500 and equilibrium quantity = 3,000.

   c. Price = P_b = .4(5000) + .6(3,500) = $4,100.

   d. The pooled equilibrium price is $4,100 and the quantity is 3,000.

   e. Zero (0) gems are sold.

   f. 3,000 lemons are sold.

   g. This is an example of adverse selection.

   h. The new equilibrium price: P_b = .8(5,000) + .2(3,500) = $4,700.

   i. The equilibrium price is $4,700. There are 4,000 gems sold and 1,000 lemons.

2. a. $PV = \dfrac{1,000,000}{1.08} = 925,925.93$

   b. $PV = \dfrac{100,000}{.08} = 1,250,000$

   c. The monopolist will not cheat. The present value of the profit from not cheating exceeds the present value of profit from cheating.

d. The present value of profit from cheating is $PV = \dfrac{1,000,000}{1.12} = 892,857.14$. The present value from not cheating is $PV = \dfrac{100,000}{.12} = 833,333.33$. So the monopolist would cheat.

e. The present value of cheating = \$925,925.93. The present value of not cheating is $PV = \dfrac{50,000}{.08} = \$625,000$. The monopolist would be encouraged to cheat.

3. a. The present value of the profit from not cheating is \$0.

b. The present value of the profit from cheating is $PV = \dfrac{100,000}{1.08} = 92,592.59$.

c. The owner of the competitive firm is likely to cheat.

d. The decision *is not* sensitive to the interest rate, because the present value of \$0 per year will always be less than \$100,000, as long as the interest rate is positive.

e. i) $PV = \dfrac{10,000}{.08} = 125,000$.

ii) $PV = \dfrac{100,000}{1.08} = 92,592.59$.

iii) The producer would decide not to cheat.

f. Entrants would commit up to the difference between the present value of profit from not cheating and the present value of profit from cheating. Hence, the maximum investment = \$125,000 - \$92,592.59 = \$32,407.40.

Answers to True-False Questions

1. *False.* In a market with asymmetric information, buyers who cannot discern quality prior to purchase will pay only the offer price for a product of *average* quality. Therefore, sellers of products of higher than average quality would suffer from the asymmetric information, and attempt to signal product quality to potential customers.

2. *True.* Adverse selection in the insurance market means that consumers that are the most willing to buy insurance are likely to be the poorest risks. Hence, reluctance to buy insurance will only encourage a pesky salesman, whereas enthusiasm may drive him/her away.

3. *True.* According to Gresham's law, an economy with a bi-metalic coinage will find that only the overvalued metal (the bad money) circulates, while the undervalued metal (the good money) is hoarded. This is an example of adverse selection.

4. *True.* If having an air bag makes drivers feel more secure in the event of an accident, they may be less careful when driving, increasing the probability that an accident will occur.

5. *True*. A vault makes a poor meat locker. If the bank shuts down, it will have a difficult time recouping its investment in the vault, which is precisely the definition of a nonsalvageable investment.

Multiple choice

1. d.

2. b.

3. c. $(P_b = .5(10,000) + .5(7,000) = \$8,500.)$

4. b. $(P_b = .2(8,000) + .8(6,000) = \$6,400 < B_g.$ So no gems are sold.)

5. b.

6. b. (Competitive firms always make zero profit in long-run equilibrium.)

7. a.

8. d.

9. d.

10. d. (As firms commit fraud they exit the industry. No firms earn economic profits, but low price entrants are still shunned.)

Chapter 15

PRICING UNDER UNCERTAINTY

• LEARNING OBJECTIVES

After completing this chapter, you should be able to

1. Explain the causes and consequences of demand uncertainty.

2. Discuss the distinction between season-opening markups and season-closing markdowns.

3. List the characteristics of goods with large seasonal variations in price.

4. Draw a probability distribution of prices.

5. Construct a demand function for a good available in several colors.

6. Find the expected price of a good sold under uncertainty.

7. Find the price that maximizes expected revenue under a single-price policy.

8. Show why a two-price policy is more profitable than a single-price policy for a differentiated good sold under demand uncertainty.

9. Identify the optimal initial and markdown prices for a two-price policy.

10. Describe the link between fashion goods and uncertainty, and explain why greater uncertainty results in greater discrepancy between the initial and the markdown prices and in a smaller fraction of total goods sold.

• CHAPTER OVERVIEW

Demand Uncertainty

Unlike previous chapters, this chapter relaxes the assumption that the firm knows the inverse demand curve for its product. Professor Pashigian introduces **demand uncertainty,** whereby sellers cannot predict the price potential consumers will pay until after buyers have decided whether to purchase a good at a posted price. The apparel industry is particularly susceptible to demand uncertainty. A department store orders garments in various sizes, colors, and styles, not knowing precisely which types of garments will be the big sellers. Based on experience, the sales manager may know that, say, different dress colors will sell for a range of prices. But the customers will decide which colors are hot and which are not. If the price is set too high only popular colors will sell; if the price is set too low the firm will sell more dresses but fail to achieve maximum revenue because the most popular colors will sell too cheaply.

Expected Value and Demand Uncertainty

Recall that we discussed the impact of uncertainty on consumer behavior in Chapter 3. The behavior of sellers is not materially different from the behavior of buyers under uncertainty. Each computes the *expected value* of the variable of interest–in this case **expected revenue** for the seller–and maximizes expected value. The **expected value** of a variable is the sum of each value that variable can have times the probability of that value. Suppose that a department store stocks dresses in ten styles. From experience, the sales manager knows that one style can be sold at $330, one style can be sold at $300, and so forth, with the least popular style selling for a price of $60. Without knowing which dress will be popular, the seller knows only the **probability distribution** of the price. Since there are 10 styles and each has a 10 percent probability of selling at each price, the probability distribution looks like a rectangle, whose width is the range prices and whose height is the uniform probability of 10 percent, as shown in **Figure 15-1**.

Figure 15-1 Probability Distribution of Prices

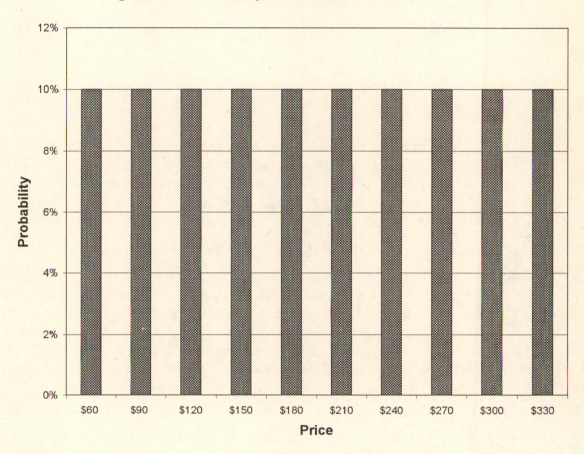

Knowing only that any dress has a 10 percent chance of selling at each price, the seller can compute only the expected price of each dress by multiplying each price by 10 percent and summing, as shown in **Table 15-1**.

Table 15-1

Price	robability	Probability times price
$330	10%	$33
$300	10%	$30
$270	10%	$27
$240	10%	$24
$210	10%	$21
$180	10%	$18
$150	10%	$15
$120	10%	$12
$90	10%	$9
$60	10%	$6
Sum	100%	$195

Note that the sum of the probabilities adds to 100 percent and that the sum of the product of price times probability yields the expected price of $195. Now, by the law of demand, any dress will sell if its price is less than or equal to the price consumers are willing to pay for that dress. If the price is set too high only the most popular dresses sell; if the price is set the price too low those popular dresses are virtually given away.

One-Price Policy and Maximizing Expected Revenue

Suppose that the store orders 30 of each type of dress for the season, not knowing which style will be popular and which style will be purchased only at bargain-basement prices. If all dresses are priced at $360, no dresses are sold, because the highest price anyone will pay is $330. So $360 is the price for which quantity demanded falls to zero. If the price is cut from $360 to $330, all 30 dresses in the most popular style are sold, but 270 dresses remain on the rack for the season. At $300, 60 dresses are sold; at $270, 90 dresses are sold, and so forth. It follows that the demand equation for dresses is $Q_d = 360 - P$. The **inverse demand function** is, simply, $P = 360 - Q_d$. By multiplying the number of dresses sold times each price yields the expected revenue, as shown in **Table 15-2.**

Table 15-2

Price	Dresses Purchased	Total Revenue	Revenue per Dress	price elasticity
$360	0	$0	na	
$330	30	$9,900	$33	-11.00
$300	60	$18,000	$60	-5.00
$270	90	$24,300	$81	-3.00
$240	120	$28,800	$96	-2.00
$210	150	$31,500	$105	-1.40
$180	180	$32,400	$108	-1.00
$150	210	$31,500	$105	-0.71
$120	240	$28,800	$96	-0.50
$90	270	$24,300	$81	-0.33
$60	300	$18,000	$60	-0.20

Note that revenue is maximized precisely where the price elasticity of demand = -1. If a sales manager can pick only one price for the entire year, the manager picks best when he or she sets the price at the point of unit elasticity, where total revenue is maximized. However, note that the one-price policy implies throwing away 120 dresses, all which could have been sold for at least $60. The **revenue per dress** is only $108, even though the dresses actually sold bring a price of $180 each. Revenue per dress is also expected revenue: the probability that a dress will sell times the price.

A Two-Price Policy

As the name implies, a two-price policy means setting a higher initial price and then marking down the remnants at the end of the season. The expected revenue of a two-price policy exceeds the expected revenue of a one-price policy, much the same as a price-discriminating monopolist, by selling at two prices, can achieve greater revenue than a single-price monopolist does. It is easiest to understand a two-price policy by working backwards. Consider the preceding one-price policy. At the end of the season, the store has 120 dresses remaining. These dresses were all priced out of the market at $180. At a price of $150, 30 of the remaining 120 dresses would sell, enhancing the firm's revenue by $4,500. At $120 each, the store would sell 60 dresses, generating $7,200, and so forth. Because 180 dresses have been removed from the market at a price of $180 each, the residual demand curve is $Q_d = 180 - 30P$. **Table 15-3** shows the remaining revenue at each price.

Table 15-3

Price	Dresses Purchased	Total Revenue	Revenue per Dress	price elasticity
$180	0	$0	$0	
$150	30	$4,500	$15	-5.00
$120	60	$7,200	$24	-2.00
$90	90	$8,100	$27	-1.00
$60	120	$7,200	$24	-0.50

It is obvious that *if the optimal first price were* $180, the ideal markdown price would be $90, precisely half the original price. Professor Pashigian shows that the single price is *not* the optimal starting price for a two-price system. Indeed, in this example, the optimal first price is 2/3 of $360, where the dress is priced out of the market. As shown in Table 15-3, at a price of $240, the store would sell 120 dresses for revenue of $28,800. In **Table 15-4**, note that the price elasticity is unitary where $P = \$120$ and the residual revenue is maximized.

Table 15-4

Residual Demand When Initial Price = $240

Price	Dresses Purchased	Total Revenue	Revenue per Dress	price elasticity
$240	0	$0	$0	
$210	30	$6,300	$21	-7.00
$180	60	$10,800	$36	-3.00
$150	90	$13,500	$45	-1.67
$120	120	$14,400	$48	-1.00
$90	150	$13,500	$45	-0.60
$60	180	$10,800	$36	-0.33

Under the single-price policy, the store generated revenue of $32,400. Under the two-price policy, the firm increased its revenue to $28,800 + $14,400 = $43,200.

The greater the degree of uncertainty about consumer taste, the greater the difference between the initial price and the markdown price. Fashion items are more likely to go on clearance than items whose demand is more predictable.

• KEY TERMS

Uncertainty about consumer tastes When sellers must stock merchandise once, before the preferences of consumer tastes are known, the sellers will suffer from uncertainty. Sellers maximize expected profit by estimating the *probability distribution* of consumer tastes, setting price to maximize revenue per item, even though some items may not be sold.

Seasonal variation The variability of some commodities, such as women and men's fashions, due to variations in weather and other unpredictable influences. Uncertainty arises because the fashion for the season will not be known until after the merchandise is stocked and consumers have revealed their preferences.

Inverse demand function for styles When preferences for a characteristic, such as style, is unknown, although the probability distribution for style preference can be determined, the seller can compute the number of items (e.g., different styles) that will be sold at each price, even though what those styles will be cannot be determined until after stocking.

Expected revenue   The sum of the probability of each quantity sold times each price. In the face of demand uncertainty, the seller will typically attempt to maximize expected revenue if the items are ordered in bulk, causing inventory costs to be a sunk cost.

Cumulative distribution of prices The function determining the quantity sold at each price; it is based on the proportion of units that consumers would purchase at a given price or a higher price.

Single-price policy   The policy of selecting a single price for a differentiated commodity in the face of uncertainty about consumer demand. The best single price occurs where the demand function is unit elastic.

Two-price policy The policy of setting the initial price above the unit elastic point on the demand curve and then selecting the markup price where the residual demand curve is unit price-elastic.

• PROBLEMS

1. Suppose that your store has ordered 4 different styles of dresses. You do not know which style consumers will prefer this year. However, you do know that one style will command a maximum price of $250, one style will command a maximum price of $200, one style will command a maximum price of $150 and one style will command a maximum price of $100. Each style has the same probability of being the most profitable, the second most popular, and so forth. You know that no dresses will sell if you charge $300 per dress.

    a.   Draw the probability distribution of prices in Chart 15-1.

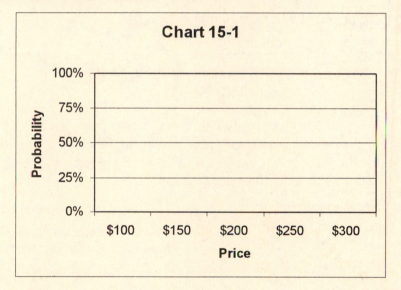

    b.   What percentage of dresses would sell if the price were $150?

    _____

    c.   Write the equation for the relationship between price charged (P) and the number of styles sold (S).

    _____

    d.   Write the inverse demand function for styles.

    _____

    e.   At what price would consumers be willing to purchase all 4 styles?

    _____

f. Write the equation relating the probability that a style picked at random will not sell.

_____

g. What is the probability that a style picked at random will not sell at $P = \$250$?

_____

h. Suppose that your store buys 10 of each style (stock = 40 dresses, total), and you decide to adopt a *single-price policy*. Fill in the table below:

Price	Quantity	Total Revenue	Expected Revenue per Dress (TR/40)
$300	_____	$ _____	$ _____
$250	_____	$ _____	$ _____
$200	_____	$ _____	$ _____
$150	_____	$ _____	$ _____
$100	_____	$ _____	$ _____

i. At which price is total revenue maximized?

_____

j. At which price is expected revenue per dress maximized?

_____

2. Can your store from problem 1 do better with a two-price policy? Let's try several strategies to see if we can increase total revenue and expected revenue per dress. Suppose that the store initially offers dresses for $250 each and then, at the end of the season, reduces them to $150 each.

a. Complete the table below.

Price	Quantity	Total Revenue	Expected Revenue per Dress (TR/40)
$250	_____	$_____	$_____
$150	_____	$_____	$_____
Total	_____	$_____	$_____

b. What is total revenue under this pricing strategy?

_____

c. What is the expected revenue per dress under this strategy?

_____

d. How many dresses remain unsold under this strategy?

_____

3. Now suppose that your store initially offers dresses for $200 each and then, at the end of the season, reduces them to $100 each.

   a. Complete the table below.

Price	Quantity	Total Revenue	Expected Revenue per Dress (TR/40)
$200	_____	$_____	$_____
$100	_____	$_____	$_____
Total	_____	$_____	$_____

   b. What is total revenue under this pricing strategy?

_____

   c. What is the expected revenue per dress under this strategy?

_____

   d. How many dresses remain unsold under this strategy?

_____

4. Now suppose that your store initially offers dresses for $250 each and then, at the end of the season, reduces them to $100 each.

   a. Complete the table below.

Price	Quantity	Total Revenue	Expected Revenue per Dress (TR/40)
$250	$_____	$_____	$_____
$150	$_____	$_____	$_____
Total	_____	$_____	$_____

   b. What is total revenue under this pricing strategy?

_____

   c. What is the expected revenue per dress under this strategy?

_____

   d. How many dresses remain unsold under this strategy?

_____

   e. Taking problems 2 through 4 together, what is the best two-part pricing strategy you analyzed? Justify your answer.

_____

_____

_____

• TRUE-FALSE QUESTIONS

For each of the following statements, indicate whether the statement is true (agrees with economic theory), false (is contradicted by economic theory), or uncertain (could be true or false; not enough information is given), and briefly explain your answer.

1. A store stocks 6 different colors of pajamas and finds that consumers have no particular color preference. The seller will maximize revenue by selling all pajamas at a price whose elasticity of demand is -1.

    _____

    _____

    _____

    _____

2. A store stocks 6 different colors of pajamas and finds that consumers have a definite but unknown color preference. The seller will maximize revenue by selling all pajamas at a price whose elasticity of demand is -1.

    _____

    _____

    _____

    _____

3. Women's clothes typically have a greater markdown at the end of the season than men's clothes do. This is because women typically do the clothes shopping and are therefore more price conscious (that is, they have a greater price elasticity of demand).

    _____

    _____

    _____

    _____

4. Whether or not a store has adopted the appropriate initial price in a two-price policy, the markdown price should be low enough to enable the store to sell all its remaining merchandise.

    _____

    _____

    _____

    _____

5. If a store manager were a clairvoyant who could forecast consumer demand prior to the beginning of the season, the store would not need a two-price policy.

_____

_____

_____

_____

• MULTIPLE CHOICE QUESTIONS

1. Which of the following types of sales result from uncertainty about consumer tastes?

   a. preseason

   b. Christmas

   c. clearance

   d. within season

2. If blouses come in 3 colors, and the most popular color sells for $100, the second most popular color sells for $75, and the least popular sells for $60, what is the expected price of a randomly selected blouse if consumer preferences are uncertain?

   a. $100

   b. $75

   c. $60

   d. $78.33

3. Which of the following goods is more likely to show up in clearance sales?

   a. white underwear

   b. beige pantyhose

   c. prom dresses

   d. navy blue blazers

4. Suppose that a buyer knows with certainty that a red dress will sell for $150 and a blue dress will sell for $125. The wholesale price of dresses is the same. What should she order?

   a. only red dresses

   b. only blue dresses

   c. 50 percent blue dresses and 50 percent red dresses

   d. 55 percent red dresses and 45 percent blue dresses

5. There are 8 colors of a shirt and the most popular 4 colors will sell for $50 whereas the other 4 colors will sell for $40. What is the probability that a shirt picked at random will not sell for $50?

   a. 0

   b. 25 percent

   c. 50 percent

   d. 80 percent

6. There are 8 colors of a shirt and the most popular 4 colors will sell for $50 whereas the other 4 colors will sell for $40. What is the expected revenue per shirt if the store prices the shirts at $50?

   a. $50

   b. $45

   c. $40

   d. $25

7. There are 8 colors of a shirt and the 4 most popular colors will sell for $50 whereas the other 4 colors will sell for $40. What is the expected revenue per shirt if the store prices shirts at $40?

   a. $50

   b. $40

   c. $25

   d. $20

8. There are 8 colors of a shirt and the 4 most popular colors will sell for $50 while the other 4 colors will sell for $40. Suppose that the store orders 100 of each color (total stock is 800 shirts). What *single price* maximizes revenue and what is revenue at that price

   a. $40; revenue = $16,000

   b. $40; revenue = $32,000

   c. $50; revenue = $20,000

   d. $50; revenue = $50,000

9. There are 8 colors of a shirt and the 4 most popular colors will sell for $50 whereas the other 4 colors will sell for $40. Suppose that the store prices all shirts at $50 initially and marks down the unsold shirts to $40 at the end of the season. What is the firm's revenue under this two-part pricing policy?

   a. $32,000

   b. $36,000

   c. $40,000

   d. $50,000

10. What is the advantage of clearance sales to a store?

    a.   Many customers wait until sale time before buying.

    b.   Retailers save on storage costs.

    c.   Consumers pay more for the items to which they attach greater value.

    d.   A firm can price discriminate between comparison shoppers and impulse shoppers.

• ANSWERS TO PROBLEMS, TRUE-FALSE AND MULTIPLE-CHOICE QUESTIONS

Answers to Problems

1. a.   The probability distribution of prices is

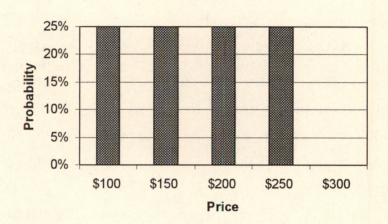

Chart 15-1a

  b.   If the price were $150, 75 percent of the dresses would sell.

  c. $S = \dfrac{300 - P}{50}$

  d. $P = 300 - 50P$

  e. $100

  f. $F(P) = \dfrac{4 - S}{4}$

  g.   75 percent.

h.

Price	Quantity	Total Revenue	Expected Revenue per Dress (TR/40)
$300	0	$0	$0
$250	10	$2,500	$63
$200	20	$4,000	$100
$150	30	$4,500	$113
$100	40	$4,000	$100

i. Revenue is maximized when price = $150.

j. Expected revenue per dress is also maximized when price = $150 because the number of dresses is fixed at 40.

2. a.

Price	Quantity	Total Revenue	Expected Revenue per Dress (TR/40)
$250	10	$2,500	$62.50
$150	20	$3,000	$75.00
Total		$5,500	$137.50

b. Under this pricing strategy, total revenue = $5,500.

c. Under this strategy, expected revenue per dress = $137.50.

d. Ten dresses remain unsold under this pricing strategy.

3. a.

Price	Quantity	Total Revenue	Expected Revenue per Dress (TR/40)
$200	20	$4,000	$100.00
$100	20	$2,000	$50.00
Total		$6,000	$150.00

b. Under this pricing strategy, total revenue = $6,000.

c. Under this strategy, expected revenue per dress = $150.

d. Zero dresses remain unsold under this pricing strategy.

4. a.

Price	Quantity	Total Revenue	Expected Revenue per Dress (TR/40)
$250	10	$2,500	$62.50
$100	30	$3,000	$75.00
Total		$5,500	$137.50

b. Under this pricing strategy, total revenue = $5,500.

c. Under this strategy, expected revenue per dress = $137.50.

d. Zero dresses remain unsold under this pricing strategy.

e. The best two-price strategy involves selling 20 dresses at $200 and selling the remaining 20 dresses at $100, which maximizes revenue at $6,000.

Answers to True-False Questions

1. *True.* With no consumer preference for color, each color of pajamas should sell for the same price. If there is no uncertainty about consumer preferences, revenue is maximized where the price elasticity of demand is -1, as shown in Chapter 1.

2. *False.* Because of uncertainty about consumer preferences, a two-price policy is likely to generate more revenue than a single-price policy where price elasticity of demand equals -1.

3. *False.* The reason for the greater markdown in women's fashions is that there is more uncertainty about tastes for women's fashions, as measured by the variability of price over the season.

4. *True.* If markdown price is to maximize revenue from the remnants, the price should be set at the point of unit elastic demand for the remaining garments.

5. *Uncertain.* The store would sell each item at the highest price it could command. If all consumers had uniform tastes for each brand, then the store would charge the highest market-clearing price for each style, and no styles would remain at the end of the season. However, if each style had a negatively sloped demand curve, the store could still benefit from a two-price policy, setting the initial price at approximately 2/3 of the maximum price for each style. Then the store would markdown the price to 1/2 the initial level late in the season.

Answers to Multiple-Choice Questions

1. c

2. d $\dfrac{\$100 + 75 + 60}{3} = \$78.33$

3. c (Tastes for prom dresses will vary most unpredictably from season to season.)

4. a

5. c

6. d

7. b

8. b

9. b

10. c

Chapter 16

CONSUMER AND SUPPLIER BEHAVIOR OVER TIME

• LEARNING OBJECTIVES

After completing this chapter, you should be able to

1. Calculate the present value of future income, for either a finite or an infinite income stream.

2. Derive an intertemporal budget constraint for a consumer using information about income in two years and the discount rate.

3. Define the marginal rate of time preference.

4. Explain the shape of indifference curves between present and future consumption prospects, and relate this shape to the degree of consumer patience or impatience.

5. Derive and explain the intertemporal utility-maximizing combination of spending in the current period, given the intertemporal budget constraint and the consumer indifference map between consumption in the present and consumption in the future.

6. Derive the demand function and the supply function for loanable funds, and identify the equilibrium interest rate and quantity of funds.

7. Explain the optimal time to sell a nonrenewable resource, given information about the price appreciation ratio and the discount rate.

8. Explain why the equilibrium current price for a renewable resource equals the present value of the future price.

9. Show and explain how a change in the interest rate affects the present and future values of a renewable resource.

10. Explain the relation between the rate of depletion of a nonrenewable resource and the interest rate.

• CHAPTER OVERVIEW

Present Value

The **intertemporal theory of consumer behavior** relaxes the assumption that the consequences of a consumer's utility maximization problem occur only in the present. Decisions made today reflect the consequences of decisions made in the past and in turn imply consequences for the future. The rational consumer considers both the present and future implications of the allocation of income among alternative goods. If present consumption is less than present income, the consumer saves and wealth increases (or debt decreases). If present consumption exceeds present income, then wealth decreases (or debt increases).

The **present value** of future income is the amount that must be invested at the prevailing interest rate, i, today to generate a specified amount of money in the future. For instance, if you require $10,000 this time next year for next year's tuition, you need to invest $9,523.81 at 5 percent interest right now. The present value of $10,000 in one year is $9,523.81, since $PV = \dfrac{10,000}{(1.05)} = 9,523.81$. In general, the formula for present value of FV dollars, received t years in the future, from a financial investment with a yield of i is $PV_t = \dfrac{FV}{(1+i)^t}$. **Table 16-1** shows the present value of a future payment of $10,000 for different maturity dates (identified in the first column) and for different discount rates (identified in the first row). Note that the present value decreases with both the discount rate and the maturity date.

Table 16-1 Present Value Calculations for Selected Discount Rates and Maturaties

Years until Payment	1%	2%	3%	4%	5%	10%	20%
1	$9,900.99	$9,803.92	$9,708.74	$9,615.38	$9,523.81	$9,090.91	$8,333.33
2	$9,802.96	$9,611.69	$9,425.96	$9,245.56	$9,070.29	$8,264.46	$6,944.44
3	$9,705.90	$9,423.22	$9,151.42	$8,889.96	$8,638.38	$7,513.15	$5,787.04
4	$9,609.80	$9,238.45	$8,884.87	$8,548.04	$8,227.02	$6,830.13	$4,822.53
5	$9,514.66	$9,057.31	$8,626.09	$8,219.27	$7,835.26	$6,209.21	$4,018.78
10	$9,052.87	$8,203.48	$7,440.94	$6,755.64	$6,139.13	$3,855.43	$1,615.06
20	$8,195.44	$6,729.71	$5,536.76	$4,563.87	$3,768.89	$1,486.44	$260.84
30	$7,419.23	$5,520.71	$4,119.87	$3,083.19	$2,313.77	$573.09	$42.13

Note that as the number of periods increases, present value decreases and approaches zero. The present value of an **annuity** is the sum of the present values of the future annual payments: $PV = \displaystyle\sum_{t=0}^{T} \dfrac{FV_t}{(1+i)^t}$. As the number of periods, T, gets larger and larger, the value of the annuity approaches the ratio of the annual payment divided by the interest rate. For instance, a **bond** promising to pay $1,000 per year in perpetuity would sell for $10,000 if the going rate of interest were 10 percent; an investor would have to put $10,000 into the investment to reap $1,000 per year at a 10 percent interest rate.

The Intertemporal Utility Maximization Problem

Whenever a consumer contemplates saving or borrowing to augment current or future consumption, he or she must trade off satisfaction from current consumption C_1, against the satisfaction from the prospect of future consumption, C_2. As in the utility maximization problems encountered in Chapters 2 and 3, the intertemporal utility maximization problem requires reconciling the intertemporal preference function, $U(C_1, C_2)$, with the **intertemporal budget constraint**, $C_2 = I_2 + (1+i)(I_1 - C_1)$. **Figure 16-1** presents the intertemporal preference function. Note that the indifference curves have the typical shape. (1) The indifference curve is negatively sloped because more consumption in each period is preferred to less consumption in that period; the only way the consumer can be indifferent is if increasing amounts of consumption in one period is associated with decreased amounts of consumption in the other period. (2) Indifference curves do not intersect if preferences are transitive. (3) Indifference curves are bowed in toward the origin due to diminishing marginal rates of substitution of future consumption for present consumption. The greater current consumption is expected to be relative to future consumption, the less future consumption a consumer would sacrifice to obtain another unit of current consumption (and vice versa).

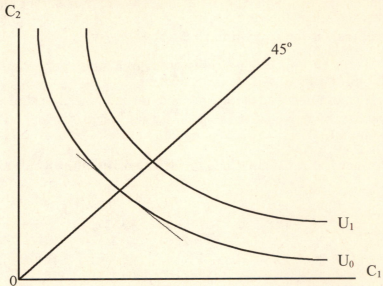

Figure 16-1 Intertemporal Preferences of a Consumer

The slope of the indifference curve between current and future consumption is called the **marginal rate of time preference** (MRTP) and measures the rate at which the consumer is willing to substitute future consumption for current consumption:

$$\text{MRTP} = \frac{\Delta C_2}{\Delta C_1}\bigg|_{U=U_0} = -\frac{\text{MU}_1}{\text{MU}_2}$$

The amount of future consumption a consumer is willing to sacrifice for another unit of current consumption depends on the marginal utility of consumption in the present to the marginal utility of consumption in the future. Of particular interest is the $45°$ line, which measures the location of equal consumption prospects, i.e., where $C_2 = C_1$. If, when consumption prospects are equal, a consumer is willing to sacrifice more than 1 unit of future consumption to acquire another unit of present consumption, that consumer is considered **impatient.** If, when consumption prospects are equal, a consumer is willing to sacrifice less than 1 unit of consumption in the future for another unit of consumption in the present, that consumer is **patient.** A **neutral consumer** would sacrifice exactly 1 unit of future consumption to obtain 1 more unit of present consumption when consumption prospects are equal.

Figure 16-2 presents the intertemporal budget constraint for a household earning $50,000 in period 1, expecting to earn $60,000 in period 2, and that can save and borrow at 10 percent interest. We obtain this diagram by plotting C_2 on the vertical axis and present consumption on the horizontal axis (future consumption is the consequence of the present consumption). The vertical intercept is maximum consumption if all current income is saved: $C_{2\max} = I_2 + (1+i)I_1 = \$60,000 + \$50,000(1.1) = \$115,000$. The horizontal intercept is this year's income plus the present value of next year's income:

$$C_{1max} = I_2 + \frac{I_1}{(1+i)} = \$50,000 + \$60,000/1.1 = \$104,545.45.$$ The higher the rate of

interest i, the steeper will be the intertemporal budget constraint. The intertemporal budget constraint must always pass through the point $(I_1, I_2) = (\$50000, \$60000)$, since the consumer always has the option to neither a borrower nor a lender be. The slope of the

intertemporal budget line is always: $\frac{\Delta C_2}{\Delta C_1} = -(1+i) < -1$.

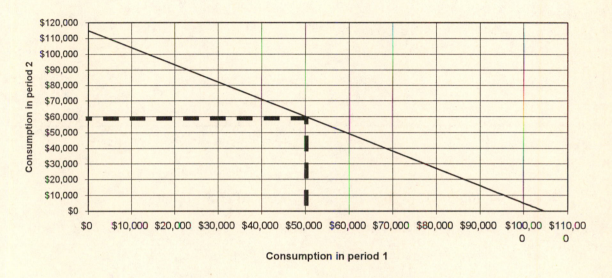

Figure 16-2 Intertemporal Budge Constraint

As in any utility maximization problem, the solution to the intertemporal utility maximization problem is reconciling consumer preferences to the budget constraint. The consumer is automatically placed on the balanced budget endowment point (I_1, I_2). From that point, the consumer will elect to save if the marginal rate of time preference is less than $-(1+i)$, as shown in the left panel of **Figure 16-3**. The consumer will elect to borrow if MRTP $< -(1+i)$, as shown on the right. If the consumers MRTP $= -(1+i)$, then current consumption would equal current income, leaving future consumption to equal future income.

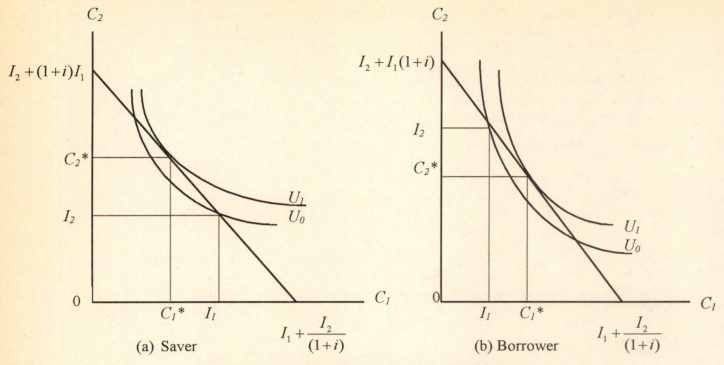

Figure 16-3 Intertemporal Utility Maximization

Changes in Income and the Interest Rate

As in the case of the one-period budget allocation problem, the intertemporal utility maximization problem can be divided into income and substitution effects. The income effect is straightforward as long as we assume that both present consumption and the prospect of future consumption are both normal goods. One important implication of this theory of choice is that **permanent income** can be increased either because future income was expected to increase by a given percentage, or because the interest income on the increase in present income is sufficient to generate that income. For example, a college professor who saw her income increase from $60,000 to $66,000 would have a 10 percent increase in permanent income. If her income doubled for one year because of a lucrative consulting job, and she invested that $60,000 at 10 percent, her permanent income would also increase to $66,000 per year.

Figure 16-4 shows the impact of an increase in permanent income on both present and future consumption. For simplicity, we imagine that the initial utility maximizing position is at point **A**, where $C_{10} = I_{10}$, so that $C_{20} = I_{20}$. The shift in the permanent income budget line could be from an increase in I_1, and increase in I_2, or from a combination of the two. What is clear is that both present and future consumption increase, since both are normal goods. If the increase in income was transitory (i.e., only I_1 increased), then the increase in future consumption will be financed out of current saving. If the increase in income will not occur until year 2, the increase in current consumption will be financed out of borrowing.

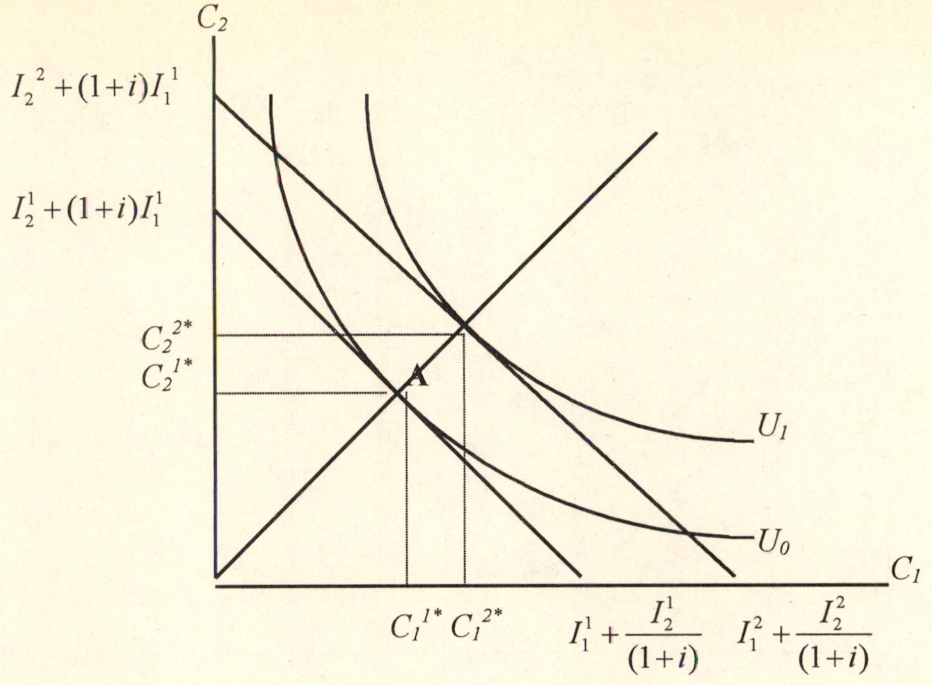
C_2
$I_2^2+(1+i)I_1^1$
$I_2^1+(1+i)I_1^1$
C_2^{2*}
C_2^{1*}
A
U_1
U_0
C_1
C_1^{1*} C_1^{2*}
$I_1^1+\frac{I_2^1}{(1+i)}$
$I_1^2+\frac{I_2^2}{(1+i)}$

Figure 16-4

A change in the rate of interest changes the relative price of present consumption in terms of foregone future consumption. An increase in the interest rate increases the relative price of present consumption; the substitution effect increases future consumption and reduces present consumption, *income remaining constant.* **Figure 16-5** presents a consumer whose initial equilibrium point occurs at the balanced budget point: $C_1 = I_1$ and $C_2 = I_2$. The increase in the interest rate causes a clockwise rotation of the budget line through the balanced budget point. Note how the consumer achieved a higher level of satisfaction by reducing current consumption to C_1' while increasing future consumption to C_2'.

When the initial point of tangency is not at the balanced budget point, a change in the interest rate exhibits both income and substitution effects. When a person is a borrower, an increase in the interest rate reduces real income. Both the income and substitution effects work to reduce current consumption, but the income effect tends to reduce future consumption, whereas the substitution effect tends to decrease future consumption. That is, when the interest rate increases, a borrower reduces borrowing or increases saving, thereby reducing current consumption. If borrowing still occurs, future consumption may fall because it costs more to finance the borrowing. If the substitution effect is strong enough to transform current borrowing into saving, future consumption will clearly increase. The exercises will work out the effect of an interest rate decrease on the behavior of a borrower.

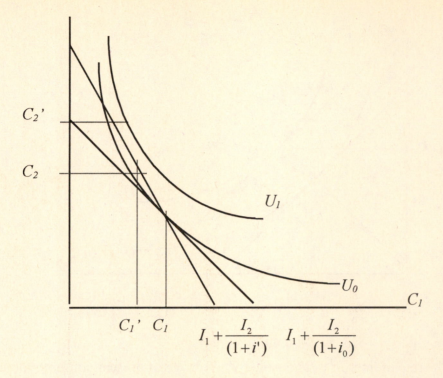

Figure 16-5

When the initial point of tangency implies saving, real income increases if the interest rate increases, and real income declines if the interest rate declines. An increase in the interest rate would discourage current consumption, but the income effect would encourage current consumption if the household were a saver. Hence, an increase in the interest rate enhances future consumption, but may also encourage current consumption, since future consumption can be financed out of higher interest income, without further reducing current consumption.

The Supply and Demand for Loanable Funds

At any point in time, some households will borrow and other households will save. As the interest rate increases, the amount that households wish to borrow tends to decrease, *ceteris paribus*. In addition to households, businesses and governments borrow for investment purposes. The **demand for loanable funds** will be inversely related to the interest rate. As the interest rate increases, the amount that households are willing to lend (e.g., by purchasing financial assets or making bank deposits) tends to increase. The **supply of loanable funds** will tend to be positively sloped. The equilibrium interest rate occurs where the quantity of funds demanded equals the quantity of funds supplied. In **Figure 16-6**, the equilibrium interest rate occurs at i_e, where the quantity of funds demanded and the quantity of funds supplied both equal F_e. An increase in the demand for funds, the supply of funds constant, would increase both the equilibrium interest rate and the quantity of funds borrowed. An increase in the supply of funds, the demand for funds constant, would reduce the equilibrium interest rate while increasing the quantity of funds borrowed.

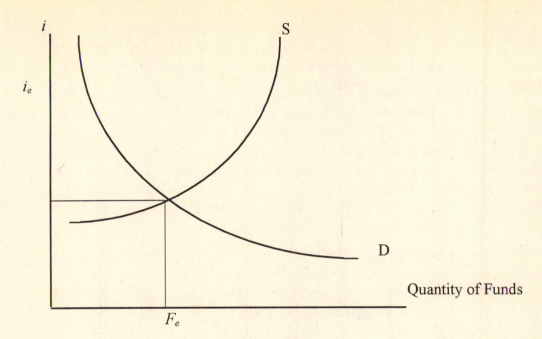

Figure 16-6

In an economy with a large number of young individuals, with low current incomes and the prospect of higher future incomes, the demand for loanable funds will be high and the supply of loanable funds will tend to be low. The equilibrium interest rate will be high as a result. As the population ages, people approach their peak earning years. Gradually, borrowing gives way to saving, which reduces the demand for loanable funds and increases the supply. The equilibrium interest rate falls accordingly. Ultimately, the age composition of the economy, as well as optimism about future income growth, have a large impact on the equilibrium interest rate.

Nonrenewable Resources and the Interest Rate

A **nonrenewable resource** is a scarce good whose stock cannot be augmented. Land itself is one of the best examples of a nonrenewable resource. Raw materials like oil, natural gas, and iron ore are others. Some resources can become renewable when new discoveries are made or when technological breakthroughs allow humans to exploit resources previously thought to be unreachable.

Many people are worried that nonrenewable resources, like oil, will not be conserved properly. Price theory provides a comforting answer. The owner of a nonrenewable resource typically seeks to maximize the present value of the stock. If the price today, P_t, equals the present value of the price in n years, $\frac{P_{t+n}}{(1+i)^n}$, the owner will be indifferent between selling now and selling in the future. If $P_t > \frac{P_{t+n}}{(1+i)^n}$, all the owners of nonrenewable resources would try to sell now, causing the current price to fall until it was equal to the present value of the future price. If $P_t < \frac{P_{t+n}}{(1+i)^n}$, all the owners would hoard their nonrenewable resources, causing buyers to bid the price up until, once again, the equality between the present price and the present value of the future price was again established. It follows that the **price appreciation ratio** must always equal $(1 + i)$.

A downward sloping market demand curve for a nonrenewable resource exists in each year. **Intertemporal market equilibrium** exists if the current price equals the present value of the future price. Therefore, the price of a nonrenewable resource must increase by i percent per year if owners are to be induced to hold their stock for another year. Otherwise, either a shortage or a surplus of the nonrenewable resource will exist in the current year, which will cause the market to equilibrate. So, if a resource is truly nonrenewable, its price will increase every year, making that resource less attractive for consumption, thereby preserving the limited supply.

If a resource is renewable, the stock can be augmented through productive activity. Inventories of renewable resources will increase if the present value of the future price exceeds the present price. Inventories of renewable resources will deplete if the present value of the future price is less than the present price.

• KEY TERMS

Present value of income The amount that must be invested at prevailing interest rates to obtain a specified future value. The formula is $PV_t = \dfrac{FV_t}{(1+i)^t}$, where PV_t is the present value of money to be received in t years, FV_t is the future value of that money, i is the interest rate, and t is the number of years until the money is received.

Intertemporal preferences The willingness of a consumer to trade future consumption prospects for more current consumption.

Intertemporal budget constraint The rate at which future consumption, C_2, can be traded for current consumption, given by the equation $C_2 = I_2 + (1+i)(I_1 - C_1)$, where I_2 is (expected) future income, I_1 is current income, C_1 is current consumption, and i is the interest rate.

Marginal rate of time preference The amount of future consumption a person will sacrifice to obtain 1 more unit of current consumption: $MRTP = \dfrac{\Delta C_2}{\Delta C_1} = -\dfrac{MU_1}{MU_2}$; the amount of future consumption a person will sacrifice to obtain another unit of present consumption equals the ratio of the marginal utility of present consumption to the marginal utility of future consumption.

Impatient consumers Consumers whose marginal rate of time preference exceeds -1 when consuming at the point where current consumption equals (expected) future consumption.

Patient consumers Consumers whose marginal rate of time preference is less than -1 when consuming at the point where current consumption equals (expected) future consumption.

Maximizing intertemporal utility This occurs when the marginal utility of present consumption equals the present value of the marginal utility of future consumption:

$$MU_1 = \frac{MU_2}{(1+i)} .$$

Demand function for loanable funds The function showing the quantity of funds demanded at each interest rate; as the interest rate increases, the amount of funds people and institutions are willing to borrow decreases, other factors remaining constant.

Supply function for loanable funds The function showing the quantity of funds supplied at each interest rate; as the interest rate increases, the amount of funds people and institutions are willing to lend increases, other factors remaining constant.

Saving The act of spending less than current income on consumption, so that the difference between income and consumption is used to reduce debt or accumulate wealth. Saving increases future consumption possibilities.

Borrowing The act of spending more than current income on consumption, so that the difference between consumption and income increases debt or reduces wealth. Borrowing reduces future consumption possibilities.

Equilibrium interest rate That interest rate that equates the quantity of loanable funds demanded with the quantity of loanable funds supplied.

Nonrenewable resources Resources whose stock cannot be augmented. What you've got is what you get.

Renewable resources Resources whose stock can be augmented through productive activity.

Price appreciation ratio The ratio of the future price of a good to its current price. In equilibrium, the price appreciation ratio for a nonrenewable resource equals $(1 + i)$.

Discounted demand function A function relating the future quantity demanded of a good to the present value of its (future) price.

Equilibrium prices over time For a nonrenewable resource, the equilibrium price appreciation equals 1 plus the interest rate, or $P_t = P_{t+n}(1+i)^n$.

• PROBLEMS

1. Fred has income of $5,000 this year, but his income will fall to $3,750 next year. The interest rate is 10 percent.

   a. If Fred continues to sponge off his parents and saves all his income this year to consume next year, what is the *maximum* consumption he can have next year?

   _____

   b. If Fred borrows as much as possible this year and sponges off his parents next year, what is the *maximum* consumption he can have this year?

   _____

c. What is the equation that relates Fred's consumption next year to his consumption this year?

_____

d. What level of consumption this year would allow him to consume the same amount next year?

_____

e. If Fred actually equates his consumption in the 2 years, what can we infer about his rate of time preference?

_____

2. For each of the following amounts of money, time periods, and interest rates, compute the present value.

a. $1,000 to be received in 1 year, with an interest rate of 10 percent.

_____

b. $1,000 to be received in 2 years, with an interest rate of 10 percent.

_____

c. $5,000 to be received in 2 years, with an interest rate of 10 percent.

_____

d. $1,000 to be received in 1 year, $2,000 to be received in 2 years, and $5,000 to be received in 3 years, all with a 10 percent interest rate.

_____

e. $1,000 forever, with a 10 percent interest rate.

_____

3. The table below shows the market demand functions for a nonrenewable resource in year 1 and year 2.

Price	Quantity 1	Quantity 2	Discounted Price, Year 2
$10	0	0	____
$9	1	1	____
$8	2	2	____
$7	3	3	____
$6	4	4	____
$5	5	5	____
$4	6	6	____
$3	7	7	____
$2	8	8	____
$1	9	9	____

a. Assume an interest rate of 20 percent, and fill in the column for the discounted price in year 2.

b. Suppose that the supply of this nonrenewable resource is equal to 9 units. What decision-making criteria should be used to allocate a stock of this nonrenewable resource between two time periods?

_____

_____

c. What should the price be each year?

i) Year 1: P_1 = _____

ii) Year 2: P_2 = _____

d. How many units of the resource should be sold each year?

i) Year 1: Q_1 = _____

ii) Year 2: Q_2 = _____

e. What is the present value of total revenue?

_____

f. The interest rate in this example is very high compared to real world rates. Why don't firms simply deplete the resource in year 1 and then put the proceeds in the bank to earn 20 percent?

_____

_____

_____

• TRUE-FALSE QUESTIONS

For each of the following statements, indicate whether the statement is true (agrees with economic theory), false (is contradicted by economic theory), or uncertain (could be true or false; not enough information is given), and briefly explain your answer.

1. An impatient consumer will never save.

_____

_____

_____

_____

2. A patient consumer will never borrow.

_____

_____

_____

_____

3. An economist is currently spending $40,000 of her $50,000 after tax income, investing the difference in government bonds at 10 percent interest. She has just been promised a raise that will increase her earnings next year to $60,000. Economic theory predicts that she will reduce her consumption this year.

_____

_____

_____

_____

4. A consumer is currently spending all of his $40,000 income and anticipates having $50,000 in income next year. The interest rate increases from 10 percent to 12 percent. This consumer will probably increase his current consumption.

_____

_____

_____

_____

5. Michelangelo's paintings represent a nonrenewable resource. Accordingly, we predict that the price of his paintings will increase with the rate of interest.

_____

_____

_____

_____

• MULTIPLE-CHOICE QUESTIONS

1. You are given the choice between $10,000 this year or $11,000 next year. The interest rate is 12 percent. You elect to take the $10,000 now. According to this example, you are

   a. not maximizing utility.

   b. an impatient consumer.

   c. a patient consumer.

   d. picking the option with the higher present value.

2. The present value of $20,000 one year from now, with a 10 percent interest rate is:

   a. 22,222.22.

   b. $22,000.00.

   c. $20,000.00.

   d. $18,181.18.

3. What is the present value of 5 payments of $1,000 each, received at the beginning of the year for the next 5 years, if the interest rate is 7 percent?

   a. $4,298.32

   b. $4,387.21

   c. $4,486.45

   d. $4,762.93

4. Suppose that the interest rate is 10 percent. What is the slope of the intertemporal budget constraint with consumption in year 2 plotted on the vertical axis?

   a. -10

   b. -1/10

   c. -1.10

   d. -0.91

5. If consumption in year 2 is plotted on the vertical axis and consumption in year 1 is plotted on the horizontal axis, a consumer with steep indifference curves displays:

   a. a high MRTP.

   b. a low MRTP.

   c. a weak preference for current consumption.

   d. both a and c.

6. A consumer selects a point nearer the vertical axis than the endowment point on an intertemporal budget constraint with consumption in year 2 plotted on the vertical axis. This consumer

   a. attaches no value to current consumption.

   b. neither borrows nor saves.

   c. is a borrower.

   d. is a saver.

7. Suppose that Bill has a choice between two jobs: Job 1 pays $40,000 this year and $10,000 next year. Job 2 pays $20,000 this year and $30,000 next year. The interest rate is 10 percent. If he wishes to maximize the present value of his income, Bill should

   a. take job 1.

   b. take job 2.

   c. be indifferent as to which job to take.

   d. obtain additional financial information before making a decision.

8. Suppose job 1 and job 2 have the same present value of income. Job 1 pays well in year 1 and poorly in year 2 and job 2 pays pretty well in both years. Which of the following is true?

   a. Select job 1 if you wish to consume more in year 1.

   b. Select job 2 if you wish to consume evenly in each year.

   c. Job selection will have no effect on consumption plans.

   d. A "patient individual" will select job 2.

9. A single owner of a nonrenewable resource could sell the entire stock this year for $100 per ton or wait until next year and sell the stock for $105 per ton. If the interest rate is 10 percent, she should

   a. sell the stock in year 1.

   b. sell the stock in year 2.

   c. sell the stock in either year–it does not matter when the stock is sold.

   d. obtain additional financial information before making decision.

10. When the interest rate increases, the discounted price demand curve will

   a. lie above the demand function.

   b. not change its relation to the demand function.

   c. lie closer to the demand function.

   d. lie further from the demand function.

• ANSWERS TO PROBLEMS, TRUE-FALSE, AND MULTIPLE-CHOICE QUESTIONS

Answers to Problems

1. a. $C_{2,\max} = \$5,000(1.1) + \$3,750 = \$5,500 + \$3,750 = \$9,250$

   b. $C_{1,\max} = \$5,000 + \dfrac{\$3,750}{1.1} = \$5,000 + \$3,409.09 = \$8,409.09$

   c. $C_2 = I_2 + (1.1)(I_1 - C_1) = \$3,750 + 1.1(5,000 - C_1) = \$9,250 - 1.1C_1$

   d. Find $C^* = 9,250 - 1.1C^* \rightarrow 2.1C^* = 9,250 \rightarrow C^* = \$4,404.76$

   e. He is a patient consumer, since $\dfrac{\Delta C_2}{\Delta C_1} = -1.1\, when\ C_2 = C_1.$

2. a. $909.09

   b. $826.45

   c. $4,132.23.

d. $PV = \dfrac{1,000}{1.1} + \dfrac{2,000}{(1.1)^2} + \dfrac{5.000}{(1.1)^3} = \$6,318.56$

e. You must invest $10,000 to get a $1,000 per year return at 10 percent interest.

3. a.

Price	Quantity 1	Quantity 2	Discounted Price, Year 2
$10	0	0	$8.33
$9	1	1	$7.50
$8	2	2	$6.67
$7	3	3	$5.83
$6	4	4	$5.00
$5	5	5	$4.17
$4	6	6	$3.33
$3	7	7	$2.50
$2	8	8	$1.67
$1	9	9	$0.83

b. Equate the present value of P_2 with P_1: $P_1 = \dfrac{P_2}{1.2}$.

c. i) Year 1; $P_1 = \$5$

   ii) Year 2; $P_2 = \$6$

d. i) Year 1; $Q_1 = 5$

   ii) Year 2; $Q_2 = 4$

e. The present value of total revenue = 5($5) + 4($5) = $45.

f. Waiting to sell yields the same revenue as selling now and investing the proceeds.

Answers to True-False Questions

1. *False.* If future income is greater than present income, an impatient consumer might still save, even though future consumption would be less than present consumption.

2. *False*. If future income is greater than present income, a patient consumer might still borrow, even though future consumption would remain greater than present consumption.

3. *False.* Present consumption is a normal good, so an increase in future income should increase both present and future consumption.

4. *False.* Consuming at the balanced budget point implies no income effect. The increase in the interest rate implies a substitution of future consumption for present consumption, so current consumption should *fall*.

5. *True*. The Michelangelo painting is a nonrenewable resource. The owner of the painting will hold that resource as long as $P_2 \geq P_1(1+i)$.

Answers to Multiple-Choice Questions

1. d
2. d
3. b
4. c
5. a
6. d
7. a
8. c
9. a
10. d

Chapter 17

WAGE DETERMINATION IN LABOR MARKETS

• LEARNING OBJECTIVES

After completing this chapter, you should be able to

1. Explain how the firm's hiring decision in the labor market is related to its profit maximizing output decision in the product market.

2. Compute the value of marginal product and marginal revenue product, and the relation of these concepts to the firm's derived demand for labor.

3. Distinguish between the scale and substitution effects of a change in the wage on the competitive firm's long-run demand function for labor.

4. Explain why the long-run demand function for labor is more elastic than the short-run demand function for labor.

5. Derive the market long-run and short-run demand functions for labor.

6. Understand the relation of individual labor supply to the individual's allocation of time between work and leisure.

7. Construct a budget constraint for an individual choosing between work and leisure.

8. Contrast the income and substitution effects of a wage change on the allocation of time between work and leisure.

9. Derive of the market supply function for labor from individual labor supply functions.

10. Determines the equilibrium wage rate and employment level in a competitive labor market.

11. Determine the short-run demand for labor of a price making firm by equating marginal revenue product to the marginal expense of labor.

12. Compute the present value of lifetime earnings.

13. Calculate the pay differential that ensures long-run equilibrium in the market for a college degree.

14. Distinguish between general and specific training, and understand who pays for each type of training, and why.

15. Understand the advantages and disadvantages of compensation schemes based on worker effort vs. worker output.

16. Explain the advantages and disadvantages of incentive pay.

17. Explain how pay structures that sort workers.

18. Understand why backloading pay will discourage shirking but leads to the necessity of mandatory retirement.

• CHAPTER OVERVIEW

In this chapter we turn toward factor markets, where households function as sellers and firms behave as buyers. Despite this role reversal, the goals of individuals and businesses continue as we have assumed all along: Firms maximize profit under competitive or monopoly market conditions, and individuals maximize utility, constrained by the options available to them.

The Derived Demand Function for Labor

We begin with the firm's **derived demand for labor.** Firms are not willing and able to hire labor out of some altruistic desire to provide income but because labor generates output, which can (the firm hopes) be sold at a profit. Indeed, just as the optimal rate of output is determined where marginal cost equals marginal revenue, the firm identifies the optimal quantity of labor services where the marginal cost of labor equals the **marginal revenue product of labor.** The marginal revenue product of labor is the amount of revenue generated by the last worker hired. When the firm is a price taker in the product market, the marginal revenue product is equal to the **value of marginal product,** which equals the price of the product times labor's marginal physical product.

Recall that the competitive firm maximizes profit by setting output so that marginal cost equals price. Recall further that, in the short-run, marginal cost equals the price of a variable factor divided by the marginal product of that factor. Translating the profit-maximizing decision in the product market to the profit-maximizing hiring decision is a simple matter of multiplying both sides of the former by the marginal physical product of labor:

$$MC = \frac{w}{MP_L} = P \rightarrow w = P \times MP_L = VMP_L$$

For a firm that is a price taker in both markets, the wage rate is the marginal cost of labor. As we have already shown, the value of the marginal product of labor is the marginal revenue generated by the last worker hired.

Plotting the quantity of labor on the horizontal axis, we multiply the marginal physical product (plotted on the vertical axis) times the price of the output to obtain the firm's demand curve for labor, as shown in **Figure 17-1**. Taking the marginal physical product, we multiply times the product price to yield the revenue generated by one additional unit of labor. At wage rate w_0, the firm hires more labor until, at quantity of labor L_0, the marginal revenue generated by the last worker equals the wage he or she costs the firm. At a lower wage rate of w_1, the worker L_0 is generating more revenue than the w_1. The firm's profits have increased (because labor now costs less per unit of time), but employment level L_0 no longer maximizes profit. Profit expands until, at employment level L_1, the value of labor's marginal product equals the marginal cost of labor (the wage rate).

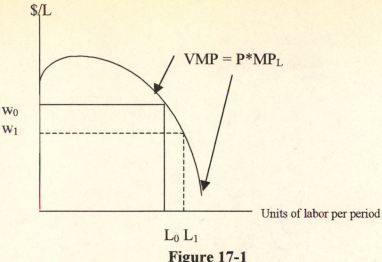

Figure 17-1

Note that the wage rate presents a horizontal supply of labor to the competitive firm; the firm can hire as much labor as it desires at the going wage, but it can hire no labor at a wage rate below the market wage. A decrease in the wage rate increases the quantity of labor hired, *ceteris paribus*. The value of the marginal product is the competitive firm's **demand function for labor**.

As with any demand function, a change in the price of the product (in this case, the wage rate of labor) changes the quantity demanded. In contrast, a change in one or more of the *ceteris paribus* conditions would cause the demand for labor to shift. In the case of labor demand, either a change in the price of the product or a change in the value of the marginal product schedule would change the demand for labor.

In the short run, when the capital to labor ratio is fixed, a change in the wage rate would simply cause a movement along a stationary labor demand curve. However, in the long run, a decrease in the wage rate would encourage the firm to substitute labor for capital. In **Figure 17-2** we trace out these two effects. The initial decrease from w_0 to w_1 causes the quantity of labor demanded to increase along short-run demand curve d_0. The **scale effect** of the wage change is shown as a movement from L_{00} to L_{01}. When the firm substitutes labor for capital, the short-run demand curve shifts to d_1. This **substitution effect** increases the amount of labor per unit of output, shown as the increase from L_{01} to L_{11} in Figure 17-2.

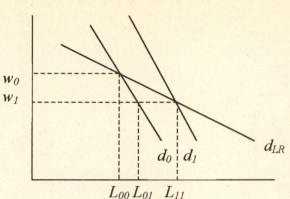

$/L

w_0
w_1

d_0 d_1

d_{LR}

Workers per time period

L_{00} L_{01} L_{11}

Figure 17-2

Figure 17-2 shows how factor substitution causes the long-run demand for labor to be more elastic than the short-run demand curve. An increase in the output price will also unambiguously increase the demand for labor. An increase in the price of capital will have two counteracting effects. As we have seen, the substitution effect will tend to increase the amount of labor used for each unit of output and so increase the demand for labor. However, the scale effect would decrease the rate of output and the demand for labor.

As in the product market, the **market demand for labor** is obtained by summing the quantity of labor demanded by all firms at each wage rate. Because each firm's demand for labor is negatively sloped, the market demand for labor is also negatively sloped. Because each firm's long-run demand for labor is more elastic than its short run demand for labor, the same follows for the market demand. The long-run market demand for labor is more elastic than the short run-market demand for labor.

The Work-Leisure Choice

We saw in Chapter 4 how the opportunity cost of time has an important influence on the household's consumption decision. In this chapter we analyze the allocation of time between work and leisure in the individual's utility maximization decision. We assume that the utility depends on the total spending on a composite good, C, and the amount of leisure time, h. As usual, indifference curves are negatively sloped, since both C and h are goods. In fact, we assume that both consumption, C, and leisure, h, are **normal goods.**

The budget line is given by the relation $C = w(H - h)$, where w is the wage rate, H is the total hours available, and h is leisure. To simplify, we assume no other income besides wages. An increase in the wage rate, real income remaining constant, would tend to reduce the amount of leisure consumed (increase the quantity of labor time supplied) because the wage rate is the price (opportunity cost) of leisure. The increase in the price of a commodity, income remaining constant, reduces consumption of that commodity, *ceteris paribus*. However, leisure is nearly unique due to the fact that as the price of leisure increases, real income increases. Because leisure is a normal good, the income and substitution effects of a wage increase tend to move in opposite directions. As shown in **Figure 17-3**, the substitution effect tends to dominate at low wage rates, while the income effect eventually takes over at higher wage rates. Plotting the wage rate on the vertical axis, and the amount of working time ($H - h$) on the horizontal axis yields a **backward bending individual supply of labor curve.**

Remember that the individual supply of labor curve shows how much labor time an individual supplies to the labor market at each wage rate. The individual labor supply curve does not indicate what market that labor is being supplied to. For instance, a student being trained as an economist might keep her student job as a cab driver until she graduates from college when she can command a high enough wage as an economist to make it worth quitting the cab drivers job. As long as labor markets allow individuals to enter in response to higher wage rates, the market supply of labor will be positively sloped, even though the individual demand curve is backward bending.

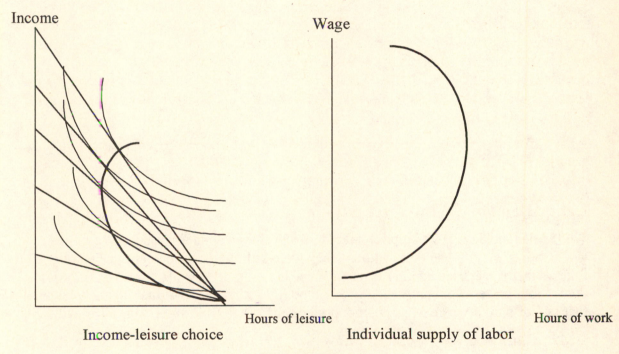

Figure 17-3

Market Equilibrium Wage Rate

We have already established that the market demand for labor curve is negatively sloped. The quantity labor demanded by firms is inversely related to the wage rate, *ceteris paribus*. The market supply of labor is positively sloped as long as workers are free to enter the market in response to higher wage rates. Only when the number of people who can supply a particular type of labor is limited either by natural talent (as in the case of entertainers or athletes) or professional associations (like the AMA) is a market supply curve for labor likely to be backward bending.

Labor markets are like product markets in that the equilibrium price is established where the quantity of labor supplied equals the quantity of labor demanded. In **Figure 17-4**, we see that at the equilibrium wage rate of w^*, the quantity of labor demanded and the quantity of labor supplied are both L^*. Total wage payments are given by the rectangle w^*L^*. The area between the supply curve and the equilibrium wage is the **supplier surplus**, the economic rent received by individuals who would supply labor at a lower wage, but are paid the equilibrium wage like everyone else. The area between the demand curve and the equilibrium wage line is the **buyer surplus**, which represents the total revenue, minus labor's share of revenue– that is paid to other (nonlabor) factors of production.

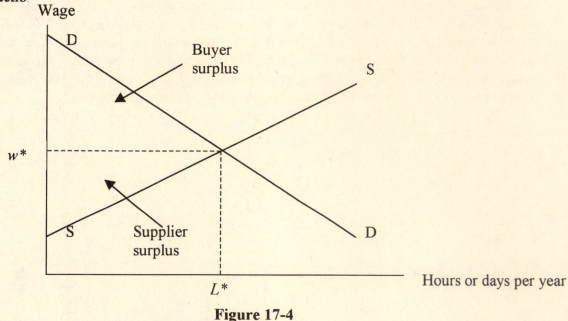

Figure 17-4

Labor Demand by the Price-Making Firm

We learned in Chapter 9 that price-making firms charge a higher price, and produce a lower rate of output than they would if they were selling under competitive conditions. It follows that since price making firms produce less output, they also hire less labor than they would if they were producing in a competitive labor market. Instead of producing that rate of output where MC = P, monopolies and other price makers produce where MC = MR. Given $MC = \dfrac{w}{MP_L}, MC = MR \rightarrow w = MR \times MP_L$.

Investment in Human Capital

Workers invest in **human capital** because the income stream of a trained or educated worker is greater than the income stream of an untrained worker. An individual is more likely to attend college if the **present value** of the earnings of a college graduate exceeds the present value of the earnings of a high school graduate. The higher the interest rate, the higher the ratio of college to high school earnings must be in order to make college a worthwhile investment, since the costs of college accrue immediately but the benefits are delayed until after graduation and beyond.

Another form of human capital investment is **on-the-job training.** On-the-job training may be either general or specific. **General training** increases the worker's marginal product in many firms. The employer will not be able to recover such an investment.

Once workers complete general training, they could raise their pay by switching employers. Therefore, employers offer general training only to workers who accept lower rates of pay. Hence **minimum-wage laws**, which preclude low rates of pay, can prohibit workers from contracting for general training with willing employers. **Specific training** increases the marginal product of workesr only in the firm offering training. The workers and the firm share in the cost of the training. Workers are paid more than the value of their marginal product during training, and less than the value of their marginal product after training. In this way, the firm can recover its share of the investment in specific training.

Compensation Based on Input or Output

Compensation based on **worker output** (piecework) is practical if the output of the worker is easy to measure. Such compensation forces the worker to bear the cost of **shirking.** Team production makes measurement of worker output difficult and leads to compensation based on **worker effort** (salaried work). Shirking may be higher for salaried workers due to monitoring costs.

A low basic salary with large bonuses for extra hours and effort will **sort** workers by intended effort. Hard workers will be attracted to the company because they anticipate high rewards for hard work. Workers planning to expend less effort will find the low basic salary unattractive and will sort into other firms.

Backloading pay means compensating a worker at the end of a time period. If the wage is *less* than the value of marginal product early and *greater* than the value of marginal product later, the worker will fear being fired and shirk less. The firm will need **mandatory retirement** since workers will wish to prolong their careers if pay is backloaded.

• KEY TERMS

Derived demand functions Demand functions generated when the willingness to pay for one good is created by the demand for another good. In the case of labor, the willingness of employers to hire workers is derived from the demand for the goods the firm produces.

Marginal revenue product The result when the marginal product of a factor is multiplied by the marginal revenue from the output market.

Marginal product The change in output due to one more unit of an input, the services of other inputs remaining constant.

Substitution effect The effect of the change in the relative price of a factor on the amount of the factor used, output remaining constant. The substitution effect is always negative.

Value of the marginal product The marginal revenue product when the firm is a price taker in the output market. Value of marginal product equals the output price times the marginal product of the factor in question.

Expansion path The location of points of tangency between isoquants and a set of isocost lines given by changes in one factor price, the price of the other factor remaining constant.

Scale effect The effect of a change in the profit-maximizing rate of output for the change in a factor price after the substitution effect has been taken into account. Typically, the scale effect reinforces the substitution effect, but there are exceptions in the case of inferior factors of production.

Work-leisure choice The utility maximization problem whereby an individual allocates time between work (income earning activity) and leisure (which, along with commodities, produces utility directly). The optimal allocation of time occurs when the marginal utility of leisure equals the marginal utility of consumption divided by the wage rate.

Human capital Investmentlike activities that generate an increase in income in the future (with some risk) after the expenditure of economic costs in the present. Education and on-the-job training are two examples of human capital producing activities.

General training On-the-job training that increases a worker's marginal revenue product for many different employers. A worker paid less than his/her marginal revenue product will seek other employment. Therefore, general training must be financed by the worker.

Firm-specific training Training that increases a worker's marginal revenue product only at one firm. The firm pays the worker more than marginal revenue product during the training period, and the worker receives less than marginal revenue product (but more than his/her next best wage offer) after training. In this way, the firm and the employer share the cost of training and each reaps part of the return.

Shirking The avoidance of effort if one believes that the probability of getting caught is small enough that the expected punishment (e.g., dismissal) is acceptably small relative to the expected payoff of successful shirking.

• PROBLEMS

1. The following table gives information on the marginal product schedule facing a competitive firm. Product price is $8 per unit and the wage rate is $200.

Workers	Marginal Product	Value of Marginal Product
1	35	_____
2	32	_____
3	29	_____
4	27	_____
5	25	_____
6	21	_____
7	17	_____
8	13	_____
9	9	_____

a. Fill in the column labeled "Value of Marginal Product."

b. How many workers should the firm hire to maximize profit?

   _____

c. Suppose that the price of the product increases to $12. What happens to:

   i) The demand for labor?

   _____

   ii) The number of workers employed?

   _____

   iii) The firm's profit?

   _____

2. Suppose that the firm in problem #1 were a price maker. Complete the following
    table and answer the questions that follow:

Workers	Marginal Product	Price	Marginal Revenue	Marginal Revenue Product
1	35	$18.25	$16.50	_____
2	32	$16.65	$13.30	_____
3	29	$15.20	$10.40	_____
4	27	$13.85	$7.70	_____
5	25	$12.60	$5.20	_____
6	21	$11.55	$3.10	_____
7	17	$10.70	$1.40	_____
8	13	$10.05	$0.10	_____
9	9	$9.60	-$0.80	_____

a. Complete the column labeled "Marginal Revenue Product."

b. How many workers would be hired at a wage rate of $200?

   _____

c. What is the value of labor's marginal product for the employment level in part b?

   _____

d. Approximately how much monopoly profit does the firm earn?

   _____

3. Chart 17-1 shows indifference curves for an individual who has a wage of $5 per hour
    and 100 hours of discretionary time available to be worked or taken as leisure each
    week.

a. Draw this individual's budget constraint, assuming no other source of earnings
    except wages.

b. How many hours are allocated to working _____ and leisure _____?

c. What is her weekly income? _____

d. Now assume she qualifies for a welfare grant of $200 per week, but she loses $1 in benefits for every $1 she earns up to $200.

   i)   Draw her new budget line between work and leisure.

   ii) What happens to the amount of time allocated to work?

_____

   iii) What happens to the amount of time allocated to leisure?

_____

Chart 17-1

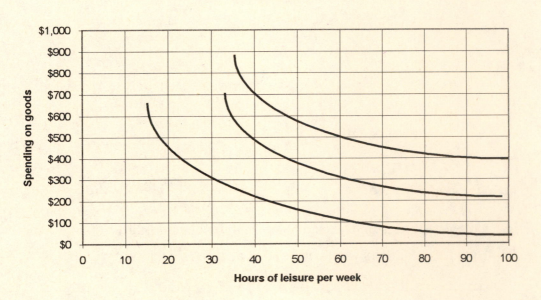

4. Suppose a college graduate earns $28,000 per year starting at the end of year 5, and a high school graduate earns $15,000 per year starting at the end of year 1. For simplicity, ignore the out-of-pocket expenses associated with a college education and the possibility of part-time work during college years. Assume that the real interest rate is 5 percent and that both individuals have infinite lives.

a. What is the present value of the high school graduate's income stream?

_____

b. What is the present value of the college graduate's income stream?

_____

c. Would a college education be a good investment?

_____

_____

d. Suppose that the real rate of interest increased to 7 percent. Would this change your answer to part c?

_____

_____

5. Suppose that only 40 percent of students who attempt college actually graduate. College graduates earn $28,000 at the end of year 5. The average college dropout earns $20,000 at the end of year 3. Is attempting a college education still a good investment at a 5 percent real rate of interest? Show how you reached your answer.

_____

_____

_____

• TRUE-FALSE QUESTIONS

For each of the following statements, indicate whether the statement is true (agrees with economic theory), false (is contradicted by economic theory), or uncertain (could be true or false; not enough information is given), and briefly explain your answer.

1. As long as the individual supply of labor is backward bending, the market supply of labor will also be backward bending.

_____

_____

_____

_____

2. When a competitive firm produces the profit-maximizing rate of output, it also hires the profit-maximizing quantity of labor services.

_____

_____

_____

_____

3. Because a price-making firm charges a higher price than a competitive firm does, the price-making firm will generally pay a higher wage rate.

_____

_____

_____

_____

4. Welfare recipients typically work fewer hours per week than do higher wage earners because they have a stronger leisure preference.

_____

_____

_____

_____

5. Workers who receive firm-specific human capital investments will typically receive less than the value of their marginal product after training is completed.

_____

_____

_____

_____

• MULTIPLE-CHOICE QUESTIONS

1. In the short run, if the price of a competitive firm's product is $15, the wage rate is $35, and the marginal product of the 10th worker is 2, the firm should

   a. hire exactly 10 workers.

   b. hire more than 10 workers.

   c. higher fewer than 10 workers.

   d. pay for general training so the workers become more productive.

2. The short-run demand function for labor by a competitive firm is

   a. the marginal revenue product curve.

   b. the value of marginal product curve.

   c. the price of the product times the marginal product of labor.

   d. all the above.

3. In the long run, if the wage rate falls,

   a. the firm substitutes capital for labor.

   b. the firm raises its price.

   c. the firm reduces the quantity of labor used for each rate of output.

   d. the firm increases the amount of labor employed.

4. The long-run demand function for labor is

    a. less elastic than the short-run demand function for labor.

    b. more elastic than the short-run demand function for labor.

    c. just as elastic as the short-run demand function for labor.

    d. more or less elastic than in the short run, depending on the industry.

5. If the income effect is less than the substitution effect of a wage change on the labor-leisure choice, the individual's supply curve of labor will be

    a. horizontal.

    b. vertical.

    c. positively sloped.

    d. negatively sloped.

6. An individual who starts receiving a nonlabor income that was not available before will

    a. work more, due to the substitution effect.

    b. work less, due to the substitution effect.

    c. work more, due to the income effect.

    d. work less, due to the income effect.

7. A monopoly has a product price of $10 and pays a wage of $20. The marginal product of the 100th worker is 10. The monopolist will maximize profit by

    a. hiring exactly 100 workers.

    b. hiring less than 100 workers.

    c. hiring more than 100 workers.

    d. doing one of the above, but the question cannot be answered without additional information.

8. Assume that the present value of the wages received by the typical college graduate equaled the present value of the wages of a high school graduate at a real interest rate of 5 percent. If the real rate of interest fell to 3 percent, we would expect

    a. more high school graduates to enroll in college.

    b. fewer high school graduates to enroll in college.

    c. the same proportion of high school graduates to enroll in college.

    d. the earnings of college graduates to rise relative to the earnings of high school graduates.

9. Who pays for general training?

    a. the worker

    b. the firm

    c. the firm and the worker

    d. it depends on the industry

10. Mandatory retirement rules may exist because

    a. they permit incentive systems to reduce shirking.

    b. the productivity of older workers declines sharply at 65 years of age.

    c. younger workers need jobs more than older workers do.

    d. older workers have less of an incentive to shirk than do younger workers.

• ANSWERS TO PROBLEMS, TRUE-FALSE, AND MULTIPLE-CHOICE QUESTIONS

Answers to Problems

1. a.

Workers	Marginal Product	Value of Marginal Product
1	35	$280
2	32	$256
3	29	$232
4	27	$216
5	25	$200
6	21	$168
7	17	$136
8	13	$104
9	9	$72

    b. The firm will maximize profit by hiring 5 workers.

    c. i) The demand for labor would shift to the right.

        ii) The number of workers employed would increase to 7, since the value of the marginal product of the 7th worker would be $204.

        iii) The firm's profit would increase, because the value of marginal product increased, but the wage rate remained constant.

2. a.

Workers	Marginal Product	Price	Marginal Revenue	Marginal Revenue Product
1	35	$18.25	$16.50	$577.50
2	32	$16.65	$13.30	$425.60
3	29	$15.20	$10.40	$301.60
4	27	$13.85	$7.70	$207.90
5	25	$12.60	$5.20	$130.00
6	21	$11.55	$3.10	$65.10
7	17	$10.70	$1.40	$23.80
8	13	$10.05	$0.10	$1.30

b. At a wage rate of $200, the firm would hire 4 workers.

c. The value of the marginal product of the 4th is (13.85)*27 = $373.95.

d. The firm's monopoly profit is 4(373.95 - 200) = $695.80.

3. a. The budget line connects 100 hours of leisure on the horizontal axis and $500 of income on the vertical axis, and is tangent to the second-highest indifference curve where leisure = 60 hours and income = $200 per week.

Chart 17-1a

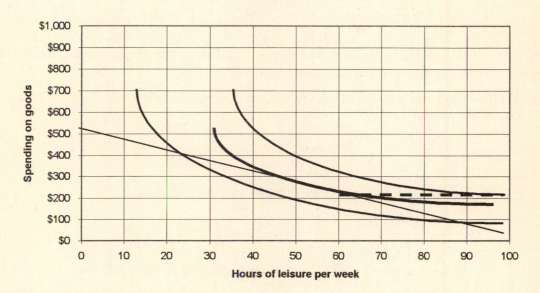

b. 60 hours are allocated to leisure and <u>40</u> hours are allocated to working.

c. Her weekly income is $200.

d. i) The budget line is horizontal from 60 hours to 100 hours of leisure at $200 of earnings.

 ii) Her time allocated to work decreases from 40 hours to zero since the effective wage rate is now zero.

iii) Her time allocated to leisure increases from 60 to 100 hourssince the opportunity cost of leisure is zero.

4. a. The present value of the high school graduate's income stream equals the present value of $15,000 in one year, divided by .05:

$$PV = \frac{\$15{,}000/(1.05)}{0.05} = \frac{\$14{,}285.71}{.05} = \$285{,}714$$

  b. The present value of a college graduate's income stream is $28,000, divided by $(1.05)^5$, divided by .05:

$$PV = \frac{\$28{,}000/(1.05)^5}{0.05} = \frac{\$21{,}938.73}{0.05} = \$438{,}774.65$$

  c. A college education is a good investment (assuming one graduates) because college graduates earn $153,060 more than high school graduates in present value.

  d. If the real rate of interest increased to 7 percent,

College graduates: $PV = \dfrac{\$28{,}000/(1.07)^5}{0.07} = \$285{,}194.47$

High school graduates: $PV = \dfrac{\$15{,}000/(1.07)}{0.07} = \$200{,}267$

Although a successful investment in college pays, the return declines to about $85,000 in present value.

5. The expected present value of a high school graduate's income stream remains constant at

$$PV = \frac{\$15{,}000/(1.05)}{0.05} = \frac{\$14{,}285.71}{.05} = \$285{,}714$$

The present value of a college dropout's earning stream is

$$PV = \frac{\$20{,}000/(1.05)^3}{0.05} = \frac{\$17{,}276.75}{.05} = \$345{,}535$$

The present value of a college graduate's earning stream remains

$$PV = \frac{\$28{,}000/(1.05)^5}{0.05} = \frac{\$21{,}938.73}{0.05} = \$438{,}774.65$$

The expected value of attending college is .6(345,535) + .4(438,775) = $382,831.

Although attending college is still a good investment, the expected return is now only $97,117-

Answers to True-False Questions

1. *False.* As long as there is free entry into the labor market, the market supply curve for labor will be positively sloped. As the wage rate increases, the entry of more individuals offering labor time will offset any tendency for the hours worked per person to decrease by those already in the market.

2. *True.* $MC = \dfrac{w}{MP_L} = P$ implies that $w = P \times MP_L$.

3. *False.* Because the price making firm produces less output, it also hires less labor than would an equivalent competitive firm.

4. *False.* Because they typically lose a $1 of welfare benefits for each extra dollar of income, welfare recipients face a 100 percent tax rate, which makes the opportunity cost of leisure zero.

5. *True.* Because firm-specific human capital investments do not increase the value of their marginal product with other firms, workers have little leverage in bargaining with their current employers for higher wages. Therefore, these workers tend to be paid less than the value of their marginal product on their current jobs, although they do receive more than their opportunity wages from their next best alternative jobs.

Answers to Multiple-Choice Questions

1. c

2. d   (Remember, $VMP_L = MRP_L$ for the price-taking firm.)

3. d

4. b

5. c

6. d

7. d   (Since the firm hires where MRP_L = wage, we cannot answer the question without knowing the marginal revenue schedule.)

8. a   (A decrease in the real interest rate will increase the present value of the earning stream for college graduates relative to high school graduates.)

9. a

10. a

Chapter 18

ECONOMIC EFFICIENCY AND GENERAL EQUILIBRIUM

• LEARNING OBJECTIVES

After completing this chapter, you should be able to

1. Distinguish between partial equilibrium and general equilibrium.

2. Trace changes in demand or supply in one market through several related markets.

3. Construct an Edgeworth box diagram, and identify the endowment point.

4. Define Pareto efficiency in exchange and explain why economic theory cannot make valid interpersonal comparisons of utility.

5. Explain how free exchange results in consumers having identical marginal rates of substitution and how this condition gives rise to the contract curve.

6. Define Pareto efficiency in production and relate efficiency to equal marginal rates of technical substitution among resources producing different products.

7. Understand why competitive markets generate Pareto efficiency in both consumption and production.

8. Derive a production possiblity curve from the location of tangencies between isoquants for different products.

9. Explain how competitive markets lead to Pareto efficiency in the product mix.

• CHAPTER OVERVEIW

Interpersonal comparisons of utility have no objective basis in economic theory. Economists cannot objectively evaluate any policy that makes one person better off while making another worse off. Yet economists agree that any policy that makes one person better off *without making anyone else worse off* would constitute an improvement in economic welfare.

A **Pareto efficient** allocation of goods is one in which any reassignment of goods that holds the utility of one consumer constant reduces the utility of the other consumer. Put another way, an allocation of goods is *not Pareto-efficient* if it is possible to make one consumer better off without making the other consumer worse off. No allocation can be efficient if unambiguous improvements in economic welfare are still possible.

Economists employ an **Edgeworth box** to analyze the distribution of goods within a two-person, two-good economy. Any point in an Edgeworth box reveals the distribution of a fixed stock of two commodities between individuals. If the **endowment point** is located at a point of intersection between the indifference curves for two individuals, voluntary exchange can improve the welfare of at least one of them, without hurting the other. Voluntary exchange will eventually move the consumption point to a point of tangency between indifference curves. The collection of all such tangency points is known as the

contract curve, since that is the location of all points where consumers exhibit equal marginal rates of substitution. Along the contract curve, no further gains from trade are possible, and the consumers have reached a Pareto-efficient allocation of commodities.

A competitive market, through the operation of Adam Smith's **invisible hand**, will produce Pareto efficiency in exchange. This is because traders independently seek to maximize utility by equating the slope of their indifference curve (MRS$_{xy}$) with the slope of the budget constraint (P_x/P_y). In a competitive market, all consumers face the same relative prices; so all consumers have the same marginal rates of substitution.

Competitive markets economize on the amount of information needed to reach a Pareto-efficient allocation. **Price controls** prevent the economy from achieving Pareto efficiency in exchange by prohibiting potentially mutually beneficial exchanges.

An allocation of factors is Pareto-efficient if any reallocation of factors reduces the output of one good, given the output of the other. Pareto efficiency in production requires the marginal rate of technical substitution (MRTS$_{KL}$) between labor and capital to be equal for the two products. Each firm minimizes the cost of production by equating MRTS$_{KL}$ to the negative of the factor-price ratio (-w/r). All firms face the same relative factor prices; so MRTS$_{KL}$ will be the same for all industries.

The **contract curve for production** shows the *maximum* quantity of Y that can be produced for each quantity of X. Plotting the rates of output of pairs of isoquants along the contract curve for production generates the **production possibilities curve.** All points on the production possibilities curve are Pareto-efficient since it is impossible to produce more of one good unless the output of the other good is reduced.

The opportunity cost of increasing the output of one good, in terms of the other good, is given by the slope of the production possibilities curve. This slope is called the **marginal rate of transformation** between Y and X (MRT$_{YX}$ = $\Delta Y/\Delta X$). The marginal rate of transformation equals the negative ratio of the marginal cost of X to the marginal cost of Y (MRT$_{YX}$ = $\Delta Y/\Delta X$ = -MC$_X$/MC$_Y$).

The marginal cost of producing a good rises, the more of that good the economy is already producing. This pattern gives the production possibilities curve its bowed-out shape.

Subsidizing the use of a factor of production by one firm or industry but not another creates a **production distortion**, and the economy will no longer be Pareto-efficient in production.

For efficiency in **product mix** to occur, it is necessary that MRS$_{XY}$ for every consumer equals the MRT$_{XY}$. Competitive markets will produce a Pareto-efficient product mix. In a competitive market, price equals marginal cost (i.e., MC$_X$ = P_X and MC$_Y$ = P_Y). It follows that the ratio of competitive prices will equal the ratio of their marginal costs. Since consumers equate marginal rates of substitution to price ratios, MRS$_{XY}$ = MRT$_{XY}$. Since monopoly firms do not equate marginal cost and price, the relative prices consumers pay will no longer reflect the ratio of their marginal costs. Monopoly distorts the product mix and also violates Pareto efficiency.

• KEY TERMS

Partial equilibrium The determination of price and quantity through the interaction of supply and demand in only one market. Changes in one market are analyzed independently of events in other markets.

General equilibrium The simultaneous analysis of the interaction between supply and demand across many markets. Here, a change in one market is traced through all the affected markets until all those markets have achieved new equilibrium states.

Consumer endowment The distribution of commodities among consumers prior to any voluntary exchanges that would improve the welfare of either or both parties.

Equating marginal rates of substitution The condition that identifies the exhaustion of mutually beneficial gains from trade. When two consumers have the same marginal rates of substitution for two commodities, any reallocation of commodities that makes one person no worse off will render the other person worse off.

Pareto efficient An allocation of goods in which the only way to make one person better off requires making someone else worse off.

Gains from trade The consequence of two people having different marginal rates of substitution from a consumer endowment. Each trade causes both parties to gain because of its voluntary nature. When gains from trade are exhausted, the allocation of commodities is considered Pareto-efficient.

Pareto efficiency in exchange Occurs when the parties to an exchange have reached a point on the contract curve where they have identical marginal rates of substitution and no further gains from trade are possible.

Competitive markets achieve *Pareto efficiency in exchange* because all consumers maximize utility by equating their marginal rates of substitution to the competitive price ratio, which is the same for all consumers.

Contract curve The location of points of tangency between indifference curves in an *Edgeworth box*.

Pareto efficiency in production occurs when it is impossible to produce more of one commodity without reducing the production of some other commodity. This condition is satisfied when producers *equate the marginal rates of technical substitution*.

Competitive factor markets achieve *Pareto efficiency in production* because all firms pay the same factor prices, and each equates the *marginal rate of technical substitution* to the common factor price ratio.

Production possibilities curve A curve generated by plotting the rates of output lying along the *contract curve for production*. Along the production possibilities curve, it is impossible to produce more of one good unless less is produced of the other good.

Marginal rate of transformation The slope of the production possibilities curve: The change in Y due to the change in X equals the negative ratio of the marginal cost of X to the marginal cost of Y: $MRT_{YX} = \Delta Y/\Delta X = -MC_X/MC_Y$.

Pareto efficiency in product mix   Occurs when the mix of goods produced is consistent with consumer demand. This efficiency is achieved when the ratio of prices of two commodities equals the ratio of their marginal costs.

Monopoly markets drive a *wedge between consumers' marginal rate of substitution and the marginal rate of substitution.* Monopolies produce too little of their commodities, causing competitive markets to produce too many of their commodities. Economic welfare would be increased if monopoly markets were constrained to produce where marginal cost equals price.

• PROBLEMS

1. **Chart 18-1** shows an Edgeworth box for consumers Adam (A) and Eve (E). Adam has an endowment of 5 fig leaves (X) and 2 apples (Y). Eve is endowed with 5 fig leaves and 8 apples.

Chart 18-1

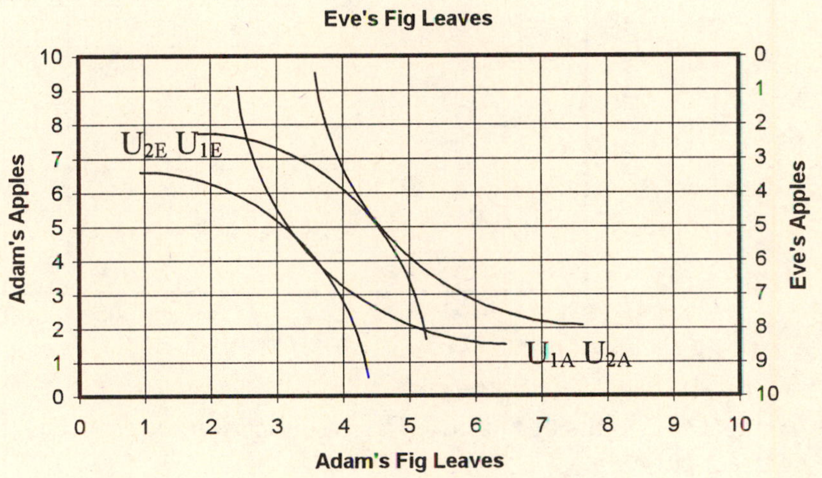

Eve's Fig Leaves

a. Label the initial endowment point "E."

b. Is point "E" on the contract curve? Explain.

_____

_____

c. Indicate, by shading, which allocations of the good are preferred by *both* A and E.

d. Suppose that Adam and Eve are free to engage in trade. What will happen?

_____

_____

_____

e. Suppose a competitive market establishes the price ratio 2X = 1Y. Will A and E trade with each other? Explain.

_____

_____

_____

2. **Chart18-2** represents an Edgeworth box for two industries producing X and Y, the industries use two factors, capital (K) and labor (L). Each isoquant is labeled with the rate of output that it represents.

Chart 18-2

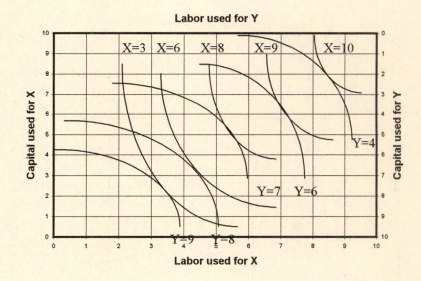

a. Connect the points of Pareto-efficient allocation of resources (the production contract curve.

b. What is the relation between the $MRTS_{LK}$ in the two industries along this contract curve?

_____

_____

_____

c. If both the X and the Y industries were competitively organized, would production end up on the contract curve? Explain.

_____

_____

_____

d. Suppose that X = 0 when Y = 10 and X = 12 when Y = 0. Use the contract curve in Chart 18-2 to draw the production possibilities curve for these two industries in **Chart 18-3**. (Hint: Plot the points given by the isoquants at their points of tangency, then connect the dots.)

Chart 18-3

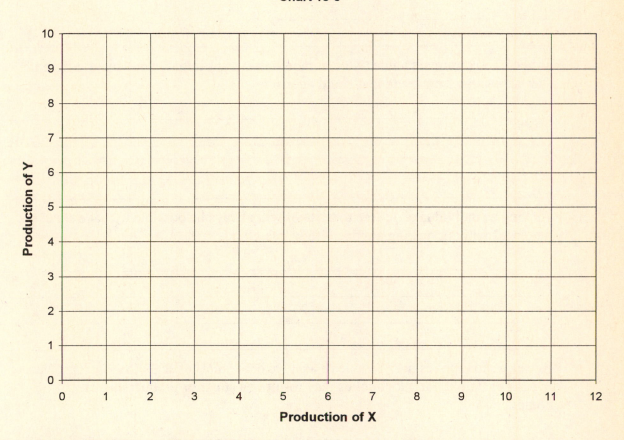

Production of Y

Production of X

TRUE-FALSE QUESTIONS

For each of the following statements, indicate whether the statement is true (agrees with economic theory), false (is contradicted by economic theory), or uncertain (could be true or false; not enough information is given), and briefly explain your answer.

1. Parents often have to make interpersonal comparisons of utility among their children: deciding where to go to vacation, deciding between braces for one and a new bike for another, or deciding who gets to choose the restaurant for a family celebration. This practice shows families decide inefficiently.

_____

_____

_____

_____

2. Although it seems a good policy to make someone better off without making anyone else worse off, if such policies have yet to be exploited, economic welfare is not being maximized.

_____

_____

_____

_____

3. When two consumers value two commodities in their initial endowment differently, there are gains from trade that could be made.

_____

_____

_____

_____

4. As long as individuals are free to trade, it will always be possible to make someone better off without making anyone else worse off.

_____

_____

_____

_____

5. Because monopolies may be able to achieve economies of scale that competitive industries would not, monopolies may result in a superior product mix over competition.

_____

_____

_____

_____

• MULTIPLE CHOICE QUESTIONS

1. An economy is Pareto-efficient in exchange if

    a. reallocation would lower the utility of at least one individual.

    b. reallocation would increase the utility of at least one individual.

    c. neither person is satisfied with the current allocation.

    d. reallocation would make both people better off.

2. Bill has 10,000 units of good X and 20,000 units of good B. Ben has 3,000 units of each good. If we take 100 units of both A and B from Bill and give them to Ben

    a. welfare will rise.

    b. efficiency will rise.

    c. the economy will move nearer the contract curve.

    d. none of the above can be proven with economic theory.

3. Bea buys both X and Y, with $MRS_{YX} = -10$, $P_X = \$50$, and $P_Y = \$5$. Bea has no more income to spend on these goods. She should

    a. buy more x and less y.

    b. buy more y and less x.

    c. maintain her current level of consumption.

    d. do none of the above.

4. If Harry's $MRS_{YX} = -4$ and Sam's $MRS_{YX} = -5$;

    a. the economy is inside its production possibilities curve for X and Y.

    b. Harry and Sam are on their contract curve for X and Y.

    c. Harry and Sam have exhausted their gains from trade.

    d. Harry and Sam are off their contract curve for X and Y.

5. Along the contract curve

    a. the marginal rates of substitution for two consumers are equal.

    b. the indifference curves of the two consumers are tangent.

    c. this two-person, two-good economy is Pareto-efficient in exchange.

    d. all of the above are true.

6. If the competitive wage is \$10 and the competitive price of capital is \$15, Pareto efficiency in production requires that in all industries
    a. $MRTS_{KL} = -2/3$.
    b. $MRTS_{KL} = -3/2$.
    c. $MP_L = 10$.
    d. $MP_K = 10$.

7. The economy is currently on the contract curve for production where output of X = 10 million and output of Y = 5 million. Which of the following statements is/are true?

    a. If industry Y expands, industry X must contract.

    b. The $MRTS_{KL}$ in industry Y = the $MRTS_{KL}$ in industry X.

    c. The economy is Pareto efficient in production.

    d. All of the above statements are true.

8. A point inside the production possibilities curve

   a. may be Pareto-efficient in production.

   b. may be Pareto-efficient in exchange.

   c. may be Pareto-efficient in the product mix.

   d. cannot be any of the above.

9. If $MC_X = 5$ and $MC_Y = 2$,

   a. $MRT_{YX} = -2/5$.

   b. $MRT_{YX} = -5/2$.

   c. $\Delta Y/\Delta X = -2/5$.

   d. (a) and (c).

10. Suppose that $MRS_{XY} = -P_X/P_Y = -5$ for two consumers and $MRT_{YX} = -5$ for two industries.

   a. There is Pareto efficiency in exchange.

   b. There is Pareto efficiency in product mix.

   c. There is Pareto efficiency in production.

   d. Both a and b are true.

- ## ANSWERS TO PROBLEMS, TRUE-FALSE, AND MULTIPLE-CHOICE QUESTIONS

Answers to Problems

1.

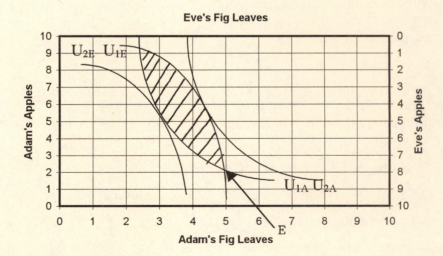

Chart 18-1a

a. The endowment occurs at point E in the above diagram.

b. This point is *not* on the contract curve, since point E occurs at a point of intersection between U_{1A} and U_{1E}. Since the slopes of the indifference curves are unequal (the $MRS_{XY,A} \neq MRS_{XY,E}$), there are unexploited gains from trade.

c. The shaded area is the "lens" bounded by U_{1A} and U_{1E}. Within that area, it is possible to make at least one person better off without making the other person worse off.

d. If Adam and Eve are free to engage in trade, either one or both can increase utility, as long as the other does not lose utility. Adam could achieve an indifference curve as high as U_{2A} or Eve could achieve an indifference curve as high as U_{2E}.

e. Adam and Eve will not trade with each other at these terms of trade. As indicated by the line $2X = Y$, through point E, Adam would have to be worse off to make Eve better off, or both would be worse off.

Chart 18-2a

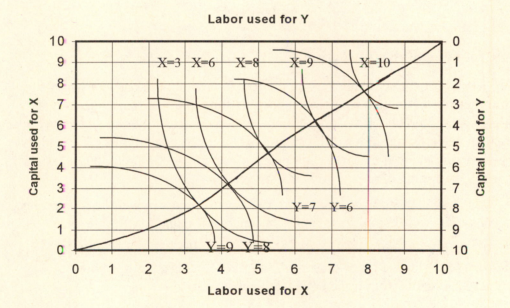

Labor used for Y

2. a. The production contract curve is shown in **Chart 18.2a**

   b. The marginal rates of technical substitution between K and L are equal along the production contract curve.

   c. If both X and Y are competitively organized, the ratio of *w* to *r* will be set by supply and demand. When firms in both industries equate the $MRTS_{KL}$ to -*w/r*, they will equate MRTS in both industries.

d. Here is the production possibilities curve for *X* and *Y*

Chart 18-3a

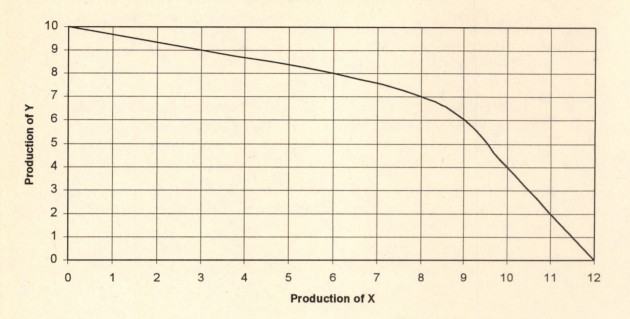

Answers to True-False Questions

1. *False*. Economic theory cannot guide interpersonal comparisons, but parents are generally altruistic enough to use such comparisons to guide family decisions: deciding were to go on vacation, deciding between braces for John and a new bike for Jennie, or determining what the menu will be for Sunday dinner. The family will be more efficient if children (and parents) can engage in mutually beneficial exchanges: swapping chores or toys, for instance.

2. *True*. It is inefficient to have unambiguous improvements in welfare unexploited, such as having laws that prohibit mutually beneficial gains from trade.

3. *True*. If MRS_{XY} is not the same for two consumers, the consumer with the lower MRS_{XY} trades X for the other person's Y until MRS_{XY} is equal for both consumers and gains from trade have been exhausted.

4. *False*. Once MRS is equal for all consumers, a Pareto efficient allocation is achieved. In that case, any reallocation that does not make one person better off will make some other person worse off.

5. *False*. Although a monopoly realizing economies of scale may produce more than a competitive industry, thus expanding the productions possibilities curve, the monopoly will produce too little of the good, causing competitive industries to produce too much of other goods. This outcome violates the optimal product mix requirement that $\dfrac{MC_x}{MC_y} = \dfrac{P_x}{P}$.

Answers to Multiple-Choice Questions

1. a

2. d (Options a, b, and c all require interpersonal comparisons of utility.)

3. c (Currently, her MRS is equal to the price ratio.)

4. d

5. d

6. a

7. d

8. b (It is still possible that the MRS is equal for all traders.)

9. b

10. d (It is possible that $MRTS_{LK,X} \neq MRTS_{LK,X}$.)

Chapter 19

EXTERNALITIES AND PUBLIC GOODS

• LEARNING OBJECTIVES

After completing this chapter, you should be able to

1. Distinguish negative and positive external effects (externalities) and explain why externalities lead to a discrepancy between the private and socially efficient output.

2. Calculate the marginal social cost of a polluting good using the marginal production cost and the marginal damage (external) cost.

3. Explain the internalization of a negative externality using a per unit tax.

4. Explain the internalization of a positive externality using a per unit subsidy.

5. Demonstrate how the Coase theorem relates the unambiguous assignment of property rights to internalizing externalities.

6. Understand why the socially correct output will be achieved regardless of which party to an externality possesses property rights or is liable for damage done.

7. Show how significant property rights nullify the conclusion that who owns property rights is irrelevant to the elimination of inefficiencies associated with externalities.

8. Define a public good and contrast public and private goods.

9. Explain why markets typically fail to provide public goods in optimal quantities.

• CHAPTER OVERVEIW

Externalities and Optimal Product Mix

An **externality** exists when a firm or individual benefits (a **positive externality**) or is harmed (a **negative externality**) by the market transaction in which he/she/it is neither a buyer nor a seller. In the case of a negative externality, the private marginal cost of production understates the **social marginal cost** by the **marginal damage** imposed on **third parties.** Negative externalities mean that the **social surplus** is less than the (private) **producer surplus** by the amount of **total external cost**.

By **internalizing** external costs, social surplus will be maximized. In the case of an externality involving one producer harming another, the external costs would be internalized by merging the two activities. For instance, a polluting paint company that increases the water purification costs for a bottled drinking-water company results in an inefficient product mix. There is too much paint produced at too low a price, and too little drinking water produced at too high a price. The paint producer would consider its pollution a production cost if the same company produced both paint and drinking water. If the government imposes a **per unit tax** equal to the marginal damage cost at the socially optimal rate of output, the socially optimal level of output would be produced.

All the rules that apply to an external cost would also apply to an **external benefit**, simply because the absence of an external cost is a social benefit. For instance, if the paint company altruistically decides to install scrubbers on its waste discharge pipes, drinking-water companies downstream would benefit from this action without bearing the cost. Again, if the paint company and the drinking water company merged, the cost of supplying clean water to the bottling plant would be considered a cost of delivering bottled water. In the absence of such a merger, the government could subsidize the paint company to produce social benefits.

The Coase Theorem

The **Coase theorem** states that a firm that generates either an external benefit or an external cost will produce the socially optimal output if (1) **transaction costs** are negligible and (2) **property rights** are clearly defined and enforced. If the agents suffering from pollution have property rights over a clean environment, they can force the polluter to pay the marginal damage cost. The assignment of liability to the polluter internalizes the cost, since the expected damage of pollution is now considered a cost of production. This results in the socially optimal rate of output. If the polluter is not liable (that is, if the firm has the property right to pollute), the "victim" of pollution must compensate the polluter for the social benefit of not polluting. Once a contract has been drawn compensating the polluter for its forbearance, the marginal damage cost (which is also the marginal social benefit) is internalized. The polluter will produce the same rate of output, regardless of whether the consequence of pollution is paying a fine or not receiving a subsidy.

Transaction costs are the costs of reaching and enforcing agreements. An important assumption of the Coase theorem is that transaction costs are very small. If transaction costs are large (e.g., a polluter harms many individuals or businesses), the private market will probably not ensure the production of the socially optimal level of output even if the right to pollute is owned by the polluter. The agreement costs among the victims, and the monitoring costs would make bribing the polluter to desist too expensive. If the agents who suffer pollution own the property rights (e.g., if any victim can sue to polluter and recover class action damages), the socially optimal rate of output is more likely. With large transaction costs, assigning liability to the agent with the lowest compliance and monitoring costs will typically result in the most efficient outcome.

Taxation of the agent causing third-party effects can be difficult if the cause of pollution is unclear. A tax can prevent the **low-cost solution** from occurring. For example, the relocation of affected parties may be a low-cost solution compared with paying a tax that forces the socially optimal output level.

Public Goods

A **pure public good** is a commodity whose consumption is **nonrivalrous and nonexclusive.** The market demand for a pure private good is obtained by the horizontal summation of the quantities demanded at each price. The demand for a pure public good is obtained by a vertical addition of the value for each unit produced. The provision of a public good is hampered by **free rider problems.** Since nonpayers cannot be excluded from consuming a pure public good, individuals try to hide their true preferences. Accordingly, the market typically fails to provide the socially optimal quantity of pure public goods: that quantity where the marginal social cost intersects the **community's inverse demand function.**

Because public goods tend to be undersupplied by the private sector, an element of **public finance** is typically involved. Through its power to tax, governments can force (supposed) beneficiaries of public goods to bear a share of the burden.

• KEY TERMS

Externality   A situation in which a firm or individual benefits from or is harmed by the behavior of other firms or individuals.

Negative externalities   Externalities that impose costs on third parties.

Positive externalities   Externalities that bestow benefits on third parties.

Third parties Economic agents (e.g., firms, households) that are neither buyers nor sellers in a market, but who experience benefits for which they do not pay, or costs for which they are not compensated.

Marginal social cost   The cost to society from the product of one more unit of output. Marginal social cost is the sum of private marginal cost and marginal damage cost.

Marginal damage cost   The marginal cost to third parties of an economic activity that generates a negative externality

Social surplus   The difference between the producer surplus and the total external costs.

Coase theorem   An idea attributed to Ronald Coase that externalities result from vague or nonexistent property rights. Formally, in a market with zero transaction costs and clearly specified property rights, externalities will be internalized and the optimal rate of output will be exchanged, *regardless of which party receives the property rights.*

Internalizing an externality   A situation when economic agents behave as if marginal damage costs were private marginal costs, thereby leading them to produce the socially optimal rate of output.

Defining property rights   The creation of enforceable legal rules assigning liability for negative externalities or the right to charge for benefits for positive externalities. A property right involves the right to exclude; e.g., the right of victims of pollution to force compensation from a polluter.

Transaction cost The cost of reaching and enforcing an agreement.

Public good   A commodity that is nonrivalrous and nonexclusive, such as national defense or a system of justice. Once one economic agent consumes a public good, all economic agents will consume it.

Nonrivalrous A condition whereby a good can be consumed by one more consumer at zero marginal cost. A movie or a sporting event is nonrivalrous as long as some seats are empty.

Nonexclusive A condition whereby the seller of a commodity cannot exclude nonpayers from enjoying the benefits of a commodity. The elimination of smallpox is nonexclusive;

once the disease is eradicated, all human beings benefit since the chance of contracting the disease is zero.

Pareto efficiency with a public good The optimal quantity of a public good is where the sum of the marginal rate of substitution between the public good and a composite private good for all consumers equals the marginal rate of transformation between the public and the private good.

• PROBLEMS

1. The table below shows cost conditions facing a polluting firm.

Quantity Produced by Firm	Marginal Production Cost	Marginal Damage Cost	Marginal Social Cost
1	$10	$1	_____
2	12	$3	_____
3	18	$9	_____
4	22	11	_____
5	27	15	_____
6	38	19	_____

   a. Fill in the column labeled "Marginal Social Cost."

   b. What is the profit-maximizing output of the firm if its goods sell at a price of $27?

   c. What is the socially optimal output for the firm at this price?

   d. What size of a per unit tax could the government levy to force the firm to produce the socially optimal rate of output? Explain.

   e. Suppose that the only "victim" of this external cost was another firm. Explain how the externality could be internalized if the two firms merged.

   f. Suppose the courts ruled that the "victim" of the external cost has the right to full compensation whenever the polluting firm pollutes. How would this result cause the socially optimal output?

g. Suppose instead that the courts ruled that the polluting firm was there first and that the second firm "moved to the nuisance", and therefore cannot collect damages. How might the socially optimal rate of output still result?

_____

_____

_____

2. The town of Weville (population = 3) will hire an economics professor to give lectures in price theory in the town square, where all 3 citizens eat their lunch every day. The question is how many lectures should be given each week and how to pay for them. The professor is willing to lecture for $30 per day, for up to 7 days a week. The table below provides the willingness-to-pay functions for Al, Babs, and Calvin, the citizens of Weville.

Marginal Willingness to Pay for Economics Lectures

Lectures per Week

	1	2	3	4	5	6	7
Al	$10	$9	$8	$7	$6	$5	$4
Babs	$20	$19	$18	$17	$16	$15	$14
Calvin	$15	$14	$13	$12	$11	$10	$9

a. Use the above information to construct the community's inverse demand function in the table below.

Lectures per Week

	1	2	3	4	5	6	7
Community's Inverse Demand Function	___	___	___	___	___	___	___

b. What is the optimal quantity of economics lectures, based on the true preferences of the citizens?

_____

c. If each citizen were assessed his/her marginal valuation for the last unit when the optimal quantity of lectures were purchased, what would be the payments for each person and what would be their consumer surplus?

	Total Valuation	Total Fee	Surplus
Al	____	____	____
Babs	____	____	____
Calvin	____	____	____
Total	____	____	____

d. Suppose that Al decides to free ride, reporting that he hates economics and refuses to pay for the lectures (even though he still will listen to them). If Babs and Calvin continue to reveal their true preference, show the revised community inverse demand function:

Lectures per Week

	1	2	3	4	5	6	7
Community's Inverse Demand Function	____	____	____	____	____	____	____

e. What happens to the number of lectures per week if Al free rides?

_____

f. Based on your answers to parts c and e, what happens to the surplus for each of the citizens?

	Total Valuation	Total Fee	Surplus
Al	____	____	____
Babs	____	____	____
Calvin	____	____	____
Total	____	____	____

g. Based only on Al's own benefits, which outcome would he prefer?

_____

h. What does your answer to part f imply about the likelihood of market failure in the provision of public goods?

_____

_____

_____

TRUE-FALSE QUESTIONS

For each of the following statements, indicate whether the statement is true (agrees with economic theory), false (is contradicted by economic theory), or uncertain (could be true or false; not enough information is given), and briefly explain your answer.

1. The distinction between positive externalities and negative externalities is not always as clear in practice as in theory.

_____

_____

_____

_____

2. The Coase theorem states that property rights are not important in solving the product mix inefficiency that results from externalities.

_____

_____

_____

_____

3. The Coase theorem is equally applicable in externalities involving consumers as it is in situations involving producers.

_____

_____

_____

_____

4. Public goods are pure externalities.

_____

_____

_____

_____

5. Unless the government produces public goods, it is unlikely that they will be produced at all.

_____

_____

_____

_____

• MULTIPLE-CHOICE QUESTIONS

1. Which of the following is an example of an externality?

   a. Al outbids Bill at an auction.

   b. A firm discharges polluted water into a stream, increasing the costs of firms downstream.

   c. A housing development moves next to a factory. The homeowner's association sues the factory and prevents it from polluting.

   d. b and c.

2. Externalities violate which condition(s) of Pareto optimality?

    a. Pareto optimality in allocation.

    b. Pareto optimality in production.

    c. Pareto optimal product mix.

    d. all of the above.

3. Firm A pollutes and raises the production costs of firm B. Which of the following actions would internalize the pollution costs?

    a. Firm A and firm B are purchased by a single proprietor.

    b. Firm B successfully sues firm A.

    c. Firm A pays firm B not to pollute.

    d. All the above.

4. The marginal production cost of coal is $50, the marginal damage cost is $10 and the price is $50 at an output of 10,000 tons of coal per week. Which of the following rates of output will maximize the coal company's profits?

    a. producing 10,000 tons per week

    b. producing less than 10,000 tons per week

    c. producing more than 10,000 tons per week

    d. shutting down and prevent further social costs

5. The marginal production cost of coal is $50, the marginal damage cost is $10 and the price is $50 at an output of 10,000 tons of coal per week. Which of the following would be best from a societal point of view?

    a. producing 10,000 tons per week

    b. producing less than 10,000 tons per week

    c. producing more than 10,000 tons per week

    d. shutting down and prevent further social costs

6. According to the Coase theorem, the socially optimal output of goods with externalities will be produced in which of the following conditions?

    a. The polluter owns the property rights and transaction costs are negligible.

    b. The polluter owns the property rights and transaction costs are positive.

    c. Property rights are clearly assigned and enforced and transaction costs are negligible.

    d. Government regulation stipulates the exact level of pollution allowed.

7. Which of the following government policies would internalize and externality?

    a. taxing a good that has a positive externality

    b. subsidizing a good that has a negative externality

    c. maintaining a system of ambiguous property rights

    d. none of the above

8. A pure public good

    a. is excludable.

    b. is nonrivalrous.

    c. is produced in optimal quantities by the private market.

    d. is all the above.

9. Which of the following is an example of a pure public good?

    a. a rock concert

    b. public television

    c. light from a lighthouse

    d. public higher education

10. Why must a government provide a pure public good?

    a. The free rider problem requires public finance.

    b. The government knows with certainty the marginal willingness to pay of each citizen.

    c. The government is more efficient than the private sector at producing a public good.

    d. Otherwise, a private firm would receive monopoly profits from selling a public good.

• ANSWERS TO PROBLEMS, TRUE-FALSE AND MULTIPLE-CHOICE QUESTIONS

Answers to Problems

1. a.

Quantity Produced by Firm	Marginal Production Cost	Marginal Damage Cost	Marginal Social Cost
1	$10	$1	$11
2	12	$3	$15
3	18	$9	$27
4	22	11	$33
5	27	15	$42
6	38	19	$57

b. At a price of $27, a profit-maximizing firm will produce 5 units of output.

c. The socially optimal output when $P = \$27$ is 3.

d. A per unit tax of $9 would result in the socially optimal rate of output.

e. If the two firms merged, the owner would treat the pollution of the first firm as a cost of production to the second, and would set the rate of output to maximize the joint profit of the two firms, producing 3 units.

f. Allowing the victim to sue for damages awards property rights to that firm. The polluting firm would internalize the expected damages and reduce the rate of output to 3 units.

g. If the owner of the "victim" firm paid the first firm $9 for each unit not produced, the polluting firm would reduce output to 3 units.

2. a. The community's inverse demand function is:

Lectures per Week

	1	2	3	4	5	6	7
Community's Inverse Demand Function	$45	$42	$39	$36	$33	$30	$27

b. Based on the true preferences of citizens, the optimal quantity of economics lectures is 6 per week.

c. If each citizen were assessed his/her marginal valuation for the last unit when the optimal quantity of lectures were purchased, here is the pattern of payments and surplus for each:

	Total Valuatio	Total Fee	Surplus
Al	$45	$30	$15
Babs	$105	$90	$15
Calvin	$75	$60	$15
Total	$225	$180	$45

d. If Al decides to free ride, and Babs and Calvin pay for the lectures, the community's inverse demand function becomes:

	1	2	3	4	5	6	7
Community's Inverse Demand Function	$35	$33	$31	$29	$27	$24	$21

e. The quantity of lectures declines to 3 per week.

f. Based on 3 lectures per week, here are each citizen's fee and surplus.

	Total Valuation	Total Fee	Surplus
Al	$27	0	$27
Babs	$57	$54	$3
Calvin	$42	$39	$3
Total	$126	93	$33

g. Based on his own benefits, Al would prefer the free rider solution.

h. The other two would envy and emulate Al, so each would hide his/her true preferences, and the *revealed* community inverse demand function would be vacuous.

True-False Questions

1. *True*. We can observe the action of a polluter from two perspectives: The pollution occurs because the polluter does not have to bear the external costs, or pollution abatement does not occur because the firm cannot charge for the external benefit of clean air.

2. *False*. Property rights are very important in solving externality problems. With ambiguous property-right assignment, the external costs or benefits will not be internalized and an inefficient product mix will result. With property-right assignment, the economic agents will internalize external benefits or costs, and a socially optimal rate of output will occur. The Coase theorem states that as long as transaction costs are negligible, it does not matter which party is assigned property rights, *as long as one of the parties is clearly assigned those rights.*

3. *False*. The conclusion of the Coase theorem rests on the observation that changes in wealth (such as having property rights vs. bearing liability for harm) does not effect the profit-maximizing rate of output. However, consumer behavior can be affected by wealth. For instance, I may charge a neighbor $100 for permission to hold a noisy party in our apartment building if the landlord listens to my complaints. However, if the landlord also goes to the party (and so bestows my neighbor with property rights), I may not be willing to pay $100 for peace and quiet.

4. *True*. Being nonexcludable and nonrivalrous, once one party pays for a public good, all economic agents consume the good in equal proportion.

5. *False*. The free rider problem requires government *finance* of pure public goods, not government production. For instance, a government could use tax revenue to hire a private lighthouse keeper.

Multiple-Choice Questions

1. d   (Bill was involved in the market, so he is not a third party.)

2. c   (It is possible that all consumers have equal MRS and that goods are produced with equal MRTS.)

3. d   4. a   5. c   6. c   7. d   8. b

9. c   (a, b and d are all excludable.)

10. a